THE CONGREGATIONALISTS

Student Edition

J. WILLIAM T. YOUNGS

Westport, Connecticut
London

The Library of Congress has cataloged the hardcover edition as follows:

Youngs, J. William T. (John William Theodore)
    The Congregationalists / J. William T. Youngs.
        p.   cm.—(Denominations in America, ISSN 0193–6883 ; no. 4)
    Includes bibliographical references.
    ISBN 0–313–22159–6 (lib. bdg. : alk. paper)
    1. Congregational churches—United States—History.
2. Congregational churches—History. 3. United Church of Christ—
History. 4. Reformed Church—United States—History. 5. Reformed
Church—History. 6. Congregationalists—United States—Biography—
Dictionaries. 7. Congregationalists—Biography—Dictionaries.
    I. Title. II. Series.
    BX7135.Y68   1990
    285.8'73—dc20   89–78411

British Library Cataloguing in Publication Data is available.

An expanded, hardcover of *The Congregationalists* is available from
Greenwood Press, an imprint of Greenwood Publishing Group, Inc.
(Denominations in America, Number 4, ISBN 0–313–22159–6)

Library of Congress Catalog Card Number: 89–78411
ISBN: 0–275–96441–8 (pbk.)

First published in 1998

Printed in the United States of America

∞™

The paper used in this book complies with the
Permanent Paper Standard issued by the National
Information Standards Organization (Z39.48–1984).

10 9 8 7 6 5 4 3 2 1

To Henry Bowden, Philip Greven, Henry May,
Michael McGiffert, and Robert Middlekauff

Mentors and friends who encouraged my interest in
Puritanism and in religious studies

In whatsoever place thou art, whether alone or abroad, by day or by night, and whatsoever thou are doing, set thyself in the presence of God, let this persuasion always take place in thy heart, that thou are before the living god.

—William Perkins

We know ourselves to be children of the Infinite; elements enter into our lives which lift us out of the realms of time and space, and reveal to us our larger parentage. It is only as we are able to draw into our life these great elements, to transfigure our human relationships and duties with the light that never was on sea or land, that life becomes significant and precious.

—Washington Gladden

CONTENTS

FOREWORD

The Praeger series of denominational studies follows a distinguished precedent. These current volumes improve on earlier works by including more churches than before and by looking at all of them in a wider cultural context. The prototype for this series appeared almost a century ago. Between 1893 and 1897, twenty-four scholars collaborated in publishing thirteen volumes known popularly as the American Church History Series. These scholars found twenty religious groups to be worthy of separate treatment, either as major sections of a volume or as whole books in themselves. Scholars in this current series have found that outline to be unrealistic, with regional subgroups no longer warranting separate status and others having declined to marginality. Twenty organizations in the earlier series survive as nine in this collection, and two churches and an interdenominational bureau have been omitted. The old series also excluded some important churches of that time; others have gained great strength since then. So today, a new list of denominations, rectifying imbalance and recognizing modern significance, features many groups not included a century ago. The solid core of the old series remains in this new one, and in the present case a wider range of topics makes the study of denominational life in America more inclusive.

Some recent denominational histories have improved with greater attention to primary sources and more rigorous scholarly standards. But they have too frequently pursued themes for internal consumption alone. Volumes in the Praeger series strive to surmount such parochialism while remaining grounded in the specific materials of concrete ecclesiastical traditions. They avoid placing a single denomination above others in its distinctive truth claims, ethical norms, and liturgical patterns. Instead, they set the history of each church in the larger religious and social context that shaped the emergence of notable denominational features. In this way the authors in this series help us understand the interaction that has occurred between different churches and the broader aspects of American culture.

Each of the historical studies in this current series has a strong biographical focus, using the real-life experiences of men and women in church life to highlight significant elements of an unfolding sequence. Every volume singles out important watershed issues that affected a denomination's outlook and discusses the roles of those who influenced the flow of events. This format enables authors to emphasize the distinctive features of their chosen subject and at the same time recognize the sharp particularities of individual attributes in the cumulative richness that their denomination possesses.

The author of this volume is a prize-winning authority on Congregationalism. His work here is further evidence of his expertise and sensitive understanding of relevant sources. One notable feature of *The Congregationalists* is the continuity which Youngs maintains in subject matter that sprawls over four centuries and two nations. While aware of generational changes in perception and idiomatic expression, he points to underlying themes that knit different epochs together to form a single, though variegated, tapestry. So colonial fathers and modern business people, schoolteachers and missionaries, combine in a rich account of one of America's earliest and most influential ecclestical groups.

Another feature is perhaps more noticeable, one that gives a characteristic signature to Youngs's interpretation of this material. As an aid to synthesizing disparate parts and providing continuity, the author emphasizes religious experience as a common denominator among different personalities. He makes no normative judgments about truth or validity. But over and over again the diaries, letters, sermons, and autobiographies resonate with shared themes. Recurrent expressions of anguish over sin, despair about redemption, joy over forgiveness, and faithfulness in worship and ethics—all these give Youngs a way to seek what Congregationalism has pursued and preserved over the years. This probing into the core of religious life and identifying it in the spiritual rather than the institutional or cultural realm, is a tour de force. The result makes for fascinating reading, informative to specialists and general readers alike. Even though most Congregationalists have given up their separate identity, pointing to the ecumenical future in joining the United Church of Christ, this volume retains their vibrant past and shows how their influence in contemporary times is still appreciable.

HENRY WARNER BOWDEN

PREFACE

"Resolved, To live with all my might, while I do live." These words, written a quarter millennium ago by Jonathan Edwards, suggest not only the quality of his life, but also a characteristic of Congregationalists throughout American history. Having begun to explore the denomination two decades ago with a book on the colonial clergy, I have been impressed while writing this book with the way that the vital qualities of Congregationalism in the 1600s and 1700s endured into the 1800s and 1900s. Many books and articles have been written about the church, some of which are described in the bibliographical essay. But surprisingly few writers have studied Congregationalism throughout the course of its history. The early Puritans are a topic of such fascination to scholars, that many have concluded that colonial America provides world enough for their studies. This is unfortunate, because so much of modern Congregationalism, and of America in general, bears the marks of the colonial past.

This continuity includes elements of diversity as well as uniformity. Considering the history of the denomination as a whole, including the recent merger by most of its members with other groups to form the United Church of Christ, one is impressed with the variety of experiences that combined to form the story of the church. But one also discovers ways that these disparate events provide unexpected links through the centuries. Congregational history is the story of a man executed in sixteenth century England for binding a book by Robert Browne; it is the tale of Jonathan Edwards standing outside in a thunderstorm to get a better view of God's lightning; it is the account of young Washington Gladden attending a revivalistic meeting in a candlelit room; and it is the story of Charles Sheldon being allowed to edit a Topeka, Kansas, newspaper for one week in 1900 "in the steps" of Christ. Each of these unique events, and many others, make up the story of Congregationalism.

In writing *The Congregationalists* I have attempted to capture some of that denominational life, mightily lived, on paper. In keeping with the goals of the Denominations in America series, I have attempted to bring together several elements. The book is a reference book, and it is an essay on Congregationalism. So at certain points I have summarized basic information about the church; at others I have attempted to provide original interpretations of particular episodes in church history or on Congregationalism as a whole. On the interpretive side, I have tried to offer new ideas about such issues, for example, as the genesis of the "visible saints" idea and the significance of Horace Bushnell.

More generally, this book stresses the continuity of Congregationalism from colonial times into the nineteenth century, and even to the present. Historians have made a cottage industry of dating the demise of Puritanism and the rise of secularism. Many would push the date back deep into the seventeenth century, some virtually to the point when the colonists stepped off the ships in New England. I do not agree, for the Puritan way of seeing God, humanity, and salvation continued to influence Americans throughout the colonial period and long afterwards.

While exploring such issues, I have had to recognize that many aspects of the denomination's history lay beyond the scope of the book. Much more could be said about such matters as the westward movement of Congregationalism during the nineteenth century or the role of the church in modern America. As both a reference work and an interpretive essay, I hope that this volume will provide a useful introduction to the church for the general reader. But I also hope that it will provoke fellow scholars to consider new ways of exploring some of the less familiar aspects of Congregational history, particularly in the nineteenth and twentieth centuries.

Throughout the book, as in this preface, I have tended to use the words *Puritan* and *Congregationalist* synonymously. History provides the link in the seventeenth century; the words were virtually interchangeable at that time. But then during the nineteenth century many people who thought of themselves as Congregationalists no longer thought of themselves as Puritans. The word *Puritan* acquired certain modern connotations that the real Puritans would have considered strange. But even though the name fell into disuse as a description of a living religious group, the spiritual sensibility of the early Puritans endured.

Any writer will leave on a book his or her own signature, or a way of practicing the historical craft and seeing reality. Some are captivated by facts; some by interpretive issues. I am interested in both, but in addition I am intrigued by the way that individuals *experienced* a relationship to what they called God. Religious issues can be so abstract that one loses sight of why they ever mattered. So there is value in learning how people *lived religiously* in the past, as well as learning what they said about such issues as how to choose ministers, or whether one could "prepare" for salvation. In an attempt to convey a feeling for the religious life of the Congregationalist, I have explored the spiritual experiences of John Winthrop, Jonathan Edwards, Horace Bushnell, and other representative figures.

I have appreciated too the help of colleagues and friends in my work. The dedication page of the book suggests that many persons have contributed directly or indirectly to its writing. Often a student's interest in a subject is nourished by the goodwill and enthusiasm communicated by other scholars. My own work on the Puritans began thirty years ago when Philip Greven, my tutor at Harvard, presided over my first extensive work on the Puritans, a senior thesis on their migration to New England. While absorbed in his important work on colonial Andover, Massachusetts, he took the time to provide good humored advice and encouragement to an undergraduate. At Berkeley I benefited from course work and dissertation guidance from two men whose own work took them deep into the Puritan world, Henry May and Robert Middlekauff. I still recall the thoughtful atmosphere of May's seminar on intellectual history and the inspiration of Middlekauff's infectious enthusiasm for Puritan studies.

Over the years Michael McGiffert has presided over the publication of many excellent articles on Puritanism as editor of *The William and Mary Quarterly*. Our many conversations have continued to enrich my experience of early American history. Finally, among the "mentors and friends" listed in my dedication, Henry Bowden has exhibited in his own work the attractiveness and variety of religious studies. As series editor of Denominations in America he deserves credit for the imaginative combination of survey history and biographical sketches that are hallmarks of this series. His comments as editor of my work on the Congregationalists have been unfailingly perceptive and encouraging.

In writing about the Congregationalists I have also benefited from the help of several bright research assistants. Norma Schmidt and Bill Johnson did good work on nineteenth century Congregationalism. Byron Care helped with the bibliography and biographies and was skillful in reading and summarizing eighteenth-century Puritan tracts. And the bibliography owes a great deal to thorough and intelligent research by Matt Redinger. I owe thanks to Richard Johnson at the University of Washington for loaning me his office one summer while I was working on the book. I have benefited from the use of that university's library and my appointment as visiting scholar by the history department. My own school, Eastern Washington University, has provided grant assistance and library office space—one of the greatest boons any scholar can receive. A research fellowship from the National Endowment for the Humanities enabled me to complete the early chapters of the book. The editors at Greenwood Press have been unfailingly helpful. Cynthia Harris provided encouragement during the years of writing, and Patricia Meyers has skillfully managed the editing and typesetting of the manuscript. My copy editor, Mary Wolf, made a number of good suggestions for the book, and my proof reader, Jay Rozgonyi, caught many of those slips of the keyboard that afflict writers even in the age of word processors and spell checkers. I am grateful to Janet Anderson for giving me permission to quote "The Real Reason," a poem by her late husband Jeremy

Anderson. Arthur Cushman McGiffert, Jr., kindly shared with me his thoughts on his long life as a Congregationalist. For other kinds of advice and assistance I am particularly grateful to Doug Adams, Harry Applewhite, Steve Coates, Pat Higgs, and Larry Winters.

My family has helped out in a variety of ways. My children, Hope and Ted, who were infants when I completed my first book on the Puritans, were themselves adept research assistants by the time I finished *The Congregationalists*. My wife, Linda, has encouraged me at every stage in the progress of the book although, admittedly, she does not share my admiration for Nathaniel Emmons. He is the nineteenth century cleric who once refused to replace a fallen board from his fence, "fearing that it would lead him to other worldly activities."

Note: Asterisks next to various names throughout the next indicate that these individuals are the subjects of entries that make up the Biographical Dictionary which appears in the expanded hardcover edition.

THE
CONGREGATIONALISTS:
A HISTORY

1
THE CONGREGATIONALISTS:
A SUMMARY OVERVIEW

In our historical imagination the Congregational church is *the* American church. Congregationalism does not owe this distinction to numbers—several other denominations claim many more adherents. And the church cannot claim a unique heritage of doctrinal consistency—it has changed considerably over the centuries. But Congregationalism is distinctive in representing to an unusual degree certain values that are widely shared in the United States.

Congregationalists fled oppression to worship freely in America; so they are associated with religious freedom. They believed that God had ordained the New World to set an example for the Old; thus they contributed to the American sense of mission. And, known often as Puritans, they believed in simplicity in worship, helping to nourish a "plain style" in American speech and behavior.

By the time most American children finish grade school, they have drawn pictures of New England Puritans in dark robes and fashioned conical Puritan hats from drafting paper. And they have heard the story of the first Thanksgiving so often that the turkey gracing the table on the fourth Thursday in November is associated in their minds with Puritans and Indians seated at long tables under the trees.

Like most other myths, the popular stories about the early Puritans are a mix of fact and fiction. The Congregationalists did come to America for religious freedom, but only for themselves. They crossed an ocean in wooden boats in order to create their *own* holy commonwealth—they were as impatient with dissenters as the Anglicans whom they fled. In the choice words of colonist Nathaniel Ward, who styled himself "The Simple Cobbler of Aggawam," members of other religious groups had "free liberty to keep away from us, and such as will come to be gone as fast as they can, the sooner the better."[1] The age of Jeffersonian liberty, based on a critical view of any denomination's pretensions to divine authority, did not blossom in the New World until long after the landing of the *Mayflower*.

Nor were the Puritans and Indians as friendly as popular images may suggest. We know almost nothing about the first Thanksgiving, but we do know that the Puritans fought two bloody wars against the Indians. After the first, an English Puritan scolded the Puritans for killing Indians before converting any. Puritan harshness towards Indians and other non-Puritans has created a second myth, opposite to the first, but equally misleading. The dark legend of the Puritans emphasizes killjoys and witch burners. Critics even claimed that the English Puritans objected to the popular sport of staging fights between bears and dogs, not because it gave pain to the animals but because it gave pleasure to the audience. Nathaniel Hawthorne in *The Scarlet Letter* characterized Puritan New England as a land where all natural instincts were banished.

Again the legend is based on half-truths. The Puritans did favor sobriety, but they advocated a careful balance of worldliness and restraint, rather than abstinence—loving the world with "weaned affections" they called it. The Puritans felt that God had given the pleasurable things of life for the enjoyment of his people; he delighted in their happiness as long as their earthly pleasures did not draw their affections away from spiritual values. They summarized this attitude with a pithy expression: "Wine is from God, but drunkenness is from the devil."

As for witches, the Salem trials of 1692 were the last great episode of this sort in the Western world. No alleged witches were burned, but nineteen were hanged and one was pressed to death. The witchcraft episode was not, however, a typical event in Congregational history. Among the Puritans the trials were criticized from the start, and within a few years most New Englanders regarded them as a lamentable mistake.

The mythic image of the early Congregationalists is larger than life and in some respects inaccurate, but even stripped of embellishments the course of the denomination's history is one of the most compelling stories in American religious history. The Puritans who came to New England in the 1630s hoped to create a "city upon a hill," a utopian religious community that would set an example for the Christian world.

This was especially true of the "nonseparating" Congregationalists who followed John Winthrop to Massachusetts Bay in 1630. While sharing many beliefs with the Pilgrims who settled Plymouth in 1620, the later Puritans considered themselves reforming members of the Anglican church, while the Pilgrims wanted simply to worship in their own way and had no expectation of changing the national church. Both groups established churches in which individual congregations held ultimate power. The people selected and ordained the ministers without any interference from bishops or synods.

Any church defines itself by those it excludes as well as by those it accepts, and the first great conflict over the boundaries of Congregationalism occurred in 1636–37 during the Antinomian crisis. Although some of the early colonists may have come to New England primarily to acquire land or to enter trade, most were intensely interested in religious matters. Inevitably some would be discontented with the new religious patterns. A few Presbyterian-minded settlers, for example, wanted a more authoritarian religious structure. But the greatest threat to Congregational harmony came from the "left," from men and women who questioned whether the Puritan preachers were stressing sufficiently the need for spiritual purity as a prerequisite for salvation.

Led by an articulate laywoman, Anne Hutchinson, who conducted religious meetings in her home, the Antinomians accused several ministers of preaching a "doctrine of works" and claimed that they had the right to determine who was truly saved and who was not. Their behavior seemed so disruptive that they were tried by the civil and the religious authorities and exiled. When Anne Hutchinson was killed by Indians a few years later, an exultant John Winthrop reckoned that the Lord had punished her for her sins.

During the period of the Antinomian controversy, the Congregationalists introduced one of their most remarkable innovations, "visible sainthood." They decided that full church membership should be limited to men and women who had undergone a conversion experience and been examined on the validity of that experience by their minister and other parish leaders. Other churches had demanded a formal profession of faith as a criterion for membership, but this testimony from the soul was part of an effort, seldom paralleled in history, to make the actual church correspond with the invisible church of saints whom Christ had saved.

The system worked well for a time. Congregationalist lay men and women came forward to describe the feelings of humiliation and acceptance that were expected in the conversion experience. But within a few years ministers were disappointed to find that fewer and fewer persons were seeking full membership in the church. Men and women raised in New England seemed less willing than their parents had been to give conversion testimony. The choice to migrate may have heightened the religious feelings of the parents; possibly the children exaggerated the piety of the parents, and expecting an unrealistic degree of spirituality, they were overly critical of themselves. At any rate, as these sons and daughters of the visible saints grew up, they began to have children, and since they, the second generation parents, were not full church members, they could not have these infants baptized.

Naturally the grandparents, good visible saints, were distressed to see their progeny forced to begin life without the mark of baptism. And the ministers were distressed to see the beginning of a new generation of children who had no formal ties to the church: their parents at least had been baptized if not yet converted. So the Congregationalists adopted another innovation, whose name seems to admit their exasperation—the "Half Way Covenant." By this rule, which became prevalent in the later part of the seventeenth century, the children of baptized Congregationalists were themselves baptized. Some historians have referred to this custom as Puritan "tribalism."

Within a few years several more innovations were adopted by various congregations. Some churches agreed to baptize all children whether or not a grand-parent had been a visible saint. Others, notably the parishes under the influence of Solomon Stoddard in the Connecticut Valley, opened communion to all men and women who understood Christian doctrine and lived moral lives. For Stoddard communion was a "converting ordinance" rather than the exclusive reward of those who had already experienced conversion. At the same time a more liberal form of Calvinistic preaching emphasized the role of human effort in salvation.

At the turn of the century, while the church was relaxing standards for admission, the ministry was undergoing several subtle changes that accentuated the sacredness of the clerical calling and emphasized the distance between laymen and pastors. Ordinations were now performed by the ministers alone without lay participation; ordination sermons stressed the importance of the clergy; and clerical associations were formed throughout New England. The Massachusetts Platform of 1705 sought to give official standing to the associations, but was never officially adopted. However, associations were still formed, and though not as authoritative as the synods of the Presbyterian Church, they did help the ministers maintain their position. In Connecticut the Saybrook Platform of 1708 gave official standing to associations.

The early 1700s were in some ways a time of secularism and religious apathy in New England. For many Congregationalists religion was more decorative than compelling, not at the center of life. But the seeds were also sown for a religious revival that would soon sweep the land. Solomon Stoddard had led revivals in the Connecticut Valley since the late 1600s. In 1727 an earthquake shook New England, and fearing for their souls many laymen rushed to become full members of the churches. In the 1730s Stoddard's grandson, Jonathan Edwards led a revival in Northampton and encouraged an interest in revivalism with his book, *A Narrative of Surprising Conversions.*

But it was an Englishman, George Whitefield, whose preaching led to a general religious revival during the 1740s. He traveled throughout New England preaching that men and women were inherently depraved and condemned to eternal damnation unless they received God's grace. Congregational preachers, inspired by the example of Whitefield adopted a new style of preaching depicting their people, in Edwards's words, as "sinners in the hands of an angry God." By the thousands earnest colonists, asked "what must I do to be saved?" and experienced the anxiety and acceptance that constituted the traditional Puritan conversion.

This, the Great Awakening, was the most stimulating, but ultimately the most troubling episode in Congregational history during the eighteenth century. The ministers at first welcomed the revival, but many were then dismayed when spiritual enthusiasm led to itinerant preaching by untrained laymen, divisions within churches between "New Lights" and "Old Lights," and withdrawals from the church by men and women who chose to become Separates, Baptists, or Episcopalians. The revival also gave impetus to Jonathan Edwards's reformulation of Calvinism, synthesizing traditional theology and the ideas of the

Enlightenment, particularly the thought of Newton and Locke. The result was the "New Divinity."

The Congregationalists entered the Era of the American Revolution divided between advocates of the New Divinity and proponents of a version of Calvinism laying more stress on human ability. Historians have argued about which kind of Calvinist more consistently supported the American Revolution, but in fact most Congregationalists, whatever their theological leanings, were comfortable with the break from England. The ministers were on the whole so avid in their support of the American cause that they were, with reason, characterized as the "Black Regiment."

After the Revolution the Congregationalists faced new challenges to their identity as a "city upon a hill." In 1700 there had been only two Baptist, one Anglican, and one Quaker church in Massachusetts; and in Connecticut there were no churches that were not Congregational. By 1800 scores of Episcopalian and Baptist churches dotted the landscape. New England was now part of a larger America that included Presbyterians, Methodists, Quakers, Catholics, and Jews—as well as many other religious denominations. One of the denominations, Unitarianism, was carved out of Congregationalism early in the nineteenth century. Many formerly Congregational parishes, particularly in Boston and its environs, became Unitarian.

Connecticut, New Hampshire, and Massachusetts still collected a tax for the support of religions—Congregationalism and others—but even that policy was abolished in all three states by 1833. Moreover, although the nation was moving west, the Congregationalists were slow in joining the movement. In 1830 nine-tenths of the Congregational churches were still in New England. In 1850 there were 224 Presbyterian churches in Kentucky and no Congregational churches.

In 1760 Ezra Stiles in his *Discourse on Christian Union* had predicted that there would be 7,000,000 American Congregationalists by 1860. The actual number was closer to 250,000. The Congregationalists suffered several disadvantages in the denominational atmosphere of the nineteenth century. Emphasizing the importance of each individual congregation and avoiding an authoritative hierarchy, they had difficulty organizing the movement of their church into new territory. Stressing the importance of a well trained clergy, they could not depend upon semi-trained itinerants to preach the gospel. Moreover, they entered into a Plan of Union with the Presbyterians in 1801 that did little for the growth of Congregationalism and was abandoned by 1850. The Congregationalists did not even think of themselves in denominational terms until about mid-century.

In other respects, however, the vitality of the Puritans was evident in the New Nation. A Second Great Awakening pumped new religious energy into the church. And the Congregationalists were in the forefront of the movement to evangelize the American Indians and the natives of Asia, Africa, and the South Seas. Their American Board of Commissioners for Foreign Missions, founded in 1810, was the first agency of its kind in the United States. Their Hawaiian mission, begun in 1820, brought New England churches to the tropics, and contributed to the Americanization of the islands. In later years Congregational ministers took the Gospel to the American West and to Asia and Africa.

Congregationalists were also leaders in American education. They founded three of the seven colleges begun in the colonial period—Harvard (1636), Yale (1701), and Princeton (1746). Later, in cooperation with Presbyterians, they founded Western Reserve (1826), Illinois College (1829), Knox (1837), Beloit (1836), Grinnell (1846), and Rockford (1849). On their own they established Williams (1793), Bowdoin (1794), Middlebury (1800), Amherst (1821), Marietta (1835), Oberlin (1833), and Mount Holyoke (1837). Congregational mission societies established three black colleges, Howard (1867), Fisk (1866), and Atlanta (1865).

Congregationalists were active in the Abolitionist movement. Congregational parishes in the Midwest were often stopping points on the underground railway. Preachers wrote tracts that influenced Abraham Lincoln and contributed to antislavery sentiment. Harriet Beecher Stowe, daughter and sister of Congregationalist ministers, wrote *Uncle Tom's Cabin*.

At mid-century Congregationalists were becoming more self-conscious about their denominational status. By 1852 the Plan of Union with the Presbyterians was completely abandoned. Missionaries had not initially thought of conversions in terms of persuading men and women to say, in effect, "I am a Congregationalist." That now changed. The first national convention of the church was assembled in 1852, the first national council, in 1871. Congregationalists became interested in their denominational history. In 1874 Leonard Bacon published *The Genesis of the New England Churches*, and at the end of the century Williston Walker published *The Creeds and Platforms of Congregationalism* and *The History of the Congregational Churches in the United States*.

With the rise of industry after the Civil War, Congregationalists were again in the forefront of social activism. Congregationalists Washington Gladden, Graham Taylor, and George Gordon were leaders of the Social Gospel movement. The denomination's enthusiasm for social reform was aided by new developments in theology. During the nineteenth century the church was increasingly reluctant to insist on a strict Calvinist or New Divinity interpretation of the relationship of a helplessly depraved man to an all powerful God. Human effort was important to the salvation of the individual and society. In 1913 the denomination adopted the Kansas City Creed, officially recognizing the movement away from the Puritan theology.

During the twentieth century the Congregational church has been in the forefront of the ecumenical movement. In 1931 the church, numbering almost a million adherents, merged with the General Convention of the Christian Church, a denomination with roughly 100,000 members, drawn largely from Baptists, Methodists, and Presbyterians in the South during the nineteenth century. The Christians espoused a noncreedal faith and proclaimed that Christian character is the only proper requirement for church membership. The amalgamated denomination was known as the Congregational Christian Churches.

A generation later discussions began with the Evangelical and Reformed church, another amalgamated body, regarding a second merger. This group was itself the product of a merger in 1934 between the German Reformed church in the United States and the Evangelical Synod of North America, consisting of German-speaking Lutheran and Reformed congregations in the Midwest. In 1957 most of the Congregational Christians joined with the Evangelical and Reformed Churches to form the United Church of Christ. Congregationalists who opposed this union created other fellowships, the largest of which is the National Association of Congregational Christian Churches.

Five years later the United Church of Christ joined with the Methodists, Presbyterians, Episcopalians, and Disciples to consider the possibility of forming a much larger United (or Uniting) Church. The Consultation on Church Union, begun in 1962, lost favor in the 1970s, and for the moment the resting place of most religious descendents of the Puritans is the United Church of Christ.

NOTE

[1] Nathaniel Ward, "The Simple Cobbler of Aggawam," in Perry Miller and Thomas H. Johnson, eds., *The Puritans* (New York, 1963), vol. 1; 227. (Aggawam was the Indian name for Ipswich.)

2

THE ENGLISH BACKGROUND

ROBERT BROWNE AND THE ORIGINS OF CONGREGATIONALISM

In the year 1580, in the English town of Norwich, a man named Robert Browne organized a Congregational church and began preaching the Gospel. By this simple act Browne broke the law, risked his life, and became founder of a new religious body, later to be known as Congregationalism.

Just as scholars argue about whether Christopher Columbus really discovered America, they disagree about Browne's contribution to Congregationalism. Other men, including the Indians "discovered" America long before Columbus. In the same way there were precedents for Congregationalism long before Browne. In fact, the Puritans proudly traced their origins to the ancient church and biblical times. Other men, following Columbus, were the first to realize that America was a new continent, and were the first to establish a Euro-American civilization. Similarly, other Englishmen, after Browne's time built Congregational churches as permanent institutions in England and America. Browne's contact with Congregationalism, like Columbus's contact with America, was serendipitous and short-lived. His story is important, none the less, in suggesting the historical milieu in which Congregationalism began.

Robert Browne was born in Tolethorpe, Rutlandshire, in about 1550. He entered Corpus Christi College at Cambridge in 1570 and came under the influence of Thomas Cartwright, a critic of the Church of England. During the next decade Browne studied and ministered among men and women who were dissatisfied with the established church. These dissenters, often called Puritans, respected the standards of doctrine, worship, and polity that could be found in the Continental Reformation and in the Bible; and they were dissatisfied with the partial reformation brought in by King Henry and his daughter, Queen Elizabeth. In particular they favored preaching that would emphasize salvation through grace, a gift from God, rather than human works; and they wanted to abolish "pagan" elements of worship, such as priestly garments and stained glass windows.

Most of the early Puritans wanted to change the church from within, seeking to practice their faith without formally separating from the Church of England. But the Anglican authorities continually limited their ability to worship freely. In Browne's first clerical position as chaplain to the family of the Duke of Norfolk, he was able to preach Puritan doctrine freely because his powerful employer insisted that his personal chaplain should be free from ecclesiastical supervision. Browne next taught school at Southwark and preached secretly to men and women who gathered in a nearby gravel pit: such was the inconvenience of religious life without the protection of a powerful patron.

Browne next returned to Cambridge and studied theology under Richard Greenham, a minister who ran a sort of theological seminary in his home at Dry Drayton. Browne began preaching in Anglican pulpits in Cambridge, and after he had served one congregation for six months, the parishioners invited him to be their minister. Knowing him, they probably shared his Puritan leanings, and Browne might well have become one of the many English ministers who quietly reformed his church while accepting a few Anglican ceremonies to keep his bishop happy.

But Browne would make no such compromise. He had come to believe that the Anglican church was a false church and that salvation must be sought in a separate organization. He could not accept ordination at the hands of a bishop without violating his principles. So he declined the post in Cambridge and moved to Norwich, the chief town in nearby Norfolk County, where he formed an illegal congregation of like-minded Christians: this was the historical antecedent of the Congregational church.

With the help of a friend, Robert Harrison, Browne extended his preaching throughout the region. In Bury St. Edmunds, according to a critical bishop, Browne ministered to common men and women who gathered in groups as large as a hundred to hear him preach in private houses. Inevitably Browne's ministry came to the attention of the bishop of Norwich. Browne was not imprisoned, but he recognized that to worship freely, he would have to migrate to Holland. With Harrison and other Norwich followers he moved to Middelburg in the fall of 1581.

Within a year Browne had written three treatises on doctrine, polity, and worship. In the words of Williston Walker, the great nineteenth-century Congregational historian, these tracts present "with great clearness the essential features of modern Congregationalism."[1] Browne argued in favor of a church of believers, and condemned the Anglicans for including all English men and women in the church. He organized his church around the pattern that he believed to have been practiced in the early churches described in the New Testament. Its members were regenerate Christians called out of a hostile world to worship together. The congregation appointed its own leaders, and each member enjoyed a direct relationship to God. The minister was ordained by leading members of the congregation rather than by bishops or fellow ministers. Moreover, the congregation wrote its own religious constitution in the form of a covenant among the founding members. Although each congregation was to be independent, Browne anticipated that the separate churches would meet together to discuss matters of common interest.

After founding the Middelburg congregation and writing his treatises, Browne fell out with his associate, Robert Harrison, and moved to Scotland with a few followers in 1583. Scottish Presbyterian authorities refused to allow Browne and his followers to worship freely, and so Browne returned to England. Once more he offended the authorities and was imprisoned. He might have been executed, but for his relationship to an English lord—and his decision in 1586 to make peace with the Church of England.

Congregationalism would have its martyrs—two of Browne's followers, John Coppin and Elias Thacker, were hanged in 1583 for distributing Browne's treatises. But Browne himself was one of those dissenters who could sustain an independent religious course for only a short time. In 1591 he became Anglican minister of Achurch cum Thorpe, where he lived obscurely for the remaining four decades of his life. He probably died without realizing that his Norwich congregation and his Middelburg treatises would be regarded as the germination of a religious denomination that would one day have adherents throughout the world.

THE ORIGIN AND MEANINGS OF PURITANISM

The obscure parson and sometime rebel Robert Browne was in some respects, then, the father of Congregationalism. The distinguishing mark of early Congregationalism was an ecclesiastical system in which each church controlled its own affairs. Every parish chose its minister, admitted church members, and administered discipline without the interference of bishops, presbyteries, or any other form of ecclesiastical hierarchy. Polity gave Congregationalism its name.[2]

But the vital force in early Congregationalism was more doctrinal than administrative—and for that matter, more spiritual than doctrinal. The sources of Congregationalism lay in the Reformation, the Puritan movement, and in Christianity itself. None of the springs of the new movement was more important than the religious sensibility that came to be known as Puritanism. During the seventeenth century Puritans supported diverse religious organizations, becoming Quakers, Baptists, and Presbyterians, as well as Congregationalists. But for several decades the two movements, Puritanism and Congregationalism, were essentially one. And the goal of the Puritan-Congregationalist movement was to establish the Kingdom of God on earth, in the hearts of men and women and in the ordering of society.

The preachers of England and New England loved to find colorful images to describe the ideal union of God and humanity. Both the heavenly Lord and the human spirit were intangible and elusive, but through compelling phrases these unseen entities could be made visible and accessible. One of the finest of these word pictures was written by Thomas Shepard, a seventeenth century Congregational minister at Cambridge, Massachusetts: "As iron put into the fire seems to be nothing but fire," he said, "so Adam, beloved of God, was turned into a lump of love, to love God again."[3]

Shepard had chosen his words carefully. He must often have watched black-smiths at work, holding metal to flame until it glowed warmly, becoming fire itself. So God, like the flames, should enter into a Christian and transform him into a spark of divinity. Achieving this condition was the primary goal of worship. Puritans believed that human beings were separated from the Lord by sin and that human happiness could be achieved only through overcoming that separation. God and humanity had been united in the Garden of Eden, and they would be reunited when Christ returned to earth. But in the mean time, men and women needed to reduce the distance between the ideal and the real. As individuals they should aspire towards personal salvation. And as members of communities they should attempt to create a more godly nation through personal virtue, family government, Christian labor, political morality, and ecclesiastical reform.

The Puritan movement began long before there were English Puritans. The aspiration towards perfect union with God finds antecedents in the lives of Paul, Augustine, Francis, Wycliffe, and other early Christians. As a specific episode in Christian history, however, Puritanism began in sixteenth-century England. When Henry VIII divorced Catherine of Aragon, broke with Rome, and established himself as head of the Church of England, he began for England an uneasy association with the Protestant Reformation. Henry destroyed the monasteries, authorized an English translation of the Bible and removed Catholic images from places of worship. He limited ecclesiastical courts, outlawed canon law, and ordered relics and images destroyed. He beheaded his one-time friend and former Chancellor, Sir Thomas More, for refusing to assent to the royal supremacy. And Henry crushed a Catholic uprising in northern England, known as the Pilgrimage of Grace, by hanging two hundred of the rebels. At Cambridge a group of Protestant reformers, including Thomas Cranmer, who became Henry's archbishop of Canterbury, met at the White Horse Tavern and discussed the writings of Martin Luther and other Continental reformers. In all of these respects Henry's England embraced the Reformation. In other ways, however, Henry adhered to traditional forms of worship and church government, much to the chagrin of more ardent reformers. His Six Articles perpetuated traditional Catholic doctrine. He followed Catholic tradition in demanding that priests be celibate, and he suppressed an English translation of the Bible written by William Tyndale.

Henry's son Edward was only nine when he became king in 1547, but his training led him to favor the Reformation. He allowed Reformed theologians, such as Peter Martyr and Martin Butzer, to become professors at Oxford and

Cambridge. With Edward's encouragement, Archbishop Cranmer prepared a liturgy in English, *The Book of Common Prayer*. The Reformed character of Edward's church was most apparent in the Forty-two Articles of Religion, issued in 1553. These included such Reformed ideas as predestination and the symbolic interpretation of the Eucharist. Finally, the English clergy began to preach more often and effectively. The reformers, beginning with Martin Luther, had emphasized the importance of the minister's delivering the Word of God to the Congregation—a radical innovation at a time when many priests did not preach at all. One of the best of the new English ministers was Hugh Latimer, who preached plain sermons that set a standard for English pulpit oratory directed towards the people.

Edward died in 1553, and his sister, Mary, came to the throne. After her father had divorced her mother, Catherine of Aragon, the frightened Mary had sometimes been treated as a bastard. She naturally sought consolation in the Catholic Church and grew up with a fervent attachment to Rome. Mary's dislike for Protestantism continued to grow during her brother's reign, when she was not even allowed to attend mass. As queen she was determined to lead England back to the days before the break with Rome. She restored five pro-Catholic bishops, deprived two thousand married clerics of their salaries, and imprisoned or exiled many Protestant leaders. Parliament repealed legislation supporting the prayer book and clerical marriage. And the convocation of Canterbury reinstituted the Catholic doctrine of transubstantiation, which interprets the bread and wine of the Eucharist as inwardly the actual flesh and blood of Christ rather than symbolic representations.

Mary's policies were popular at first, for Protestantism had taken only a weak hold in England during the previous two decades. She might have been a popular queen if she had been willing to organize a national church in England along Catholic lines. But she sought a complete return to the past, and this alienated many of her countrymen. Those who had benefited from the dissolution of the monasteries worried that she would make them return their new lands. Those fearing clerical oppression opposed her choice of Papal Legate Reginald Pole as archbishop of Canterbury. Nationalists disliked her marriage to Philip II of Spain and her unsuccessful military campaigns in Europe on behalf of Catholic monarchs.

Most of all Mary made enemies by burning some three hundred religious dissenters. The victims of Mary's purge ranged from simple artisans and their wives to the archbishop of Canterbury, Thomas Cranmer. Mary hoped that their deaths at the stake would rid the realm of Protestantism, but many of the victims died so bravely and so full of zeal for the Reformation that they were regarded as martyrs. Thomas Cranmer, who had previously signed a recantation of his Protestant views, held his offending hand to the flames. Bishop Hugh Latimer told Bishop Nicholas Ridley as both were about to be burned, "We shall this day light such a candle, by God's grace, in England as shall never be put out."[4] Sympathetic crowds gathered to watch the executions and carefully wrapped the victims' ashes in shrouds. With these deaths the Protestant cause gained new adherents; it became the cause of virtue, courage, and nationalism. When Mary died on the morning of November 17, 1558, and coincidentally her archbishop of Canterbury died a few hours later, few English men and women lamented their passing.

Henry's other daughter, Elizabeth, came to the throne in 1558 after Mary's death. She realized that the only way to avoid religious turmoil was to steer a moderate course between Catholicism and extreme Protestantism. Under the Elizabethan Settlement of 1559 the church again broke from Rome and adopted a reformed prayer book; in 1563 the Thirty-nine Articles, based on Edward's Forty-two Articles, set forth the main elements of Anglican doctrine. The most important of these measures was *The Book of Common Prayer*, which is substantially the book created by Thomas Cranmer and adopted by Edward's church in 1552. Its literary elegance and doctrinal moderation made it, in Sydney Ahlstrom's words, "the quintessential expression of Anglicanism."[5]

The Elizabethan Settlement included much to encourage an English reformer. As orthodox a Protestant as Cotton Mather would remark, a century later, that Elizabeth's Thirty-nine Articles were consistent with the Westminster Confession, one of the principal statements of Congregational beliefs. But some Englishmen felt that Elizabeth's reforms did not go far enough. Those reformers who in the late sixteenth century protested against the remaining Catholic elements in the church became known as "Puritans," a derisive name based on their seemingly excessive demands for a pure church. As so often happens with such expressions, the dissenters gloried in their nickname, and it stuck.

The Puritans opposed clerical vestments, making the sign of the cross in baptism and communion, confirmation, kneeling at communion, using the term *priest* to signify a minister, the saints' days, bowing at the name of Jesus, organs, and singing in parts. All of these observances seemed popish to them. The vestments put too much emphasis on the minister, taking attention away from God, and saints' days focused worship on people rather than upon God.

In addition the Puritans insisted on an educated preaching clergy. They held that the essential element in Christian worship was the delivery by the minister of the Word of God. Moreover, the the Puritans believed that the minister's primary obligation was to his own flock; no bishops and archbishops should supervise his activities. Above all the Puritans sought to intensify religious life within each English parish, and ultimately, within each English family. To this end they favored the widespread distribution of the Bible, particularly the Geneva Version of 1560, which had been translated by Miles Coverdale and other English Protestants who became exiles during the reign of Queen Mary.

For several decades the Puritans tried unsuccessfully to win support for their reforms. During the 1560s and 1570s they sought to persuade Parliament to abolish clerical vestments and to adopt a Presbyterian form of government, placing control of the church in local congregations and ministerial associations rather than in an episcopal hierarchy. But Parliament upheld the status quo. At Cambridge, Thomas Cartwright, the Lady Margaret Professor of Divinity, delivered lectures in 1570 favoring Presbyterianism. He was removed from his post and went into exile in Geneva. During the years 1586–88 John Field led a a movement to win nationwide support for Presbyterianism. His death in 1588 ended the attempt.

Despairing of victory a few Englishmen decided to start secret Reformed congregations of their own rather than wait upon a universal reformation. Robert Browne's abortive efforts to reform the church at Norwich—"reformation without tarying for anie," he called it—was simply one expression of the desire to create in England a different sort of church than the Anglican establishment.[6]

Most English reformers, however, could not accept such piecemeal attempts at reform. They believed they must reform society as a whole, not simply preserve themselves as a holy remnant. In 1603, when James I ascended the throne, many Puritans felt that their time had at last arrived. James had been raised in Presbyterian Scotland, and would, it was hoped, carry on the Reformation in England. He even met with Puritan representatives at Hampton Court in 1604 and promised to make some changes in the liturgy and the ministry.

But otherwise his reign was a disappointment to the reformers. He demanded that the Puritans conform to the Church of England. And the new archbishop of Canterbury, Richard Bancroft, was even more hostile to the Puritans than his predecessor and drove many of them from their pulpits. Under Bancroft's regime William Ames, the foremost Puritan theologian of his time, was forced into exile for refusing to wear clerical vestments and use the sign of the cross in baptism.

The early history of Congregationalism was, thus, a history of successive defeats in the arena of national policy. And yet in another sphere, that of personal conscience and conduct, Puritanism fared well late in the sixteenth and early in the seventeenth centuries. At Oxford and Cambridge, Puritans held sway in several colleges, and Emmanuel College was founded at Cambridge by Sir Walter Mildmay in 1584 as a nursery of Puritanism. There and elsewhere Puritan theologians such as Laurence Chaderton, William Perkins, and John Preston taught their students a distinctively Puritan view of the relationship between humanity and God. These pupils, in turn, took the message to the English people.

Although they could not openly attack Anglican ceremonies, the Puritan graduates of Oxford and Cambridge could preach Puritan doctrine in the great churches of London and the remote corners of the realm, and in so doing they could alter the complexion of English society. Their central theme was a Protestant description of God, sin, and salvation.

Puritans described God as the creator and supreme ruler of the universe, so far above his creation that he was unseen and incomprehensible. He was like the weather in that no person could predict or guide his course. Men could not look upon the Lord any more than they could stare at the sun. And yet his very remoteness gave cause for admiration. As one minister wrote: "We admire the luster of the sun the more in that it is so great we cannot behold it."[7]

Despite God's mysterious character, the Puritans felt that he was not detached from human life; he filled the world with his being, guiding human history by divine providence. The Lord was both infinitely remote and infinitely present. He could appear in nature, as he did when Anne Bradstreet in frontier Andover, Massachusetts, saw a beautiful sunset and wrote: "More of heaven than earth was here."[8] And if viewed properly, the whole earth testified to God's existence. Thomas Shepard declared: "Can we when we behold the stately theater of heaven and earth, conclude other but that the finger, arms, and wisdom of God hath been here?...Who taught the birds to build their nests, and the bees to set up and order their commonwealth? Who sends the sun post from one end of heaven to the other, carrying so many thousand blessings to so many thousands of people and kingdoms? What power of man or angels can make the least pile of grass, or put life into the least fly if once dead?"[9]

For the Puritans God was the source of life, strength, wisdom, and happiness. He gave human existence its purpose and exhilaration. And yet many men and women failed even to recognize God's existence. Most were "notorious worldlings, that look no higher than their barns, no farther than their shops." The Puritans regarded this absorption in the world as the essence of sin.

Sin was wrong because it distracted people from God. The sinner was "a dead corpse, lying rotting and stinking in the grave."[10] Sinners might appear to be alive: frolicking in the tavern, fornicating with whores, cheating in business. But they were dead in the thing that mattered most—their relationship with God. Thomas Hooker, a seventeenth-century minister, described the sinner's plight: "Shame takes away my honor, poverty my wealth, persecution my peace, prison my liberty, death my life, yet a man may still be a happy man, lose his life, and live eternally: But sin takes away my God, and with him all good goes."[11]

The Puritans believed that most men and women ruined their lives by chasing after the wrong objects. From morning until night they sought worldly pleasures. Good meals, fine clothes, elegant houses: these were their gods. But such things could not even satisfy men's material needs. "Thy clothes may warm thee," declared Thomas Shepard, "but they cannot feed thee; thy meat may feed thee, but cannot heal thee; thy physic may heal thee, but cannot maintain thee; thy money may maintain thee, but cannot comfort thee when distresses of conscience and anguish come upon thee."[12]

God was the source of all that was good, but sin separated people from God. The human story might have ended there, but for a third element, salvation through Christ. To Puritans, people were by nature "dead in sin." Cut off from God, they deserved only misery in this world and eternal damnation hereafter. But for humanity's sake, Christ, the Son of God, had died upon the cross, taking upon himself the sins of the world. God was willing to forgive and redeem those men and women who believed in Christ.

Puritans gave many sermons explaining the mystery of redemption. One could not win salvation simply by doing good deeds. Redemption came only when grace entered a believer's soul and allowed him or her to see the Lord. Men and women could prepare for grace by lamenting their sins and praying for pure hearts. But salvation came only through the free gift of God.

Puritan saints so disciplined their minds that they waited continually upon the gift of grace. In this expectation they could be stern and introverted, fearful of frivolity and worldliness. They were taught to consider that there was "a snare...in every lawful liberty." They needed to ask themselves: "May I not sin in my mirth, in my speaking, in my sleeping?"[13]

This austere self-control led to the Puritan reputation for excessive sternness. We should not, however, exaggerate the Puritan opposition to pleasure. Puritans tried to pursue a moderate path in all things. They would "be merry in the Lord, and yet without lightness."[14] The things of the world were there to be enjoyed, but not to excess. One or two glasses of wine at dinner, for example, were fine, but drunkenness was not. The Puritans disapproved of sexual relationships outside of marriage. Between husband and wife, however, connubial bliss was not only allowable, but positively expected. In Massachusetts Bay judges sometimes scolded lethargic husbands of wives in court for not having sexual intercourse often enough with their spouses!

Men and women were free to enjoy food and drink and lovemaking as long as they recognized that these earthly comforts must be subordinate to a greater pleasure in God. All other joys were transitory, but this was eternal. "This God is a joy in sadness, light in darkness, life in death, heaven in hell," said Shepard. "Here is all thine eye ever saw, thine heart ever desired, thy tongue ever asked, thy mind ever conceived. Here is all light in this sun, and all water in this sea, out of whom, as out of a crystal fountain, thou shalt drink down all the refined sweetness of all creatures in heaven and earth forever and ever. All the world is now seeking and tiring out themselves for rest; here only it can be found."[15] Perry Miller, the foremost Puritan scholar, summarized this piety in a suggestive phrase: "Men were made believers by an inward gladness."[16]

The main object of the Puritan religious life was to achieve "inward gladness" by making the spiritual journey from the natural condition of sin to the supernatural state of grace. A central element in Puritan sermons was the tale of the saint's difficult progress to redemption. The soul was portrayed sometimes as a hardy warrior fighting for a cause and sometimes as a poor pilgrim lost in the desert or confined in jail. In a famous analogy, John Cotton likened the convert's journey to grace to a man's walking into a body of water. First he "wades in the rivers of God his grace up to the ankles." Then he goes in up to his knees. Grace refreshes his legs, but the rest of his body is still untouched and thus corrupt. The man goes on until finally he is afloat in God's grace. "There is such a measure of grace," says Cotton, "in which a man may swim as fish in the water, with all readiness and dexterity."[17]

Stories like these abound in Puritan sermons. They can be likened to folk tales because of their dramatic quality and their appeal to the common people of England and New England. The Puritan saint was expected to walk through life as if on a journey to heaven. "In whatsoever place thou art," Puritans were told, "whether alone or abroad, by day or by night, and whatsoever thou art doing, set thyself in the presence of God."[18] Long before some "Pilgrims" made the physical journey to New England, Puritans thought of themselves as pilgrims. They lived in the world, but they attempted to set their hearts on heaven. This piety led to distinctive modes of behavior.

In seeking frequent communion with God, Puritans ideally began each day by praying silently in their beds. Then the father, as head of the household, would pray and read from Scripture before the whole family. These services would be repeated in the evening, and during the day the devout Puritan would try to find more time for prayer and meditation.

Puritans regarded the whole Sabbath day as the Lord's own time. They frequently attended long church services in the morning and the afternoon, and they set aside the rest of the day for reading Scripture, discussing the sermon, meditating, and other forms of devotion. One of their primary grievances against King James was that he encouraged his people to devote their Sundays after church to sports, such as soccer. James believed that such exercises would strengthen his people and make them better soldiers. The Puritans, however, were devoted first to Christian warfare against sin and regarded the king's suggestions as an abomination. One can imagine them listening in dismay to the howls of neighbors engaged in village soccer on Sunday.

Through family worship and honoring the Sabbath, Puritans demonstrated their love of God. Their piety also required virtuous conduct in secular affairs. Above all they regarded their vocation as a holy duty. Housewifery, farming, trading, and other enterprises were ordained by the Lord. A person should work hard and serve their community and God in their callings. Merchants, for example, should not cheat their customers or charge them more than a "fair price." The purpose was not to enrich oneself, but to serve humanity.

Because Puritanism encouraged hard work and orderly conduct, it has sometimes been associated with capitalism. Certainly many Puritans did become wealthy because of their diligence and efficiency. They even regarded their riches as signs of God's approval. But we must not conclude that Puritanism led easily to materialism. The Puritans did not endorse wealth as an end in itself and sternly opposed the gaudy display of riches. As in other matters, they sought to pursue a moderate course, regarding wealth with detachment. Attractive as it might have been, prosperity was not to interfere with their relationship to God.

A PURITAN MICROCOSM: JOHN AND THOMASINE WINTHROP

In such precepts we can see the broad contours of Puritan piety and the emergence of a historical movement, with its essential doctrines and its code of behavior. Let us consider how these elements entered into the lives of two typical Puritans, John and Thomasine Winthrop. In the story of their brief life together we can gain a fuller appreciation of the character of Puritan piety.

John and Thomasine were both children of East Anglian gentry families. In the mid-sixteenth century John's grandfather, Adam, had purchased a church property known as Groton Manor, when Henry VIII sought to further the Reformation and enrich himself by dissolving the monasteries. A second Adam Winthrop, John's father, inherited the manor. John Winthrop was born in 1588, the year that the English defeated the Spanish Armada.

The land where the Winthrops lived was in the southern part of Suffolk, not far from the border with Essex. The gently rolling country was covered with rich farmland, green marshes, ponds, and forests of oaks, beeches, and willows. Noted for its mutton, beef, butter, and cheese, it was a pastoral land—though the white gulls that flew over the Groton ponds reminded people that the sea was only a few miles away.

John was raised on the manor until the age of fourteen, when he went to Cambridge to attend Trinity College. He stayed at Cambridge for only two years, returning to Groton when nearly seventeen to help his father run the manor. He so impressed his parents with his maturity that they consented to his marriage to Mary Forth, the twenty-year-old daughter of a neighboring gentleman. John and Mary lived together for ten years until her death in 1615, when she left him with four children.

Although John lamented Mary's death, in those days a bereaved spouse seldom remained single for long. Marriage was a practical as well as a personal and romantic relationship, for a wife's help was essential in raising children and overseeing a household. Shortly after he lost Mary, John began to court Thomasine Clopton, whom he undoubtedly knew already. She was the daughter of William Clopton, the squire of a nearby estate. The couple married in the autumn of 1616.

Thomasine was a good wife, "industrious," "plain hearted," and "patient of injuries." She showed her love of God in public and private worship, and cared for John's children as if they were her own. John was so attracted to her that he would recall, after her death, that their affection "had this only inconvenience, that it made me delight too much in her to enjoy her long."[19]

During their year together John and Thomasine spent most of their time in the prosaic work of managing their country estate. The Winthrop Papers and descriptions of other households allow us to draw a picture of their daily life. On a typical spring day they would awake with the crowing of the cock. They would dress quickly in their chilly room and hurry downstairs to a warm fire prepared by the servants. John's four children would soon arrive and huddle near the flames warming themselves, while the servants came in from the kitchen. Each morning John read to the family from the Bible and offered a prayer asking for God's favor in the day ahead.

Over breakfast John and Thomasine might discuss the day's activities with the children and servants. After they finished the meal, John would likely tour the manor to see that all was in order, inspecting cattle and pigs and supervising his servants in the fields or woodlot. On many spring mornings the air was damp and cold, but there were pleasant days when the sun broke through the clouds to the east and the wind bore the scent of salt water off the North Sea. Since most physical labor at Groton was carried out by servants, John could devote time to studying the Bible and other religious works. We may imagine him retiring to his study after touring the manor.

Thomasine would supervise the domestic chores, seeing that rooms were dusted, floors swept, butter churned and meals prepared. She might attend personally to a garden of flowers, vegetables, and herbs. While men supervised grain cultivation, English women usually tended radishes, beets, carrots, cabbage, cucumbers, onions, melons, parsley, cloves, and other garden crops.

At supper the family might discuss the day's events. John would again read from the Bible, and they would sing a Psalm. That spring, Thomasine learned that she was pregnant. In bed she and her husband might discuss the new baby, John wondering whether she felt well and Thomasine worrying about the older children's reaction to a new brother or sister. John might tell her, as he later wrote in his diary, that his children already loved her like a mother.

On the surface, life at Groton Manor seems a kind of agrarian paradise. The family was close; everyone was well fed, clothed, and housed; the men and women spent their days in honest toil. John and Thomasine believed, however, that they must not become too absorbed in the pleasures of day-to-day life. Instead they should think constantly about their relationship to God.

John Winthrop's interest in religion began at an early age. When he was ten, he came to have "some notions of God," but he characterized himself as being "lewdly disposed," "wild and dissolute," and dominated by a "voluptuous heart."[20] This does not mean that he spent his time drinking, whoring, and stealing. The only youthful sin he specifically mentions in his later writings is the theft of two books when he was a small boy. When John referred to himself as possessing a "voluptuous heart," he was probably describing the course of his imagination rather than his actual behavior. But although such activity may not qualify as dissolute today, this failure to master his desires grieved John. He believed that a good Christian would discipline his heart and think about God in all his free moments. Sin was present, he believed, in "all such works as are done to fulfill the will of the flesh rather than of the spirit."

By the age of eighteen John Winthrop was deeply concerned with his spiritual condition. Now for the first time the Word came into his "heart with power." He would walk for miles to hear a good sermon and developed a reputation for giving good spiritual advice to others. But he also became proud, and, since he realized that without Christ's grace none of his good works would save him, he began to despair that perhaps he was only a hypocrite.

Throughout his twenties John's religious life consisted of alternating periods of assurance and doubt. He abandoned hunting and cards because he felt that they interfered with his spiritual life. He attempted to devote more time to prayer, meditation, and religious reading, but frequently failed to meet his own high standards of behavior. He accused himself of having become too frivolous in his relationships with friends and worried that he ate and drank more than was appropriate. Once he condemned himself because during a church service he began thinking about a journey he was about to take into Essex, and soon his heart was "possessed with the world."

John Winthrop sought to "tame his heart" by regulating his diet, singing Psalms while traveling, and reading tracts. But he found that complete abstinence from the pleasures of the world left him "melancholy" and "dumpish." He found that complete asceticism was as destructive to his spiritual equilibrium as excessive worldliness. So he tried to find a moderate course between these two experiences.

The goal of John's constant self-regulation was a "felt" relationship with Christ. Puritans believed that God should be experienced emotionally as well as understood mentally. For John such moments of spiritual illumination were rare but compelling. In 1612, for example, after comforting an old man with spiritual advice, John went to bed and dreamed that he was with Christ. "I was so ravished with his love towards me," he writes, "...that being awakened it had made so deep an impression in my heart, as I was forced to unmeasurable weepings for a great while."

Despite such experience of ecstatic acceptance by God, John Winthrop often felt that he was too concerned with the world. His religious life was a constant struggle to "tame" his heart to a complete service to God. On the manor he was responsible for overseeing a complex economy, planting crops, buying and selling livestock, gathering rents, and a dozen other duties. Important as these activities were, however, when he wrote about his own life or went to bed at night, his greatest worry was often whether his rebellious heart had indulged too much in the world.

We know less about Thomasine's religious life than we do about John's. But it is apparent that she, too, was a serious Christian and believed that salvation came through God's grace. John later praised her for her reverent attention to religious services at home and in church, and noted that she avoided "all evil" herself and reproved sin in others. Undoubtedly, on many evenings after they had discussed crops, children, or servants, they ended the day by praying or reading Scripture.

John and Thomasine thus spent their days attending to matters temporal and spiritual. The year 1616 progressed from season to season. In the summer there were bright days interrupted occasionally by sharp storms of thunder and lightning. Then came the time to harvest and thresh the wheat. In October, grey clouds darkened the skies; crisp night air and geese flying overhead announced the approach of winter. The hearth with its crackling fire drew the family to it in the morning. John and Adam fished their main pond, catching carp for dinner. In preparation for winter the family salted fish and pressed apples into cider to store in the cellar.

Thomasine was less active now. She spent time preparing for the new baby, making blankets and a bunting. With fewer chores she spent more time playing games with the children and helping them read. In November she had difficulty moving and sleeping comfortably. Then on Saturday, November 30, she felt that her time had arrived.[21] John summoned a midwife, who came to the house with several neighbor women, and encouraged Thomasine. They heated kettles of water while Thomasine bore her pains patiently, asking constantly about the child. People would later remark "how careful she was" for the life of the baby during her travail. At last the infant was born, a tiny girl. She was washed by the women and then placed alongside her mother. John now entered the chamber and sat beside Thomasine and their daughter. He offered prayers of thanks for the baby's safe delivery.

That night John slept in a separate room, leaving Thomasine under the watchful eye of a "keeper," a woman who made sure that mother and child were well. On the following morning, a Sunday, John arose early and came to the room. When Thomasine awoke, he sat with her, and prayed for the continuing health of mother and daughter. After breakfast John, his parents, and the other children went to church. Later on Sunday, the child weakened, and on Monday morning she was dead. John later recorded that Thomasine took the child's death with "patience," by which he meant that she accepted the loss as God's will. In view of Thomasine's earlier concern for the child, people now "marvelled" at her ability to accept its death.

But John had little time to think about the loss of his infant daughter, for his wife now grew ill with a violent fever and cough. The next morning these symptoms were allayed, but her mouth was sore, she grew hoarse, and her throat bled. John began to fear for her life. On Wednesday he sent for his cousin, a doctor. When Thomasine heard that a physician was coming, she told John she expected to die. People were frequently not told the truth about their ailments, for fear of upsetting them, but Thomasine did not wish to be deceived.

"John," she said, "when cousin Duke comes, I hope that he will deal plainly with me and not fill me with vain hopes."

Forced by his wife to see her danger, John began to cry. Thomasine was moved by his tears and begged him "to be contented"—to accept her condition with patience—"for you break my heart with your grievings."

John replied, "I can do no less when I fear to be stripped of such a blessing."

Forgetting her pain, Thomasine now sought to comfort her husband. John later recalled, "Always when she perceived me to mourn for her, she would entreat and persuade me to be contented, telling me that she did love me well, and if God would let her live with me, she would endeavor to show it more." She urged him to pray for her and stay near.

At noon, Thursday, the doctor arrived, and after examining Thomasine he declared her condition dangerous. When John told her this, she was "no whit moved at it, but was as comfortably resolved whether to live or to die." In this condition of resignation, of willingness to accept life or death from God, she fell asleep. At midnight she awakened, feeling that death was near, and called John to help her prepare. She wanted also to see her ministers and other friends and so desired "that the bell might ring for her."

In the early morning hours the neighbors came one by one to talk by candlelight "quietly and comfortably" with Thomasine. The bell began to toll. John tells us that "some said it was the four o'clock bell, but she conceiving that they sought to conceal it from her, that it did ring for her, she said they needed not, for it did not trouble her." The ringing of the bell was a traditional way of telling a community that someone was critically ill. It allowed men and women in and around Groton, who already knew of Thomasine's difficulty, to visit her or say prayers or simply be concerned.

Certain now that she would die, Thomasine called in all her family one by one to give them her final advice. Her parting words to her sisters included admonitions to serve God, marry for religious rather than worldly considerations, avoid lying, and raise their children well. Then she spoke to her mother, noting that she, Thomasine, was the first child her mother would bury and praying that her mother would not be "discomforted." Her mother, a pious woman, replied, "I have no cause to be discomforted. You will go to a better place, and you will be with your father again." The thought must have helped her mother, but Thomasine, perhaps overly self-righteous now, noted that she would go to God and hence she would be with "a better father than her earthly father."

Then she spoke to members of John's family, thanking his parents for their kindness and blessing the children. She spoke to the servants, praising some and scolding others and encouraging them to behave well and observe the Sabbath. Finally, she told the woman who had served as her keeper not to blame herself for what had happened.

Thomasine was still in great pain. Her breasts were so swollen that her friends cut her waistcoat to give her some relief. She uttered many prayers and exhorted those around her to prepare to die, telling them that they did not know "how sharp and bitter the pangs of death were." She asked God to "bless good ministers, and convert such ill ones as did belong to him, and weed out the rest."

It was apparent now that "God had given her victory" in her spiritual struggle. In the afternoon her pains lessened, and she told John she expected to live for another twenty-four hours. Through the afternoon and into the evening he read the Scriptures to her. Thomasine was attentive, remarking on his texts and asking John "earnestly" to read on whenever he paused. "This is comfortable," or "this is a sweet Psalm," she would say.

In the evening the Reverend Sands came and prayed. Thomasine took him by the hand and bid him farewell. Then John retired, leaving his wife in the care of a woman who continued to read to her late into the night. Thomasine frequently asked about John, and at two in the morning he came to her again.

It was now Sunday, and at times Thomasine had doubts again about her conversion, saying that the devil wanted her to cast off her "subjection" to her husband. At noon when others were at dinner, John and Thomasine continued to talk. John assured her of Christ's love for her and told her "how she should sup with Christ in paradise that night." From Groton Manor in Suffolk, England, she would actually go into the presence of Abraham, Isaac, Jacob, and the other prophets, apostles, and saints. This thought so encouraged Thomasine that she said "if life were set before her she would not take it."

Thomasine and John conversed throughout the afternoon. He told her that the previous day had been the first anniversary of their marriage and that now she was going to Christ who would "embrace her with another manner of love." She misunderstood him and replied, "O husband, I must not love thee as Christ."

After a while she could no longer speak, but lay back with her eyes "steadfastly" upon John, as he spoke to her about the promises of the Gospel and the "happy estate" she was "entering into." If he paused, she would signal him feebly with her hands, urging him to continue. At five o'clock on Sunday afternoon, a minister came to pray with her. At the end of the prayer she sighed and fell "asleep in the Lord." Three days later, she was buried beside John's first wife in Groton chancel. Her child was taken from its tiny grave and laid by her.

During the days that followed, John Winthrop thought often about the course of his life.[22] A small sin committed many years before troubled him. As a boy visiting a house, he had spied two books. Reasoning that the owner had thrown them away, he took them with him. The memory of that act grieved him, especially in times of affliction. Now, troubled once more, he made "satisfaction" for the books, probably by paying something or returning them to the owner.

In January 1617 Winthrop attended a court session, usually an occasion for entertainment as well as business. This time, however, he felt detached from the worldly pastimes of his colleagues. Later, on a trip to London he noted that although he used to "lose all my time in my journeys, my eyes running upon every object, and my thoughts varying with every occasion," now he passed the time in prayer, Psalm singing, and meditation.

Later in life John would identify this period as his time of greatest piety—he felt powerfully that Christ accepted and loved him. This was not merely an intellectual conclusion, but rather a pressing conviction of Christ's presence. "I was not grown familiar with the Lord Jesus Christ," he wrote. "He would oft tell me he loved me. I did not doubt to believe him. If I went abroad, he went with me; when I returned, he came home with me. I talked with him upon the way, he lay down with me and usually I did awake with him. Now I could go into any company and not lose him."

The story of John and Thomasine Winthrop shows how Puritanism entered daily life. The Winthrop history is on one level an account of prosaic secular events—tending an estate, governing a household, bearing a child, and enduring death. It is also, however, the story of a Christian pilgrimage. Through prayer, Bible reading, and meditation John and Thomasine tried to bring God into their daily lives. Perhaps they were never able to glow continually with God's love like the iron in the blacksmith's fire, described by Thomas Shepard. But they were able to view the end of life as a transformation rather than a termination. Here was the moment when the longed-for union with God could become a reality.

In their daily lives and in their confrontation with death, John and Thomasine Winthrop embodied the Puritan ideal of seeking to live "in the presence of God." During the years when James I ruled England, Puritan piety shaped the course of life in many English households. Thousands of families like the Winthrops were willing to nourish their Puritan piety at home without concerning themselves greatly about reforming the nation as a whole. Certainly they disliked the episcopacy, the King's *Book of Sports*, and the "popish" elements of the church service. But Puritan ministers were generally free to preach as they wished, and in obscure parishes or areas ruled by sympathetic bishops they could even modify the service and preach without clerical vestments. With such encouragement Puritan families like the Winthrops could practise their piety freely, worrying less about bishops and kings than about their own inner lives.

NOTES

[1] Williston Walker, *The Creeds and Platforms of Congregationalism* (Boston, 1960), 12.

[2] The account that follows is based on the author's essay, "The Social Impact of Puritanism," in Geoffrey Barraclough, ed., *The Christian World* (London and New York, 1981), 201-14.

[3] Thomas Shepard, *The Sincere Convert* (Boston, 1853), 19.

[4] John Bartlett, *Familiar Quotations* (Boston, 1980), 156.

[5] Sydney Ahlstrom, *A Religious History of the American People* (New Haven, 1972), 90.

[6] Robert Browne, *A Treatise of Reformation without Tarying for Anie* (Middelburg, Holland, 1582).

[7] Shepard, *Sincere Convert*, 14.

[8] Anne Bradstreet, "Contemplations," in Perry Miller and Thomas H. Johnson, eds., *The Puritans* (New York, 1938), 564.

[9] Shepard, *Sincere Convert*, 10.

[10] Richard Rogers, *A Garden of Spiritual Flowers* (London, 1667), [3].

[11] Thomas Hooker, "A True Sight of Sin," in Perry Miller, ed., *The American Puritans* (New York, 1956), 159.

[12] Shepard, *Sincere Convert*, 15.

[13] Shepard, *Sincere Convert*, 84.

[14] Richard Rogers, *Seven Treatises* (London, 1610), preface.

[15] Shepard, *Sincere Convert*, 15-16.

[16] Perry Miller, *The New England Mind: The Seventeenth Century* (New York, 1939), 63.

[17] John Cotton, *The Way of Life* (London, 1641), 104-5.

[18] William Perkins, "A Grain of Mustard Seed," in Perkins, *Workes* (London, 1616), 642.

[19] John Winthrop, "Death of Thomasine Clopton Winthrop, 1616," in Samuel Eliot Morison, et al., eds., *Winthrop Papers* (New York, 1968), vol. 1, 190. The account which follows relies particularly on the Winthrop Papers and Edmund S. Morgan, *The Puritan Dilemma: The Story of John Winthrop* (Boston, 1958).

[20] John Winthrop describes his early religious life in "John Winthrop's Christian Experience" and "John Winthrop's Experiencia," in *Winthrop Papers*, vol. 1, 154-61, 161-69.

[21] The story of Thomasine Winthrop's childbirth and death is from John Winthrop's account, "Death of Thomasine Clopton Winthrop, 1616."

[22] John Winthrop's "Experiencia, 1616–18," in *Winthrop Papers*, vol.1, 190-215.

3
THE NEW ENGLAND WAY

PURITANISM IN OLD AND NEW ENGLAND

The reformers failed to change the formal structure of the Anglican church, but they worked within that structure to change the religious lives of the men and women who heard their sermons. Many preachers with Puritan leanings put on vestments and followed Anglican forms of worship when they expected a visit from the local bishop, but otherwise, they often conducted worship as they saw fit. Through their preaching they created in England thousands of Christians whose religious lives, although formally within the Anglican communion, bore a distinctly Puritan character. By 1620 many of these Puritans believed that history was on their side. Their influence was already felt throughout the realm, especially in London, East Anglia, Lincolnshire, the West Riding, the Midlands, and the Southwest. Although Puritanism did not appeal exclusively to any class, it was particularly attractive to artisans, small merchants, lawyers, yeomen, and lower gentry of the countryside. Its emphasis on self-discipline and hard work and its suspicion of worldly pomp were especially congenial to middle-class English men and women. But there were also upper-class English people who, for reasons of their own, favored the reform movement.

These men and women, high and low, had begun to make England a Puritan nation. During the 1620s, however, official resistance to their ideas became more rigid. Charles I came to the throne, and with the help of William Laud, who became archbishop of Canterbury, he suppressed the Puritans. Laud was determined that the discipline, organization, and ceremonies of the Anglican church should reflect what he called "the beauty of holiness." Laud's idea of religious beauty seemed to many English men and women to presage a return to Rome. King Charles married a French Catholic princess, and England refused to assist the Protestant side in the Thirty Years' War, which began in 1618. In doctrine the church began leaning towards Arminianism, which stressed the role of human choice in conversion—a belief anathema to the Puritans.

The doctrine of predestination, the view that God alone had the power to determine who was saved, was outlawed at Oxford and Cambridge in the 1620s. Throughout the land church altars were raised and set off from the congregations, a gesture suggesting a Catholic idea of the power of the priesthood. Laud visited many churches seeking out recalcitrant Puritans, imprisoning the Puritan bishop of Lincoln and punishing men such as William Prynne, who criticized his policies. Using the Star Chamber, the Court of High Commission, and regional ecclesiastical courts, he applied the full authority of church and state to discourage dissent.

What could the Puritans do? They might seek relief in Parliament, but in 1629 Charles dismissed Parliament and began to rule without it. Few Puritans contemplated revolution at this early date, but many now found life in England unbearable. How could one "live in the presence of God" when the Antichrist seemed to have taken control of church and state? In this seemingly hopeless situation, some English men and women looked westward to the lands across the Atlantic, which appeared now to have been set aside by God as a refuge for oppressed Christians.

William Bradford and the Pilgrims were the first to go to America. They had left England in 1607 to begin a new life in Holland, but then they became disenchanted with life on the Continent. They could worship freely, but their children seemed likely to become more Dutch than English. The Pilgrims decided the only place where they could be both English and Puritan was in the New World. But still the decision to migrate did not come easily. The Pilgrims initially imagined America as a hostile wilderness where there were "only savage and brutish men which range up and down."[1]

After a difficult voyage of sixty-six days during the autumn of 1620, they arrived at Cape Cod where they "fell upon their knees and blessed the God of Heaven." But the voyage was only the beginning of their difficulties. Along the sandy shore of Massachusetts Bay they could expect, in Bradford's words, "no friends to welcome them, nor inns to entertain or refresh their weather beaten bodies; no houses or much less towns to repair to, to seek for succor."[2] During the harsh first winter in New England, half of the *Mayflower* colonists died. The sixty survivors planted crops, built houses, and began Puritan life in the New World. They called their infant colony Plymouth Plantation.

During the fall of 1621, when the crops were in, they held a feast of thanksgiving, establishing a precedent for the annual Thanksgiving celebration that would become in the nineteenth century a distinctive American holiday. The Puritans themselves, however, never held regular annual feasts. If they experienced good fortune, they gave thanks to God. But if they encountered hardships, they held fasts to acknowledge their sins. A set thanksgiving holiday would have seemed to them an empty ritual. God—and not the calendar—gave them their occasions for feasting.

William Bradford became governor of Plymouth Plantation, and with several hundred other colonists who came to New England during the 1620s, he established the first permanent Puritan settlement in America. In the mean time, the political situation in England had worsened, and many more Puritans began to consider migration. Among them was John Winthrop and a group of his friends, who obtained a charter in 1629 to establish the Massachusetts Bay Colony.

On March 29, 1630, Winthrop set sail in the *Arbella*, leading a fleet of seven ships and a thousand Puritan immigrants to America. The trickle of migration that had peopled Plymouth soon became a torrent. During the next decade more than thirty thousand English men and women migrated to New England. They came for many reasons, not the least being the promise of land. But the leaders and most of the followers in the migration were motivated primarily by the desire to create a Puritan commonwealth. Many, like Winthrop, had to convince themselves that they were not deserting England by coming to America. They claimed that they were still English and even members of the Church of England. But they believed that in America they could establish a society so faithful to the rules of God that other people would see and imitate them. They would reform the Old World by temporary exile in the New. In a sermon delivered at sea aboard the *Arbella* Winthrop urged his fellow passengers to be "knit together in the bond of brotherly affection." Even as the ship bore these Puritans away from England, Winthrop assured his audience that they would not be cut off from their fellow countrymen. "We must consider," he said, "that we shall be as a city upon a hill, the eyes of all people are upon us."[3]

Thousands of other Puritans shared Winthrop's vision of the holy commonwealth. During the 1630s they peopled not only Massachusetts Bay, but established other colonies in Connecticut, Long Island, and even the Caribbean. Through their organization of church, state, town, and family, they gave their communities a Puritan stamp. For the first time in their lives, men like John Winthrop and Thomas Shepard actually were able to create religious institutions consistent with their own views of God's will.

Far from the interference of bishops, the Puritans founded Congregational churches, virtually autonomous bodies governed by the members of each parish rather than by an episcopal hierarchy. No ornate images drew the people's attention away from the Word of God. Instead, the church structures were plain wooden buildings, known sometimes as "the Lord's barns." All the citizens were expected to attend church on the Sabbath, but only a small group of visible saints were allowed to take communion and vote in church affairs. These same saints elected representatives and the governor. The Puritan governments passed laws supporting the church, sanctifying the Sabbath, preventing vice, and enforcing Christian charity in business. The ministers, in turn, preached sermons reminding the people of their duty to uphold the rulers. So that educated ministers might never be lacking, Harvard College was founded in 1636.

If the Puritan church and state sought to stand in the presence of God, so too did those smaller units of Puritan society, the town and the family. During the seventeenth century the typical New England village had no more than a few hundred residents, who governed themselves in town meetings attended by most of the adult males. In many villages the typical family reflected the strength and cohesiveness of Puritan society. In Andover, Massachusetts, for example, public records indicate that fathers exercised firm control over their children for many years after adolescence. Men did not tend to marry until they were in their mid-twenties, and women in their early twenties. Even after marriage young men settled on their father's farms, not owning land of their own until middle age. Puritanism, with its emphasis on godly discipline, contributed to the patriarchal quality of life in Andover and other New England villages.[4]

During the 1630s many of the leading figures in the Puritan movement, especially among the ministers, left England. But in the 1640s the prospect of a new holy commonwealth in England loomed before the reformers. In 1640 Charles I, needing funds to quell a revolt in Scotland, convened Parliament, ending eleven years of personal rule. It was soon apparent that the members of that long-slighted body were more interested in reforming England than in fighting Scotland. Charles dissolved Parliament again only to face further criticism from a newly elected Parliament. In 1641 the members of the "Long Parliament" voted in favor of the Grand Remonstrance, a bill containing some two hundred reforms, including abolition of the notorious courts of Star Chamber and High Commission, extinction of the Episcopal hierarchy, and recasting of the order of worship. Within a year the breach between Charles and the Puritan-dominated Parliament had resulted in Civil War. In 1643 Parliament negotiated a military alliance with Scotland, the Solemn League and Covenant, promising to refashion the church in England following the example of "the best reformed churches" and the Word of God.

During the turbulent years that followed, Puritans would come to govern all of England. But first they needed to create and govern an army. Under the influence of its foremost leader, Oliver Cromwell, the Puritan army became not merely the agent of change, but also its embodiment. Within the army the Puritan ideal of standing, in William Perkins's phrase, "before the living God" became a principle of martial discipline.

Cromwell was eminently suited to emerge as the foremost spokesman of the Puritan revolution. Like John Winthrop he may be described as a "typical Puritan." He was the son of a country gentleman who had acquired his estate through the dissolution of the monasteries. As a young man, Cromwell endured a long period of self-doubt—almost a prerequisite for Puritan sainthood—and considered himself "the chief of sinners." When he was about thirty, however, he felt that God had forgiven his sins and accepted him as one of his own chosen people.

Cromwell was soon active in the Puritan movement. In 1628 he argued in Parliament against the episcopacy and the prayer book. He favored a preaching clergy and gave money to support Puritan lecturers who operated on the fringes of the established church. As a member of the Long Parliament, he favored the Grand Remonstrance and later implied that he might have joined the migration to America if the bill had not passed. He began his service in the Puritan, or "Roundhead," army as a minor cavalry officer. Cromwell soon rose to leadership in the cavalry, creating a force that tipped the balance for Parliament in several battles. His men showed a remarkable combination of religious zeal and military efficiency. Cromwell believed the army should put into practice in its own ranks the Puritan discipline for which it fought. Accordingly he fined soldiers who swore and imprisoned those who drank excessively. He urged Parliament to dismiss officers whom he considered profane and favored the promotion of honest, devote Puritans, preferring "a plain russet-coated captain that knows what he fights for and loves what he knows" to a gentleman who lacked enthusiasm for the cause.

In 1649 after Parliament had prevailed over the Royalists and executed Charles I, Oliver Cromwell was the most powerful man in England. But the next nine years proved that it was more difficult to rule England than to defeat her former rulers. The revolution had given heart not only to moderate Puritans, but also to thousands of men with diverse visions of the ideal society. In 1647 many of these "masterless men," as Christopher Hill calls them, joined ranks in the Leveller Movement and attempted to win the army over to a program of radical reform, including universal suffrage and a written constitution. They were thwarted when the officers, including Cromwell, reasserted control of the army. But they continued to agitate for their reforms, and their spiritual heirs, the Diggers, began to establish a collection of democratic "commonwealths" by taking over unused lands and creating tiny republics of their own.

These political reformers regarded the Protestant emphasis on the equality of people before God as implying equality on earth. Other reformers found additional meanings in the Protestant notion of humanity's proximity to God. Under the leadership of George Fox, the Quakers emerged as a new religious body, emphasizing direct and often ecstatic communion with God. Quakers had no need for ministers, believing that, in a congregation of the faithful God could speak through any member. Other sects even abolished the Bible, regarding it as an unnecessary intrusion into the felt relationship with God.

Such fervent feelings of God's closeness also led to diverse forms of millenarianism—to the notion that the Lord would soon appear in history to redeem a fallen world. Fifth Monarchy Men claimed that Christ himself would soon rule in England. American Puritans inadvertently fed these expectations in the 1640s by beginning to convert Indians to Christianity. Many Europeans believed that the Native Americans were actually descendants of the Ten Lost Tribes of ancient Israel; the Bible had promised that the conversion of the Jews would come before the millennium. Minds feverish with the expectation of God's imminent arrival could easily construe Puritan preaching in distant wigwams as an antecedent to the Lord's arrival on earth.

Cromwell sought to steer a moderate course among the various religious factions, allowing many the liberty they fought for. During his Protectorate, Congregationalists, Presbyterians, Quakers, and even Anglicans and Catholics worshipped with some degree of freedom. Nevertheless, through his major-generals Cromwell imposed a Puritan seal on English life. By closing ale houses, suppressing cock fights, and imposing other reforms, they sought to color English society with the somber hues of Puritan moral discipline.

Ironically, Puritanism as a political movement may be said to have brought about its own decline in England. Many citizens grew weary of the extremes of authority and chaos—the rule by major-generals and the turmoil of sectaries. After Cromwell's death in 1658, the nation slipped almost inevitably into the frame of mind that made possible the Restoration of the Stuart monarchy in 1660 in the person of Charles II. By the Act of Uniformity of 1662, the Congregationalists became "non-conformists," and hundreds of their ministers lost their posts. The New England colonies were left as the only region in which Congregationalists could worship freely. What had become of the New England experiment? To what degree had the American Puritans succeeded in developing a Congregationalist commonwealth and righteous citizens?

THE PURITAN ENCOUNTER WITH GOD

Twenty years after the Restoration, in June, 1680, a pious Dutch traveller, Jasper Danckaerts, sailed past Cape Cod on his way to Boston, where he would "examine the country" and evaluate its reputation for "special devoutedness." His ship passed through a storm of wind and rain in the middle of Massachusetts Bay, lumbered through a "considerable rolling sea" at the mouth of Boston Harbor, and came to rest at the foot of Milk Street, where Danckaerts disembarked and began to explore the Puritan citadel.[5]

The Dutchman's curiosity about early New England finds its counterpart three hundred years later among historians and literary scholars, who have made the study of Puritans, in Paul Seaver's phrase, a "scholarly industry."[6] So much has been written about Puritanism that scholars appear determined to overcome the limitations of historical distance and actually travel, like Danckaerts, to seventeenth-century Boston, bringing with them the research tools of history, anthropology, literature, psychology, and sociology. Since obstacles more formidable than a mild storm and a rolling sea prevent that voyage, they would at least reconstruct the whole society and learn every vital statistic, every town and church history, the patterns of every economic, social, and religious activity.

In the aggregate, modern accounts of New England describe a vital interaction between intellectual and social forces. And yet the question Jasper Danckaerts asked 300 years ago—was New England characterized by "special devoutedness"—demands further consideration. We know a great deal about formal religious behavior in New England, but little about inner spiritual life. The distinction between formal and experiential religion was clear to Jasper Danckaerts shortly after he arrived in Boston. His ship captain took him to meet his father, whom they discovered at home conducting family worship in his kitchen. As

Danckaerts and the captain watched, the patriarch uttered a prayer "loud enough to be heard three houses off." As if, the visitor added disparagingly, "that made it good." All the while a fine meal was cooking over the fire, and soon everyone sat down to dinner. Danckaerts was convinced by this incident and by his visits to church, where the people were "very worldly and inattentive," that New England's religion consisted merely in outward observances.[7] Was Danckaerts right? What was the character of spiritual life among the early Puritans—what was the nature of their "encounter with God"?

To gain perspective on the Puritans' experience, we will consider several modern descriptions of religious experience. In their revolt against the liberal theologians, who tended to identify God with human progress, many twentieth-century theologians have stressed God's remoteness. Karl Barth described God as "wholly other," so distant from man that he can never be addressed or described with assurance. And Martin Buber speaks of God's "unincludable otherness."[8] While describing the distance between man and God, theologians have also celebrated the points of contact between humanity and deity. Buber held that men and women can have "living experience" of the divine. In *The Idea of the Holy* Rudolph Otto described the felt presence of God as the *mysterium tremendum*. "The idea of it," he said, "may at times come sweeping like a gentle tide, pervading the mind with a tranquil mood of deepest worship....It may become the hushed, trembling, and speechless humility of the creature in presence of—whom or what? In the presence of that which is a *Mystery* inexpressible and above all creatures."[9]

Otto believed that the felt presence of the divine mystery, or as he called it, the "numinous," could be stimulated by a concrete object such as a cathedral, poem, or painting, or could grow without external stimuli. In his view, as in the writings of many other twentieth-century theologians, the encounter with God is compelling and often disturbing. But while emphasizing God's unpredictability, these theologians argue that experiences of the divine undergird religious institutions, influencing doctrine, worship, and polity. "The great images of God fashioned by mankind," wrote Martin Buber, "are born not of imagination but of real encounters with real divine power and glory." Or as psychologist William James wrote: "The founders of every church owed their power originally to the fact of their direct personal communion with the divine."[10]

Three ideas stand out in these descriptions of the relationship between God and humanity. First, God is remote and hidden from people; he is a mystery, a "wholly other" being. Second, in any human encounter with God there is an element of surprise, riveting a person's attention to a new reality; in Paul Tillich's words, God "breaks into the temporal, reversing the expected course of things."[11] And third, the relationship between God and human institutions is unstable; faith requires the creation of images, institution, and doctrines, but these representations of God become empty without the continuing presence of the Lord.

The encounter with God may be understood as a spiritual relationship to a living deity or as a psychological condition in the mind of the believer. In either case the encounter constitutes a fundamental element in human experience; it exists independent of doctrine and polity, but justifies the creation of formal religious structures. What role did it play in American Puritanism? To what degree was the religious life of New England Congregationalism characterized by "encounters with God"?

Puritan descriptions of God correspond to modern accounts of the Lord's inaccessibility. Puritans held that God was both inscrutable and all-important. He was not, as some "ignorant folks" thought, "an old man sitting in heaven." He was a distant figure, so mysterious that "our wisest conjecture of him is as uncertain as the prognostication is of the rain, snow, and wind."[12]

But even though God was elusive, human beings were called to recognize his existence. Puritan sermons are full of earthy images, designed to make the spiritual life concrete. A single Puritan sermon alludes to dead men, houses, musical instruments, doors, grass, wildflowers, disease, counterfeit coins, mud puddles, and a pig. Despite God's distance from humanity Puritans held out the possibility of spiritual intimacy. "Spiritual life is nothing else," wrote John Preston, "but a conjunction of the soul with the spirit of God."[13]

Puritan sermons were devoted largely to describing the spiritual life: explaining what it was, urging people to examine themselves to see whether they were leading it, distinguishing true spirituality from mere formalism. The essence of the spiritual life was that it had to be from God. Puritan men and women must not merely follow the rules laid down by the Lord, they must walk in the presence of the deity, first undergoing a conversion experience and then leading a Christian life out of a deeply felt relationship to God. To follow God's rules without experiencing a relationship to him was like being faithful to a spouse one had never met. One could do so from duty, but not from love. The rules were intended to support a felt relationship. "A man knows what he loves," wrote Preston, "love is a very sensible and quick affection. When a man loves anything, when he loves his wife, loves his friend, loves his son, loves his sport, his recreation, he knows he loves it, he hath a sense of that love in himself."[14] Men and women should worship a present God, a God who met with them, conversed with them, soothed their fears, excited their piety.

So the Puritans were told, and yet they often had difficulty in feeling God's presence. As a young man Thomas Shepard, later pastor of Cambridge, Massachusetts, was vexed with God because his prayers seemed monologues rather than conversations. He prayed to God, "that if he were as his works and word declared him to be, he would be pleased to reveal himself by his own beams, and persuade my heart by his own Spirit of his essence and being."[15] If God is real, Shepard seemed to be saying, let him make himself known.

Despite such periods of spiritual vexation, Puritans occasionally did feel that God revealed himself to them "by his own beams." These moments were as real theologically and psychologically as their churches and schools, their roads and houses. By using Puritan letters, diaries, and sermons we can distinguish at least four circumstances in which Puritans encountered what they called God: providential events, meditative communion, "walking with God," and spiritual dreams.

PROVIDENCE

God, Puritans said, ruled the world by his providence, determining the course of events for men and nations. Often he used events to communicate with human beings, punishing the wicked and rewarding the virtuous. But in their daily lives, men and women often overlooked God's presence. A pleasant day, a good meal, a warm house, and other such blessings were so common as to be taken for granted.

Sometimes, however, Puritans lived through events so startling that they felt the very hand of God upon them. Such was Thomas Shepard's experience on his first attempt to reach New England in 1634. He and his family boarded the *Hope of Ipswich* late in the year. During their second day on the North Sea, they ran into a storm that drove the ship with fierce winds and mountainous waves toward Yarmouth Roads, an area of shallow water off the English coast. Seeing sand spits ahead, lethal under the pounding surf, the crew cast out one anchor, then another, only to have both give way. In desperation the captain cut away the mast and cast out a last, small anchor—but the ship drove onward. The sailors pointed to the place where they expected to be overturned, too far from shore for anyone to survive in the surf. Hundreds of people lined the walls of nearby Yarmouth, watching the helpless ship. Recognizing that nothing could be done, the captain asked for prayers, and Shepard assembled the crew on the tossing deck while another minister, John Norton, gathered the passengers below. "We went to prayer," says Shepard, "and committed our souls and bodies into the Lord that gave them."

Then, as they were preparing to die, the wind abated, and the last anchor held, bringing the ship to rest "just when it was ready to be swallowed up of the sands." The amazed Shepard saw that the anchor "cable was let out so far that a little rope held the cable, and the cable the little anchor, and the little anchor the great ship in this great storm." He felt "if ever the Lord did bring me to shore again, I should live like one come and risen from the dead."[16]

God's providence seldom touched men and women so dramatically as in the deliverance of the *Hope of Ipswich*, but colonial sermons and diaries are full of accounts of seemingly miraculous episodes: a man saved from drowning, a woman recovering unexpectedly from a serious disease, a profane man tumbling into the sea, a rainstorm ending a drought. Many such events passed without exciting the spiritual life, but most men and women could recount two or three times in their lives when the Lord had seemed to reach out and shake them with his providence.

MEDITATION

Other encounters with God were psychological rather than physical. Through meditation and prayers, Puritans attempted to converse with their Lord. In silence or out loud, alone in the bed chamber or in the middle of a congregation, men and women used prayer and meditation to reflect on their lives, their ambitions, and their relationship to God:

I have sinned; may God forgive me.
My child is ill, and I would have her well.
May our ship arrive safely in New England.
How can I find salvation?

In such thoughts and petitions men and women addressed the Lord. Often these were formal exercises, but occasionally God seemed to be standing by the petitioner, listening, coaxing, chiding, encouraging. As a young man, Thomas Shepard often went out into the fields outside of Cambridge to contemplate his spiritual condition, taking with him "a little book" to write down what he learned. In this period of intense spirituality he often felt that God communicated with him, helping him to shape his thoughts. In the fields he found "the Lord teaching me somewhat of myself or himself or the vanity of the world." He seemed to learn lessons from Christ "before any man preached any such thing to me." Similarly, John Winthrop could recount having "a very sweet meditation of the presence and power of the Holy Ghost in the hearts of the faithful."[17] Neither Shepard nor Winthrop claimed that God spoke to them an audibly, but in such moments their thoughts seemed to be guided by the Lord.

WALKING WITH GOD

In a third kind of religious activity, "walking with God," Puritans tried to lead their lives as if they were in God's presence. Raising children, cooking meals, harvesting crops, and other daily activities were to Puritans vocations ordained by God, and should be stimulated by faith. The virtuous man must not "wrap his faith in a napkin and let it lie dead."[18] God would assist the spiritual person, nourishing his or her virtuous acts, just as he encouraged pious thought.

In practice, a sense of God's companionship in the daily life was as elusive as any other encounters with the deity. John Winthrop often complained that he felt spiritually dead while performing the "outward duties" of Christianity. But he also knew moments when the "unspeakable comfort" of communion with Christ filled him with "joy, peace, assurance, boldness."[19] Such periods of deep religiosity filled the forms of Christian duty with the felt presence of the God in whose names those forms were established.

DREAMS

The Puritans also experienced the divine in the world of dreams and visions. Such encounters were the least systematic of their religious experiences and are seldom mentioned in Puritan sermons, but they appear to have occurred regularly. One night in 1642 when Thomas Shepard was praying for his poor parishioners in Cambridge, Massachusetts, he suddenly realized that God's glory enriched his whole congregation, rich and poor alike. The Lord, he said, "gave me a sweet glimpse of his glory this night upon this occasion to see myself and mine and all his people infinitely happy in having God ours though we had all wants." Shepard was a minister, devoting his life to his New England townspeople. In that brief "glimpse," or vision, he saw his people actually united to God.[20]

Such dreams of proximity to God were apparently common in early New England. John Winthrop reported that a Puritan layman dreamed that upon "coming into his chamber, he found his wife (she was a very gracious woman) in bed, and three or four of their children lying by her, with most sweet and smiling countenances, with crowns upon their heads, and blue ribbons." This vision into the world of spirit made the father feel that his family would be "fellow heirs with Christ" in the Kingdom of God.[21]

Puritans were taught to be suspicious of dreams; the devil as well as God could prey on the imagination, and too much attention to dreams seemed a foolish habit. When reporting the dream about the garlanded children Winthrop noted that "no credit nor regard" could be given to dreams "in these days."[22] Nonetheless he did record the incident. As personal experiences, dreams were compelling; like other spiritual encounters they enabled men and women to feel that they were experiencing the reality of God.

During moments of illumination in providential events, meditation, daily activity, and dreams Puritans thus experienced a relationship to what they called God. Such episodes can be ascribed to psychological and sociological forces, or they can be regarded theologically as moments of contact with the living God. As personal historical events they were deeply moving, whatever their original source. Puritan doctrine taught men and women to seek direct communication with God, and Puritan experience taught that such contact was possible. These encounters were part of the psychological reality of early New England.

They did not, however, occur in a predictable fashion. Puritan ministers taught people to anticipate a permanent union with Christ in the conversion experience, but religious life did not resolve itself into a clear distinction between preconversion and postconversion experience. John Winthrop, for example, had periods of strong religiosity before the events he identified as his conversion, and he had periods of spiritual deadness during the years following. The encounter with God was imperfectly called up or organized by the church. A doctrinal sermon might fail to excite piety, while an unexpected dream could take a Puritan into the presence of God. In short, Puritan spiritual experience consisted of intense but intermittent encounters with God.

Thus, the Puritan encounter with God was both important and elusive. For all their fame as diarists, only two early Puritan New Englanders, Thomas Shepard and John Winthrop, left extensive descriptions of their religious lives, and even these are fragmentary. Most letters from early New England deal with terrain, politics, society, and the church, rather than the inner life. Even a contemporary observer such as Jasper Danckaerts could record only the outer side of Puritan piety. He reported that a constable sent out to enforce Sabbath closing laws in the taverns got drunk himself, but he could not know whether on other occasions the same constable conversed with God in thoughts and dreams.

Since Puritans were never certain when they would feel themselves near to God, they made a virtue of the longing for grace. "A sure sign of grace is to see no grace, and to see it with grief," wrote Samuel Clark. "The greatest part of a Christians' grace," said Thomas Shepard, "lies in mourning for the want of it."[23] Puritans tried to create in New England an environment in which people and God would walk together and looked forward to a spiritual future when Christ would appear among them, his chosen people. But the commonwealth was imperfect; the apocalypse never arrived; and their encounters with God were intermittent. They discovered, as Richard Sibbes had written, "The spirit of Christ...sometimes bows strongly, sometimes more mildly, sometimes not at all. No creature hath these winds in a bag to command."[24]

Neither a contemporary observer such as Jasper Danckaerts, nor modern scholars, nor the Puritans themselves could fully chronicle the mysterious course of human spirituality. But the encounter with God did leave impressions on the historical consciousness and traces on the historical record. The history of those spiritual episodes in early New England is important, because, in the final analysis, they are what Congregationalism, and for that matter all religions, are about.

VISIBLE SAINTHOOD AND ANTINOMIANISM

Spiritual encounters were elusive, but the Puritans tried to make them more accessible. Although Congregational ministers often warned their people about the great distance between God and humanity, they tried to bring their people, while on earth, into what Cotton Mather called the "suburbs of Heaven."[25] The church was organized along biblical lines, the state was ruled by church members, the people heard godly sermons on the Sabbath. People were taught a "devotional discipline"—the use of spontaneous and systematic prayer, daily scripture reading, private meditation, and family prayer—to bring God into their daily lives. Religion must not be merely a Sabbath matter. In 1657 Richard Mather told his congregation in Dorchester, Massachusetts, that they must perform their religious duties amid, "your eating and marriage,...your buying and selling, your plowing and hoeing, your sowing and mowing and reaping, your feeding cattle and keeping sheep, your planting orchards and gardens, your baking and brewing, your building houses and outhouses, your fencing in ground or other business whatever."[26]

Other Reformation sects were as idealistic as the Congregationalists, but none went as far in attempting to identify the living church with the men and women God actually choose for salvation, the visible saints. In order to become a full member of a Congregational church—and thus to gain the right to take communion, present one's children for baptism, and take part in the government of church and state—the communicant had to present a narrative of religious experience to his or her minister and congregation.

The origins of this practice have never been fully explained. Visible sainthood was not a requirement for membership in Reformed churches on the Continent, and the idea does not appear in early Congregationalist writing. Many churches required "testimonies of faith," in the sense of an examination on a set creed, but the Puritans went one step further in requiring a testimony of *personal* religious *experience*. By 1640 the requirement was common practice throughout the Puritan churches of New England. And yet, the evolution of the new practice left hardly a mark in Puritan letters, diaries, or tracts. It developed so naturally and with such a consensus of support that it can be called an unthinking decision.

But although the Congregationalists did not leave a record of their reasons for requiring a conversion narrative for full church membership, they did write many accounts of the conversion process. Some are proscriptive accounts in religious tracts; some are personal accounts by converts. Descriptions of the conversion process varied. One minister might emphasize God's role in beginning the process. Another would stress man's preparatory acts. There were also differences in numbering the stages of conversion. But ministers tended to agree that three experiences, or stages of conversion, were fundamental.

The first was humiliation, an experience of sorrow for having sinned against God. The second was justification, a sense of having been forgiven and accepted by God through Christ's mercy. The third was sanctification, an enduring ability to lead a godly life out of an inward gladness in doing God's will.

Conversion began as a spiritual crisis in which a person became acutely aware of his or her own sinfulness. As John Preston put it, God's course was "to pull down before he build."[27] During conversion something new was thought to enter a person and something old was thought to be replaced. The self-sufficiency and egotism of the natural man or woman, which made it possible to ignore God and to indulge his worldly appetites, was destroyed by self-doubt.

The second stage in conversion, often known as "adoption" or "justification," came when a person recognized that salvation was possible only through Christ. The Puritans held that a sinner's own efforts to reform could not in themselves win God's approval. But God was willing to forgive sinners who believed that Christ had died for them. "Faith is a wonderful grace of God," wrote William Perkins, "by which they elect to apprehend and apply Christ and all his benefits unto themselves particularly."[28]

Once justified the convert was ready for the third stage of conversion, known as "sanctification." The regenerate person was expected to lead a godly life because grace, implanted and nourished by God, had entered the soul. The convert's attraction to the life of Christ could be compared to the pull of a magnet: "As there is in the iron a certain natural quality to follow the lodestone," wrote John Preston, "so there is in the saints towards Christ."[29]

The theory of conversion was well developed long before the first Congregationalists arrived in New England. But the requirement of a personal testimony as a condition of church membership evolved in the new land. No synod met to introduce religious tests, nor are there any written documents indicating an agreement among the churches to evaluate spirituality. The innovation came about during and after the period of the "Antinomian crisis." Its sources were a curious blend of religious radicalism and social conservatism.

Antinomianism, the belief that the moral law is of no use because faith alone is necessary to salvation, had been present in Protestantism since the early days of Luther's Reformation in Germany. As a doctrine it was particularly loathsome to most reformers because it began with an emphasis on the spirit—which all Protestants shared—and took that emphasis to extremes that threatened both church and state. In 1534 John Beukels, a leader of an Antinomian revolution in Münster, Germany, ran naked through the town and announced a new order with himself as messianic king. All books except the Bible were to be burned; swearing, adultery, and backbiting must be punished by death; and men were *required* to take more than one wife. In such ways the emphasis on the spirit, advocated by the Reformation, took bizarre forms in the actions of religious zealots.

No American Beukels brought bloodshed to the Puritan colonies, but among the early immigrants were some who were more radical than the Puritan leaders. In 1634 a woman named Anne Hutchinson arrived in Massachusetts Bay, and some orthodox Congregationalists thought they saw in her a religious radical who threatened to bring chaos to the holy commonwealth. She came to Boston with her husband and children following her minister, John Cotton, across the ocean.

In 1635 Anne Hutchinson began holding private meetings at her house on weekdays, where she summarized the previous week's sermons for the benefit of women who had been unable to attend church. Hutchinson was intelligent and articulate, and soon dozens of people, men as well as women, began to attend her meetings. At first there was nothing extraordinary in her meetings. Lay men and women were encouraged to participate in the religious life of the church, even to "preach" to their families and friends. Hutchinson admired John Cotton, who emphasized in his sermons the role of faith in salvation. So her teachings were consistent with his.

But in the fall of 1635 John Wilson, who was Cotton's associate at his parish in Boston, returned from England and began to share the pulpit with Cotton. Like many other Puritan clergymen, Wilson preached the doctrine of "preparation." According to this theory a person could prepare for salvation by attending church, reading the Bible, leading a moral life, and other conscious acts. Wilson did not claim that good deeds merited salvation—that would have been heresy—only that they helped a sinner prepare for God's saving grace. In contrast, Cotton emphasized the unanticipated quality of God's redeeming grace.

Both ministers believed that salvation came through grace alone, but Anne

Hutchinson believed that Wilson's emphasis on good deeds undermined the fundamental doctrine of salvation by faith. During the summer of 1636 she used her private meetings to criticize John Wilson and other ministers who, she claimed, were preaching a "covenant of works" rather than a "covenant of grace."

By now her meetings were attracting scores of participants, including William Aspinwall, William Coddington, John Coggeshall, and Henry Vane, who were among the most powerful citizens of Massachusetts Bay. But other citizens, among them John Winthrop and John Wilson, were alarmed by Hutchinson's preaching. In her emphasis on the mystical experience of grace she appeared to threaten public order in church and state. The pursuit of grace had brought thousands of Puritans to New England; but the moderate leaders of New England—and their Puritan God—favored order as well as spirituality.

As Anne Hutchinson's belief in her own rectitude grew stronger, she became increasingly critical of ministers who did not measure up to her own standards of grace. Alarmed at her popularity and radicalism, the colony's leaders summoned her to a meeting with the clergy at John Cotton's house in December, 1636. There she made new enemies by questioning whether many of the ministers were converted. In August, 1637, a synod convened at Newtown to discuss the crisis. The assembled ministers drew up a list of 82 "errors" promulgated by Anne Hutchinson and her supporters. The difference between Hutchinsonian ideas and Puritan orthodoxy is implicit in the "Catalogue" of errors and refutations adopted by the ministers. For example:

"*Error* 1. In the conversion of a sinner, which is saving and gracious, the faculties of the soul, and workings thereof, in things pertaining to God, are destroyed and made to cease....

"*Error* 2. Instead of them, the Holy Ghost doth come and take place, and doth all the works of those natures, as the faculties of human nature of Christ do.

"*Error* 4, 5. That those that be in Christ are not under the law, and commands of the word, as the rule of life. *Alias*, that the will of God in the Word, or directions thereof, are not the rule whereunto Christians are bound to conform themselves, to live thereafter."[30]

These and other "errors" listed by the ministers at Newtown were obnoxious to orthodox Puritans because they suggested that human minds and earthly laws were replaced by divine impulses after conversion. One of the most appealing features of Puritanism is the effort to balance the love of life and the love of God. The God who gave the precept of moderation also gave the gift of wine. The God who punished sinners, also took on human form and experienced human suffering. The God of the Puritans did not destroy the humanness of humanity; he met with people, conversed with them, illuminated them. In conversion the human soul was elevated, not obliterated.

Antinomianism was obnoxious to Puritan aesthetics and to Puritan politics. In the view of orthodox Puritans, antinomians saw themselves as gods, elevated by conversion above the laws of their nation and the limitations of their humanity. They thought themselves fit to pass judgment on their nominal superiors in church and state. Similar pretensions to spiritual autonomy had led to chaos and bloodshed in Europe. Leaders like John Winthrop were determined that the same thing would not happen in New England. The people must recognize that even the best of Puritans could only dwell in the "suburbs of heaven" while on earth, not in heaven itself. And while living in those suburbs they must recognize the authority of their magistrates and ministers.

In November, 1636, the general court of Massachusetts Bay banished two supporters of Anne Hutchinson—John Wheelwright and William Aspinwall. Next they tried Anne Hutchinson. She shocked the court with the spirit of her testimony. When Governor Winthrop demanded that she present biblical evidence for her course in preaching and then questioned the relevance of a passage that seemed to support her position, she remarked contemptuously, "Must I show my name written therein?"[31] It was a clever remark, but hardly appreciated in a society where women were expected to show a certain deference to men. Hutchinson was a formidable adversary, but she sealed her own fate when she claimed to have received direct personal revelations from God. The rulers in Massachusetts Bay could not afford to allow men and women the right to set themselves up above church and state on the basis of the claim that God spoke through them. Anne Hutchinson was banished. She moved with her family to Rhode Island, joining other Antinomian exiles in a region that would serve as a kind of "safety valve" for Massachusetts.

In Puritan New England the Antinomianism of Anne Hutchinson was unacceptable. Her threat ended with her removal, but there remained the possibility that other religious renegades might come to the colony, claiming again the spiritual authority to set themselves above their rulers. During this period of religious turmoil, the Puritan ministers evaluated the spiritual condition of their people and developed strict requirements for church membership. Communicants were examined by their ministers, church elders, and other full members of the church to determine whether they had experienced saving grace. The standard against which they were judged was the three stages of grace described by the ministers: humiliation, justification, and sanctification. Had Anne Hutchinson been exposed to such a test she would probably have failed, for the candidate was expected to remain humble even after conversion. Hutchinson's assurance that God spoke directly to her and encouraged her to pass judgment on the ministers would have been regarded as a sign of obdurate pride.

The Puritan emphasis on visible sainthood thus helped establish a kind of Congregational "middle way" between the extremes of the Anglican emphasis on works and the Antinomian emphasis on grace. The conversion requirement for full church membership attested to the Puritan belief in salvation by grace. But the careful evaluation of conversion by trusted church members enabled Puritans to separate those they regarded as sincere converts from those they regarded as religious fanatics. The practice of identifying "visible saints" thus served the Congregational yearnings for spirituality—and for order.

THE CONVERSION EXPERIENCE: IMAGE AND REALITY

The practice of designating visible saints served, thus, a conservative cause, keeping piety under control. It may have discouraged Antinomian tendencies. But it did not make spiritual experience any more accessible. In actual practice the process of conversion seldom followed exactly the path suggested by the theory of conversion. Just as the Puritan encounter with God took forms that were not always predicted by doctrine, so too the conversion experience varied with each communicant. The writings of Thomas Shepard suggest something of the complexity of the interaction between Puritan experience and Puritan ideology. In his autobiography Shepard describes the conversion process by which, as he said, "the Lord began to call me home to the fellowship of his grace."[32] At the time, in the early 1620s, he was a student at Cambridge.

The first stage of Shepard's conversion experience follows roughly the pattern described in Puritan sermons and tracts. He began the account by describing himself in his early years at Cambridge as a person who neglected God and devoted himself to "lust and pride and gaming and bowling and drinking." He came to lament this situation after he passed out from drunkenness one night and had to be carried to a room by his friends. When he awoke the next morning, he was ashamed and confused. He went outside and "spent that Sabbath lying hid in the cornfields where the Lord...did meet me with much sadness of heart and troubled my soul for this and my other sins."

This initial experience dampened Shepard's "lust," but it did not complete his conversion. After his day in the cornfield, Shepard listened to a series of sermons preached by John Preston, which he said, opened "the secrets of my soul." He learned that the first step towards spiritual regeneration was regret for his sins. But although he had recently felt sorrow for his drunkenness, he found it difficult to regard himself as totally depraved. He attempted to discipline his mind to produce the right attitude. He considered the "evil of sin" and the "beauty of Christ." He often went into the fields to meditate, and there, he said, "I did find the Lord teaching me somewhat of myself or himself or the vanity of the world."

Despite these efforts, however, he found that he was still unable, as he said, to "feel sin as my greatest evil." Recognizing these flaws, he began finally to fear the "terrors of God." "I did see God," he says, "Like a consuming fire and an everlasting burning, and myself like a poor prisoner leading to that fire." In this condition Shepard finally recognized his inability to help himself, and so he came to experience total humiliation. This feeling came over him late one Sunday evening. He had been taught that he could only know God when he perceived his own limitations. Now he was seeing those faults. "I found the Lord helping me," he wrote, "to see my unworthiness of any mercy and that I was worthy to be cast out of his sight,...and then and never until then I found rest." After praying he went to supper and late that night "the terrors of the Lord began to assuage sweetly." Prior to this time Shepard had been unable to feel God's greatness and his own sinfulness. Now the recognition of his own inadequacy brought him to a feeling of his need for God.

With these thoughts Shepard may be said to have completed the first stage of the Puritan conversion experience. God, man, and meditation had brought him to a recognition of his own inadequacy and his need for God. The second stage followed more easily. Having recognized his "own constant vileness," Shepard realized his need for help. He wrote, "I saw the Lord gave me a heart to receive Christ with a naked hand, even naked Christ, and so the Lord gave me peace." Thus a sense of unworthiness had led to a sense of his dependence on God, and realizing that dependence, he had become worthy of salvation through Christ. This completed the process of justification, the second stage in his conversion.

We might expect that after experiencing his dependence upon Christ, Shepard would continue to be aware of his relationship to God through the remainder of his days. And there were many times in the years ahead when he felt that God was near to him. But frequently he had no feelings of grace. When his first-born child died shortly before his departure for New England, he considered that he had been punished for his "unmortified, hard, dark, formal, hypocritical heart." When he was at sea on the way to America and his ship was battered by a storm, he viewed this event as a sign that God wanted to awaken him—"My heart lying long out of the Lord."

Shepard was acutely aware of the many times that the demands of his ministry or his family drew his attention away from God. He once wrote "either there is no life of Christ [in me], which is most sad, or if there be any I crucify it and disfigure it and put it to open shame, which is most sad also." Such periods of doubt were interspersed with moments of grace, when Shepard felt the love of God. But much of his life—even after the events which he regarded as his conversion—was lived without the *felt* presence of what he called God.

When we compare Shepard's spiritual experience with the image of conversion presented in Puritan doctrines and tracts, we can recognize the prescribed pattern of humiliation-justification-sanctification. But the experience, significant though it was, was less complete than a Puritan might hope. In achieving a condition of humiliation, Shepard frequently had to be satisfied with a sense of regret at *not* feeling regret for sin. William Perkins might describe the Puritan saint as "iron" drawn to the "lodestone" of Christ, but Shepard realized that in his own spiritual life, the attraction to heavenly things was only periodic.

John Winthrop's conversion provides another example of the somewhat loose relationship between Puritan ideology and experience. As we have seen, in 1616 and 1617 after the death of his second wife, Thomasine, Winthrop became acutely aware of his relationship to Christ. As was common among Puritans, his bereavement made him think more about God. "Although the loss of my wife was to me a grievous thing," he wrote, "yet God, in his more than fatherly mercy, drew my mind from being too attentive upon it, by giving me cause to look into myself, and...showed me mine own nakedness and unworthiness."[33] In this period of acute sorrow Winthrop gained an insight into the nature of Christ's love, and with that insight came his experience of justification.

During the early months of 1617 he devoted many hours to meditation and to reading such works as William Perkins's *A Treatise Tending unto a Declaration Whether a Man be in the Estate of Grace*. Such activities nourished some feelings of piety in him. But his most intense spiritual awakening followed a seemingly trivial event. He chose one day to reread the love letters that his first wife had written him. In doing so he was struck by two things: the affection in the letters—and the poor orthography! As he read them, he found himself loving her all the more tenderly because of the imperfections in her writing. With this thought in mind, he suddenly realized that here was the spirit in which Christ loved and accepted sinners. A person could not present himself perfectly to Christ and should not expect to do so, for Christ loved a person despite his imperfections. "He accepts with all favor the sincere simplicity of the heart," wrote Winthrop, "and covers all imperfections with the skirt of his love."

This sense of being accepted despite his failings gave Winthrop an unusual sense of peace. He believed that his sins had been "washed away" by Christ. There follows in Winthrop's journal a lyrical passage in which he compares Christ to a spouse. Thou didst "wash me in the ever flowing fountain of thy blood," he writes, "Thou didst trim me as a bride prepared for her husband." In the months and years ahead, Winthrop's life continued to fluctuate between periods of spiritual deadness and spiritual fullness. But later, when he offered a testimony of his faith to his church in Massachusetts, he would identify this time as the period of his conversion.

Several points stand out in these examples of the conversion experience. Shepard and Winthrop each struggled towards a personal understanding of the relationship to God. In each case the conversion experience occurred only after long periods of meditation and self-examination. In each case there was an element of the unexpected, erratic, even the bizarre in their conversions. Shepard made a "breakthrough" after coming to an intellectual conclusion—that his recognition of his *inability* to feel his own sinfulness was in itself a sign of humiliation. In Winthrop's case neither a sermon nor meditation was the immediate occasion for his sense of adoption by Christ; the stimulus was a casual reading of his first wife's love letters.

During the late 1630s the New England Congregationalists tried to take the disparate experiences of Winthrop and Shepard and hundreds of other Puritans and evaluate them in a formal way to determine who among the settlers had actually experienced regeneration. The few conversion testimonies that survive from that era have the same quality as Winthrop's and Shepard's accounts. In each case a profound sense of unworthiness preceded the feeling of acceptance and salvation. But the details vary considerably from person to person, indicating the importance of subjective elements in the conversion experience.

CONSOLIDATION: THE CAMBRIDGE PLATFORM AND THE SAVOY DECLARATION

Those who could chronicle in their own lives these feelings of remorse and redemption were the leaders in church and state during the early years of New England's settlement. They built new towns, pushed the frontier inland thirty or forty miles from the sea, and settled the Connecticut River Valley. In 1636 Thomas Hooker led a group of Puritans to Connecticut and established a new colony, following substantially the same pattern in politics and religion as existed in Massachusetts. Other Puritan settlements took root along the coast in New Hampshire and Maine. Puritans from Connecticut settled in eastern Long Island and New Jersey. And colonists from Massachusetts settled in Virginia and later, after being expelled from Virginia, in Maryland. At the end of the century a group of settlers from Dorchester, Massachusetts, settled near Charleston, South Carolina. In 1752 some of these Carolina Congregationalists migrated south to Midway, Georgia. These settlements were remote outposts of a denomination that was otherwise heavily concentrated in the colonies of Massachusetts, Connecticut, and New Hampshire.

During the 1640s several New England divines wrote descriptions of the Congregational polity. These tracts were written not so much to consolidate practice in the New England churches as to enter debate with Presbyterians in England on the proper form of church government. Thomas Hooker's *Survey of the Summe of Church Discipline* won the approval of a ministerial meeting in Cambridge in 1645. The original version was lost when the ship carrying it to England went down at sea, but a rough second draft was published shortly after Hooker's death in 1647. Williston Walker declared that Hooker's preface to this work is "as clear a presentation of Congregational principles as has ever been given in the brief space of little more than a page of print."[34]

As new threats to the Congregational Way appeared in England and America, Puritans felt the need for a more authoritative statement of their beliefs. In England Presbyterians had gained the upper hand and might force their ideas about church membership and government upon the New Englanders. In Boston several Presbyterians, led by Robert Child, presented a petition to the general court in May, 1646, demanding a redress of grievances. They were particularly critical of the Congregational restriction of church membership to the visible saints and the restriction of the franchise to those who were full church members. Child and his followers threatened to appeal to England if they did not gain satisfaction in Massachusetts.

Puritans also felt threatened by a more radical interpretation of baptism and church membership promulgated by Baptists in England and Rhode Island. Taking the logic of visible sainthood one step further, the Baptists claimed that not only communion, but also baptism should be available only to those who had experienced a work of redemption. Baptist tracts began to arrive in Massachusetts, and several ministers, including John Cotton and Thomas Hooker wrote refutations. Additionally, the Massachusetts General Court passed legislation in 1644 against criticizing the validity of infant baptism.

Such events make it clear that the independence of the congregations existed only within the borders of a consensus about fundamental issues. One minister could take a somewhat original position on, say, the issue of preparation, and he would not be persecuted. Congregations and their pastors were allowed a degree of independence in some matters. This was the characteristic for which Congregationalism was named: the right of the individual parish to govern itself and worship God in its own way. But the circle of Congregational flexibility existed within a larger sphere of religious intolerance. Normally careful not to trample on the rights of the individual congregation, and constitutionally suspicious of higher authority, the Congregationalists seemingly forgot these scruples when they encouraged the state to punish heretics like Anne Hutchinson.

The Puritan notion of flexibility simply did not apply to certain religious ideas and practices. Catholics would not have been tolerated, nor were Quakers or Baptists. In later years Puritans would be criticized for hypocrisy. In one stereotype they came to America for religious freedom, but as soon as they arrived they began persecuting others.

This criticism, though popular, is based on a superficial understanding of Puritanism. It rests on an understanding of religious freedom that gained acceptance in the western world long after the Puritan Migration. The Puritans came to America to worship freely, but not to establish religious freedom as an absolute value. Like most Europeans at that time, they believed that God expected his people to establish one true church. The true church of the Puritans was more flexible than many, but none the less its boundaries were patrolled by the state, just as religion was supervised in contemporary France or Italy or Spain.

The Puritans would willingly accept the statement that they were intolerant, saying that they were only intolerant of heresy—as God would have it. Nathaniel Ward, who served as minister of Ipswich, Massachusetts, and drew up the first codification of the colony's laws in 1641, wrote a passionate defense of Puritan intolerance in 1645. In *The Simple Cobbler of Aggawam* he claimed that religious liberty creates chaos. "If the devil might have his free option," he wrote, "I believe he would ask nothing else but liberty to enfranchise all false religions and to embondage the truth." After graduating from Emmanuel College, Cambridge, in 1618, he had studied on the Continent, where he had seen the effects of religious diversity: "I lived in a city where a Papist preached in one church, a Lutheran in another, a Calvinist in a third....The religion of that place was but motley and meager, their affections leopard-like." In his view tolerance simply diluted true religion by allowing false religions to thrive. "Poly-piety," he argued, "is the greatest impiety in the world." Quoting Augustine, Ward said, "No evil is worse than liberty for the erring." With tolerance "the roof of liberty stands open" and "light heads" are free to spread their heresies. Ward proclaimed proudly that the "roof" of intolerance was secure in New England: "I dare take upon me to be the herald of New England so far as to proclaim to the world, in the name of our colony, that all Familists,

Antinomians, Anabaptists, and other enthusiasts shall have free liberty to keep away from us; and such as will come to be gone as fast as they can, the sooner the better."[35]

During the 1640s Congregationalists faced a problem that would trouble the denomination into the twentieth century: how to temper independence with uniformity. Faced with challenges to Congregational orthodoxy, the general court issued a call in 1646 for a synod to draw up a comprehensive description of New England beliefs and practices. The statement would not be authoritative, for the ultimate power rested in individual congregations, but it would encourage uniformity among the churches, and it would declare to critics in England and dissenters in New England that the American Puritans had indeed established a holy commonwealth, based on religious principles that were widely held.

The synod met in Cambridge in 1647 and 1648 and agreed on most issues. The only major point of difference between the delegates grew out of Richard Mather's proposal to extend infant baptism to the grandchildren as well as the children of visible saints. This idea would soon grow in popularity, but it was too radical for the majority at the synod. The Cambridge Platform, adopted in 1648, favored a church whose power centered in congregation that were joined together in voluntary covenant and led by visible saints. Their confidence that they had created a church based on biblical precepts resounds in this passage from the Psalms, quoted on the title page of the platform: "One thing have I desired of the Lord that will I seek after, that I may dwell in the house of the Lord all the days of my life to behold the beauty of the Lord and to inquire in his temple."[36]

The platform is in part a refutation of objections to Congregational practices. Critics had complained that because full membership in New England's churches was restricted to relatively few communicants, the great body of Christians was left outside the church, and therefore there was no way of "calling in of ignorant and erroneous and scandalous persons." That objection was easily answered, for all the settlers were subject to church discipline and most attended church, whether or not they were full members. The visible saints ideally contributed to the congregation as a whole: "A little leaven laid in a lump of dough, will sooner leaven the whole lump, than the whole lump will sweeten it." And they could be compared to good stones in a wall: "We...find it safer to square rough and unhewn stones before they be laid into the building, rather than to hammer and hew them, when they lie uneven in the building." With "leaven" and "well-hewn stones" as the basis of the church, the ministers could "call in" other colonists by preaching to them—for all settlers were "required by wholesome laws" to attend religious meetings. And ministers, lay elders, and other church members could further counsel non-members to live godly lives.

The ministers alone had the authority to preach and to administer the sacraments—baptism and communion. But they were assisted by lay "ruling elders," who helped make decisions on admission of new members and excommunication of "notorious and obstinate offenders, renounced by the church." The ruling elders also ordained the ministers, visited the sick, and saw "that none in the church lived inordinately out of rank and place" or worked "idlely in their callings." Other laymen served as deacons, who administered church funds for communion, charity, and other purposes. All the church officials were chosen by the visible saints.

One of the most important functions of the ministers and elders was to admit new members to the church. The stipulation that the member profess faith and repentance meant more than simply subscribing to a creed; it meant in practice that the candidate must describe a personal experience of faith and repentance in such a way "as may satisfy *rational charity* that these things are there indeed." Although the candidate must expose himself or herself to a critical examination of their feelings, the probing must be gentle. "Severity of examination is to be avoided," the platform declares. "The weakest measure of faith is to be accepted in those that desire to be admitted into the church: because weak Christians if *sincere*, have the *substance* of that faith, repentance, and holiness which is required in church members, and such have most *need* of the ordinances for their confirmation and growth in grace." Christ was said to have approved such charity: "The Lord Jesus would not quench the smoking flax, nor break the bruised reed, but gather the tender lambs in his arms, and carry them gently in his bosom."

The solicitude for the candidate that is apparent in these comments on the examination carried over to the description of the candidate's public testimony of faith. The convert would ideally relate his or her conversion experience in front of the whole congregation, but this requirement could be waved: "In case any through excessive fear, or other infirmity, be unable to make their personal relation of their spiritual estate in public, it is sufficient that the elders having received private satisfaction, make relation thereof in public before the church, they testifying their assents thereunto." In practice this meant that statements of faith by candidates were sometimes read by someone else to the church at large.

This solicitude for the convert must have grown out of experience with Puritans who were grappling for an understanding of that most complex of spirits, their own souls. We have seen how elusive the conversion experience was for such Puritan leaders as John Winthrop and Thomas Shepard. Surely among ordinary lay men and women it was equally difficult. The voice of God did not come to Congregational New Englanders with such clarity and force as it came to Paul on the road to Damascus. And so the Puritans would be charitable to candidates for church membership, insisting on only the tiniest trace of "smoke" in the "flax" of personal devotion.

The Cambridge Platform was the definitive statement of New England Congregational polity and emphasized these basic principles: (1) the creation of local churches from visible saints, (2) the complete autonomy of those churches, including their right to choose and ordain officers, (3) ministerial standing based on congregational election, (4) the consent of church members as a requirement of church admissions and censures, (5) synods and councils for advice, but not for authoritative statements, (6) the mutual support of church and state, and (7) lay membership based on visible sainthood.

The Platform consolidated Congregational thought on polity. At later synods the Congregationalists adopted a doctrinal statement, drawing on two English documents, the Westminster Confession of Faith and the Savoy Declaration. The later document was based on the earlier Westminster Confession and grew out of a conference of Congregationalists in 1658, near the end of Oliver Cromwell's reign. Because of the disruption of English Congregationalism brought about by the restoration of the monarchy in 1660, the Savoy Declaration did not achieve prominence in England. But in America it was adopted by Congregationalists in synods in Massachusetts (1680) and Connecticut (1708), and it was reaffirmed by a council in 1865 representing Congregational churches throughout the United States. Among the churches this and other creedal statements had binding power only in so far as individual congregations adopted it, but the Savoy Declaration was accepted as the basis for many church creeds.

The Savoy Declaration begins by asserting that the "light of nature, and the works of the creation and providence,...manifest the goodness, wisdom, and power of God."[37] The declaration then describes the all-powerful deity: From the beginning of time God ordained "whatsoever comes to pass." Most important he predestined some men and women to salvation, others to damnation: "Some men and angels are predestined unto everlasting life, and others fore-ordained to everlasting death."

This was the most difficult doctrine in all of Protestantism: how could a just God condemn to eternal damnation men and women who had never had a chance to save themselves because of predestination? The number of the saved was so certain and definite, "that it cannot be either increased or diminished." The Savoy Declaration disposes of the common objection that this doctrine makes God the author of sin by simply denying that this is the case.

According to the declaration, in order to bring salvation to humanity God established two covenants. The first was a covenant of works, whereby men and women could achieve salvation through their own good deeds. But it was never fulfilled, not even once, because of the fall of Adam. That fall involved all of humanity: "Man by his [Adam's] fall having made himself uncapable of life by that covenant." God then instituted a new contract, the covenant of grace, which was made possible by the life and death of "the Son of God, the second person in the Trinity." Christ "did, when the fullness of time was come, take upon him man's nature, with all the essential properties and common infirmities thereof, yet without sin, being conceived by the power of the Holy Ghost, in the womb of the Virgin Mary of her substance." In his death the Lord "underwent the punishment due to us," and so became a mediator for men and women who believe in him.

The Savoy Declaration draws a comforting picture of the Christian life. The convert should be able to attain assurance of salvation; and through that assurance "his heart may be enlarged in peace and joy in the Holy Ghost." The convert need never despair of salvation, even when faced with doubts or temptation, for he or she could not lose the favor of God. But still the Christian should beware of "carnal security" and should be "always watchful" for the coming of the Lord.

The declaration was written after Congregationalists had worshipped freely in America for almost four decades and in England for almost two. It drew upon other earlier doctrinal statements in England and America. It also reflects the experience of men like John Winthrop, Thomas Shepard, and the thousands of other Puritans in Old and New England who had sought grace, but found that even in their best moments they could come no closer to God than "the suburbs of heaven." Part of the strength of the Congregational church in its early years lay in its synthesis between a religious idealism that sought union with God and a humility that recognized the distance between God and man. The saints would not live without periods of error and self-doubt; a fuller union with God lay in an unknown future. And while the convert dwelt on earth, all he or she could do was to be watchful for the coming of Christ, and hope that in the hour of judgment God would approve of the people's faithful efforts—in the midst of their "sowing and mowing and reaping"—to create on earth holy communities, holy churches, and holy lives.

NOTES

[1] William Bradford, *Of Plymouth Plantation* (New York, 1959), 25.

[2] Bradford, *Plymouth Plantation*, 61.

[3] John Winthrop, "A Model of Christian Charity," in Perry Miller, ed., *The American Puritans* (Garden City, N.Y., 1956).

[4] For Andover, see Philip J. Greven, Jr., *Four Generations: Population, Land, and Family in Colonial Andover, Massachusetts* (Ithaca, N.Y., 1970).

[5] Bartless Burleigh James, ed., *Journal of Jasper Danckaerts* (New York, 1913), 254-55, 270, 252.

[6] Paul Seaver, *The Puritan Lectureships: The Politics of Religious Dissent, 1560–1662* (Stanford, California, 1970), vii.

[7] James, *Journal of Jasper Danckaerts*, 255, 274, 263.

[8] Karl Barth first set forth his view of God in *The Epistle to the Romans* (Geneva, 1919). Two of Martin Buber's best known works are *Eclipse of God* (New York, 1952) and *I and Thou*, 2nd ed. (New York, 1958).

[9] Rudolph Otto, *The Idea of the Holy* (London, 1924), 12-13.

[10] Buber, *Eclipse of God*, 14; William James, *Varieties of Religious Experience* (New York, 1958), 42.

[11] Paul Tillich, "Vertical and Horizontal Thinking," in Hiram Hadyn and Betsy Saunders, eds., *The American Scholar Reader* (New York, 1960), 129.

[12] [William Perkins], *The Foundation of Christian Religion* (London, 1591), no page; John Preston, "A Sensible Demonstration of the Deity," in *Sermons Preached*

before His Majesty (London, 1631), 80.

[13] John Preston, *A Sermon of the Spiritual Life and Death* (London, 1630), 2; Robert Bolton, *A Discourse about the State of True Happiness* (London, 1612), 1.

[14] John Preston, *The Breastplate of Faith and Love* (London, 1630), 24.

[15] Thomas Shepard, *Certain Select Cases Resolved* (London, 1648), 142.

[16] Shepard, "Autobiography," in Michael McGiffert, ed., *God's Plot: The Paradoxes of Puritan Piety* (Amherst, Massachusetts, 1972), 57-60.

[17] Shepard, "Autobiography," 42, 45; John Winthrop, "Experiencia, 1616–18," 196.

[18] Preston, *Breastplate of Faith and Love*, 139.

[19] Winthrop, "Experiencia, 1616–18," 204.

[20] Thomas Shepard, "Journal," in McGiffert, *God's Plot*, 160.

[21] James Kendall Hosmer, ed., *Winthrop's Journal: "History of New England," 1630–1649* (New York, 1959), vol. 1: 121.

[22] Hosmer, *Winthrop's Journal*, 121.

[23] Samuel Clark, *The Saint's Nosegay, or a Posie of 741 Spiritual Flowers* (London, 1642), 49; Shepard, "Journal," 198. This thought recurs often in Puritan literature. "As hunger is a sign of health in the body," wrote Samuel Clark, "so is spiritual hunger of health in the soul." And in phrasing reminiscent of Shepard he said, "The greatest part of a Christian man's perfection in this life, consisteth rather in will than in work, and in desire and endeavor more than in deed." *Saint's Nosegay*, 50.

[24] Richard Sibbes, *Bowels Opened, or a Discovery of the Near and Dear Love, Union, and Communion betwixt Christ and the Church* (London, 1639), 9.

[25] Quoted in Charles E. Hambrick-Stowe, *The Practice of Piety* (Chapel Hill, N.C., 1982), 285.

[26] Quoted by Perry Miller, *The New England Mind: From Colony to Province* (Cambridge, Massachusetts, 1953), 15.

[27] John Preston, *The Saints Qualifications* (London, 1633), Introduction.

[28] William Perkins, "A Treatise Tending Unto a Declaration, Whether a Man be in the Estate of Damnation, or in the Estate of Grace" in Perkins, *Works* (London, 1608–30), vol. 1: 365.

[29] Preston, *Saints Qualifications*, 486.

[30] "A Catalogue of Erroneous Opinions," in David D. Hall, *The Antinomian Controversy, 1636–1638* (Middletown, Connecticut, 1968), 219-20.

[31] Quotation from Martin E. Marty, *Pilgrims in Their Own Land* (Boston, 1984), 81.

[32] The quotations on Shepard's conversion are from his "Autobiography," 40-44, 46, 61, 75.

[33] The quotations on Winthrop's conversion are from his "Experiencia, 1616–18" 191-92, 202-4.

[34] Walker, *Creeds and Platforms*, 142.

[35] Ward, "The Simple Cobbler," 96-100.

[36] The Cambridge Platform was published in Cambridge, Massachusetts, in 1649. It appears in Walker, *Creeds and Platforms*, 194-237.

[37] "The Savoy Declaration" in Walker, *Creeds and Platforms*, 354-408.

4
DECLENSION AND AWAKENING

THE PURITAN LEGACY OF A DYING FATHER

During the winter of 1694 an unknown Bostonian took quill in hand and began writing a book of religious advice to his young children. In large letters he penned a title page: "The Legacy of a Dying Father—Bequeathed to His Beloved Children." The father wrote that he had "seriously considered the brevity of life, and the uncertainty of all earthly comforts" and realized that he might die before his children reached maturity, leaving them without "a father to dandle you upon his knee, to comfort, support, and council you; a father to pity, to pray, and provide for you." The author was not expecting to die soon, but as a good Puritan he reminded himself that his life was in God's hands. This thought intensified his own religious life, and motivated him to write. He admitted that many books of advice to children had already been written, but he considered "that the dying words of a father do frequently lay more deep impression on their surviving children than the sayings of others." So he wrote his "legacy," he told them, in the hopes that it would "be of some good unto you, when after my head is laid in the silent dust."[1]

We do not know who wrote the "Legacy." The very anonymity of the author is significant, however, for it suggests the widespread influence of Puritan religious thought. The pronouncements of the ministers, the declarations of clerical and lay delegates at Cambridge and Savoy, the books that came off the presses in Boston and London—these and other formal religious discourses influenced not just a ministerial elite, but a whole people. Samuel Sewall, a great Congregational layman, once remarked that he had "sucked in" a belief in witchcraft with his mother's milk. He and thousands of other Puritans could as easily say that they imbibed a whole cluster of religious ideas with their Congregational upbringing. The "Legacy" provides an excellent example of the fact that those ideas went from ministers to the laity to children of lay persons, influencing the whole of New England culture.

The father began by telling his children to "know the God of your father, to serve him with a perfect heart and willing mind." God would hear their prayers, he said, "for the Lord searcheth all hearts, and understandeth all the imaginations of the thoughts: if ye seek him, he will be found of you, but if you forsake him, he will cast you off forever." They should never engage in any action in which they could not comfortably seek God's blessing. The father described prayer as "a holy conference with the living God," which "gives you admission into the stateroom of heaven if guided by the hand of faith." Prayers are "the spiritual breathings of a gracious heart." The children should also read the Bible, knowing it is the Word of God. "You may better be without the sun in the firmament than be without your Bible."[2]

He counseled the children always to attend church. "Religion never thrived more," wrote the father, "than when the Sabbath hath been most strictly kept." Christians, he said, should look forward to attending church and should "spend not more time in decking your body, than in adorning your soul." He advised his children to take notes on sermons; note taking "will not only keep you from sleeping, but be of singular advantage unto you as to family repetition." The father also urged his children to regard the sacraments seriously. They had been baptized, and that fact meant that they had a special obligation to seek God and salvation. When the time came for them to take communion, they should consider the sacrament in good Congregational fashion as a memorial of Christ's sacrifice: "Let your eyes be steadfastly fixed on the bread broken, and wine poured...being lively emblems of ye body and blood of Christ."[3]

In their daily lives, the father emphasized, good Christians should always behave as if God were watching their every act. The doctrines of predestination and salvation by grace should not lead them to ignore the obligation to "do good." Some of the most compelling phrases in the "Legacy" note the precariousness of life as an inducement to do good:

The neglect of one duty may hazard your everlasting well being.

I would advise you at no time to lie down in any condition, but what you are willing to die in.

It is your probation time, and as your actings are here so will it be with you in eternity.

No sooner did you begin to live, but you began to die.[4]

The author of the "Legacy" described activities that did not conform to his idea of life lived in the felt presence of God. Too many men spent their time "walking up and down the streets from house to house and tavern to tavern, spending their time, broaching of news, wasting their estates, etc." "Our present age," he said, "is strangely infatuated with invented fopperies." He was particularly critical of gaudy clothing and makeup. He did not like low-cut dresses, and he had these choice words about cosmetics: "They which love to paint themselves in this life otherwise than God created them, may justly fear that at the resurrection he who made them will not then know them."[5]

Some of these statements conjure up the stereotype of the Puritan as killjoy. But other passages support view that within the boundaries of moderation, Puritans enjoyed life. The father told his children: "I hate a stoical sourness that will not admit of a cheerful behavior." And he gave his sons this advice on choosing a wife: "Let her be one whom you can really love."[6]

Still, worldly pleasures should be enjoyed with moderation:

When the moon is fullest the further it is from the sun—the silver trumpet sounds a retreat from God.

Contentment comes not from the abundance of what a man hath, but in the moderating of his desires.

The more full the branches are of fruit, the more they bend themselves.[7]

The "Legacy" was written during the time when Benjamin Franklin was a boy. It is easy to imagine him receiving similar advice from his father, his friends, and his minister. Franklin's famous adage, "Early to bed, early to rise, makes a man healthy, wealthy, and wise," was a catchy phrase advocating diligence. Franklin may have invented the wording, but not the concept. "Keep good hours," the author of the "Legacy" advised. "Rise early, improving all opportunities of gaining knowledge and experience." And "defer not until tomorrow of doing that which ought to be done today."[8] But in Franklin's adages there is an important difference. Franklin urged men and women to live the fullest possible lives because life on earth was important in and of itself. What was lost in Franklin's advice is the conviction felt by the early Congregationalists that they were living in the presence of an all-powerful and ever-present God—that their lives were surrounded by eternity.

This was the message of the English theologians whose ideas formed the basis of early Congregationalism; this was the spirit in which the Puritan woman Thomasine Winthrop faced death; and this was the conviction underlying the creation of "holy commonwealths" in New England. The "Legacy" of an unknown New Englander to his children shows the continuity of that spirit. But in the latter half of the seventeenth century there were also changes in the religious character of the Congregational churches, challenges to the ideals of the founders and to the unity of the faith.

THE HALF-WAY COVENANT

The first major religious problem faced by the Puritans after the Antinomian crisis was the question of the status of the unconverted sons and daughters of the saints. Their parents were visible saints, and the children had been baptized and educated in the Christian faith. Most of them studied the Bible, listened to sermons, led moral lives, and raised their children as Christians. Some could claim to have experienced the change of heart that their parents described as conversion. But many could not.

Why were there fewer conversion experiences among second generation New Englanders? There are several reasons. The children's historical experiences were less conducive to dramatic religious feelings than those of their parents. The immigrants had tested their faith by adhering to a persecuted creed in England and by creating new religious communities in the American wilderness. In comparison the lives of their children and grandchildren were prosaic.

It is also possible that the children held back from communion because they exaggerated the faith of their fathers and mothers. God was elusive, even among the pious first generation of New Englanders: "The greatest part of a Christian's grace," Thomas Shepard had said, "lies in mourning for the want of it." But such imperfect and very human men and women as Shepard and Winthrop were portrayed to later New Englanders as superhuman. Their reverence for their ancestors may have led second and third generation New Englanders to hope to experience religious emotions with a steadiness and power that was rare even among the founders of the faith. The founders had to live up to God, their descendents had to live up to both God and the founders—which was harder to do!

At any rate, as the number of baptized but "unconverted" adults grew, the religious and political leaders of Massachusetts and Connecticut began to worry. They did not expect every New Englander to be a full member of the church. They rejected the membership ideas of Presbyterians, Anglicans, and other groups that favored geographically defined church membership: in Presbyterian Scotland all citizens were, de facto, full members of the Presbyterian church, and in Anglican England all citizens were expected to be full members of the Anglican church. The New England Congregationalists did create a territorial church in that Congregationalism was the only religion allowed during the early years of settlement, all citizens were expected to attend church and support the minister, and the state occupied itself with the welfare of the church. But at the same time Congregationalism was a believer's church, or a sect, in the sense that certain privileges were available only to the visible saints. The most important of these were communion, baptism for one's children, and the right to vote and hold office.

This curious wedding of state church and sectarian church required a continual supply of citizens who were saints. Although the ministers preached a doctrine of predestination and warned their people that salvation was available only to a saintly few, in practice they encouraged all of their people to experience salvation, and they assumed that among the people of New England many more would be saints than in England or Europe. Thus every New Englander was either a saint or a potential saint.

As time passed, however, the proportion of saints dwindled. Ministers continued to call their people to salvation, as they had in the past. But they also began to consider ways that the unconverted as well might be drawn closer to the church without abandoning the idea of visible sainthood or embracing a territorial conception of church membership. The clergy did not open baptism and communion to all New Englanders, nor did they invite the baptized but unconverted sons and daughters of the saints to the Holy Supper. But some ministers allowed the unconverted children of the saints to have their own children baptized. In this way they increased the number of men and women whose baptismal experience placed upon them a special obligation to support the church and seek salvation.

Congregational baptismal practice had already exhibited an element of tribalism. Simply by virtue of their blood line, the children of the visible saints were admitted to baptism, a sacrament that was denied to others. (The Baptists claimed that their sacramental practices were purer in that they restricted both communion and baptism to those who had experienced conversion.) For some Congregationalists the next logical step seemed to be to extend the bloodline of baptism to the grandchildren of the saints.

The discussion of this innovation, which acquired the derisive name "Half-Way Covenant" during the nineteenth century, began slowly. While sensing a need to broaden the baptismal covenant, ministers and lay men and women were reluctant to accept an innovation that apparently diluted the membership standards of the honored founders of New England. One of those founders, Richard Mather, argued for the Half-Way Covenant in 1648 during the debates over the Cambridge Platform, but as we have seen, he was in the minority at the time.

The individual churches still had freedom, however, to choose their own baptismal standards. Just before his death in 1649 Thomas Shepard announced that he favored the Half-Way Covenant. Six years later Richard Mather persuaded his Dorchester congregation to accept the innovation—but just a year later, in 1656, they had second thoughts and abandoned the Half-Way Covenant. That year the Massachusetts General Court called for a ministerial meeting to consider the baptismal issue. In 1657 thirteen ministers from Massachusetts and four from Connecticut met together in Boston and recommended that men and women who had been baptized and subscribed to their church covenant be allowed to have their children baptized. In the words of the ministers: "In case they [the children of the saints] understand the grounds of religion, are not scandalous, and solemnly own the covenant in their own persons, wherein they give up both themselves and their children unto the Lord, and desire baptism for them, we (with due reverence to any Godly learned [person] that may dissent) see not sufficient cause to deny baptism unto their children, these reasons for the affirmative being proposed to consideration."[9]

This formal endorsement of the Half-Way Covenant encouraged local congregations to adopt the innovation. But since this was a ministerial assembly rather than a synod (with lay delegates) and since each New England congregation was free to accept or reject the advice of the assembly, opposition to the Half-Way Covenant continued. Desiring a more authoritative statement, the General Court of Massachusetts ordered the formation of a synod "to discuss and declare what they shall judge to be the mind of God, revealed in his word." In particular they asked, "Who are the subjects of baptism?" The synod convened in Boston in 1662, with eighty lay and clerical representatives including John

Wilson, John Eliot, and Richard Mather and his son, Increase Mather.[10]

The synod was sharply divided on the issue of baptism, and had to meet three times before drawing up a statement, but in the end the supporters of the Half-Way Covenant prevailed. The preface to the findings of the synod is a careful reaffirmation of the fundamental principles of Congregationalism. The delegates declared, "That one end designed by God's all-disposing providence, in leading so many of his poor people into this wilderness, was to lead them unto a distinct discerning and practise of all the ways and ordinances of his house according to Scripture-pattern." Although the members of the synod thus declared their respect for the Puritan pioneers, they hastened to add that the founders had not known the whole truth—that more truth might be discovered. "He that hath made the path of the just as a shining light," they wrote, "is wont still to give them further light, as the progress of their path required further practice, making his word a lantern to their feet, to show them their way from step to step, though haply they may sometimes not see far before them."[11]

The members of the synod considered that they were following a "right middle way of truth" between those who were "too strict" and others who were "too lax and large" in determining who should be baptized. God did not approve of the "lax" way of admitting all to baptism, for then some would be admitted whose parents were not under the "yoke of Christ's discipline." But "on the other hand," they declared, "we find in Scripture that the Lord is very tender of his grace; that he delighteth to manifest and magnify the riches of it, and that he cannot endure any straightening [limiting] thereof....Hence when he takes any into covenant with himself, he will not only be their God, but the god of their seed after them in their generations."[12]

Here was the essence of Puritan tribalism and of the Half-Way Covenant. Simply by virtue of being born of full church members and by living in godly households, the baptized children had a special relationship to God. In the hierarchy of religious worth they were one step below those who had experienced conversion. But they were a full step above other New Englanders who attended church, yet were neither converted nor the descendents of the converted. And these other residents of Congregational New England were, in turn, much closer to God than men and women in Rhode Island and Virginia and England and other regions that did not even follow God's ordinances in worship.

The results of the synod of 1662 were recommended to the churches of Massachusetts by the general court. But the delegates did not anticipate that every church would immediately accept the Half-Way Covenant. The members of the synod had themselves declared, "We are far from desiring that there should be any rigorous imposition of these things." They did not expect a uniformity of practice and urged the parishes of New England to be tolerant of each other: "Let not him that practiseth despise him that forbeareth, and let not him that forbeareth judge him that practiseth."[13]

Practice did certainly vary during the years immediately following the publication of the results of the synod, but the atmosphere in New England was hardly characterized by "forbearance." A "pamphlet warfare" erupted that resulted in so many statements for and against the Half-Way Covenant that, according to scholar Perry Miller, "nobody can figure out how the typesetters and equipment in Cambridge kept up with the schedule." Charles Chauncy, the President of Harvard, and an opponent of the Half-Way Covenant led the attack with a tract titled *Anti-Synodalia Scripta Americana.*

On several occasions the debate over the covenant entered politics. Connecticut churches tended to be even more sympathetic to the Half-Way Covenant than those in Massachusetts. The Connecticut General Court, however, was reluctant to take a stand. In 1662 the colony had received a generous new charter by which it annexed New Haven—until then a separate colony and the home of one of New England's most conservative clerics, John Davenport. Fearing to antagonize the conservatives in the new territory, the Connecticut legislature in 1669 simply instructed the local churches to follow their own inclinations.

Religion and politics mingled in Massachusetts when John Davenport accepted a call to Boston's First Church. In his new parish he found that a large minority favored the Half-Way Covenant. When they sought his permission to form a new church, he refused. But they gained the support of a ministerial council and the colonial magistrates and founded Boston's Third Church.

Davenport died soon afterwards on March 13, 1670, at the height of the controversy over the Half-Way Covenant, but his supporters in the general court managed to pass a resolution criticizing the ministerial council that had encouraged the dissidents to secede from the First Church. The next year reform-minded clergy and laymen campaigned for delegates who would support their position in the general court. Their candidates came to control the court, and in 1671 the delegates withdrew their criticism of the ministerial council.

The opponents of the Half-Way Covenant suffered another defeat that year by the conversion of Increase Mather to the new standard. The son of Richard Mather, one of the earliest supporters of the innovation, Increase had led the opposition during the Synod of 1662, but now he changed his mind. Charles Chauncy, the President of Harvard, underwent another sort of conversion that indirectly weakened opposition: he decided that neither the grandchildren, nor even the children, of the visible saints should be baptized until they had experienced conversion. "Unless thou believest with all thy heart, thou mayest not be baptized," he said during the debates over the covenant.[14] His ideas led him beyond the recognized bounds of Congregational diversity. Following his beliefs to their logical conclusion, he became a Baptist.

The various congregations of New England were, if possible, even more inventive than the authors of the pamphlets on the Half-Way Covenant in deciding how to handle the question of church membership and baptism. Some churches adhered to the original standard. Richard Mather's church, for example, did not adopt the Half-Way Covenant until 1677, seven years after his death. For reasons that have never been fully explained, many congregations were more conservative than their ministers on the question of baptism. Some churches carried the original baptismal standards into the eighteenth century.

Other churches adopted the Half-Way Covenant, some requiring the parents to "own the covenant"—that is declare their acceptance of the covenant of their particular church. Others simply required that the parents be orderly Christians. Still others made baptism available to all infants, whether or not their parents or grandparents had been baptized. A few churches went still further, and opened not only baptism, but communion as well to the unconverted, in some cases requiring that they be descended from visible saints and in others not even demanding that. Their justification for such liberality was that both baptism and communion were "converting ordinances," capable of assisting the unconverted on the way to salvation.

Richard Mather had distinguished between half-way and full members of the church with the simple statement: "It is one thing to be in the covenant and in the church in respect of external state, and another thing to enjoy all the spiritual and eternal benefits of such a relation."[15] The founders had sought to unite the external and the spiritual church through identifying visible saints. But the compromises that had begun with the baptism of the saints' children allowed sincere Congregationalists to regard all of the churches ordinances as available to all serious Christians. This "external" involvement in the church could itself be regarded as a means to conversion. Following this logic, Northampton's Solomon Stoddard, who was for many years the leading minister in the Connecticut River Valley, argued that just as sermons were means of conversion, so too communion was a means God sometimes used to communicate saving grace. Many years later Williston Walker wrote, "The root of Stoddardeanism is to be found in the dual and inconsistent theory of those founders as to church-membership, by experience and by birth. It is the complete demonstration of that original incongruity."[16]

But the issue was more than one of experience versus birth as criteria for participation in the ordinances. The underlying problem was where to draw the line between church privileges available to all New Englanders, and privileges available only to the visible saints. The issue was made all the more complicated by disagreement as to whether the saints earned the privileges or the privileges made the saints. For example, Congregationalists debated whether communion should be available only to converts because they alone deserved it, or should be available to everyone because communion was a means of engendering converts. Congregationalists had a good idea of what separated them from Anglicans or Baptists, but among themselves they accepted a great deal of diversity on the membership issue. Most New Englanders embraced the position that their society should be divided into full members, half-way members, and others. (And almost everyone was some sort of communicant—unconverted and unbaptized New Englanders generally attended the Congregational churches on Sunday along with the visible saints.) But at the extremes some people opposed even half-way membership for the grandchildren of saints, and others wanted to open both baptism and communion to all sober citizens. By 1700 Congregational New England was a patchwork of different religious practices in matters of baptism and communion.

RELIGIOUS DECLENSION

The division over the Half-Way Covenant was the most serious breach in Congregational unity during New England's first century. But it was part of a larger, if less tangible, issue. The early Puritans had sought to create *holy* commonwealths in the New World. But many New Englanders were now asking themselves whether they could still claim that they were especially holy— favored by God and uniquely covenanted to do his will and reap his rewards. Could they claim that they were, in their daily lives, more godly than other Englishmen?

During the 1660s and 1670s the Puritans began to criticize themselves for failing to live the righteous lives demanded of a chosen people. Their failure to experience regeneration in sufficient numbers was only one sign of a more general failure. The more scrupulous New Englanders found many signs of moral decline. Merchants took advantage of their customers, charging more than their products were worth. Stylish ladies and gentlemen followed London fashions in clothing, apparently caring more for showy costumes than for pure hearts. Citizens who should have been "knit together" in communal love continually argued with one another.

Ministers began to preach many sermons, known as "jeremiads," castigating the people for their sins. Their titles suggest a sense of communal failure: *Nehemiah on the Wall* (Jonathan Mitchell, 1667), *New England's True Interest Not to Lie* (William Stoughton, 1668), *New England Pleaded With* (Urian Oakes, 1673), and *The Day of Trouble is Near* (Increase Mather, 1673). The jeremiads were surprisingly well received among the people who had allegedly fallen from grace. The most popular of all at the time was a jeremiad in the form of a poem, written by a Puritan minister, Michael Wigglesworth.

Called The Day of Doom, the poem begins by describing a sinful people, unaware of the judgment about to come their way:

> Still was the night, Serene and Bright, when all Men sleeping lay;
> Calm was the season, and carnal reason thought so 'twould last for ay.

These "vile wretches" were accustomed to "wallowing in all kind of sin," and yet they "lay secure." Then suddenly, "At midnight brake forth a Light, which turn'd the night to day." Graves flew open, and men and women stood before Christ. Some, clad in white, he chose for salvation:

> Christ's Flock of Lambs there also stands, whose Faith was weak, yet true;
> All sound Believers (Gospel receivers) whose Grace was small, but grew.

These, the saints, stood at Christ's right hand, "At Christ's left hand, the goats do stand." These were apostates, idolaters, blasphemers, and more:

Sabbath-polluters, Saints persecutors, Presumptuous men and Proud,
Who never lov'd those that reprov'd; all stand amongst this Crowd.

The poem goes on to describe the "fearful doom" of these sinners, whose "pain and grief have no relief." Then Wigglesworth returns to the saints and their blessed life in heaven:

For God above in arms of love doth dearly them embrace,
And fills their sprights with such delights, and pleasure in his grace.[17]

Michael Wigglesworth's "Day of Doom" was America's first "bestseller." Why were the Puritans so willing to admit—almost to relish—their own failings? Perry Miller has suggested that the jeremiads (whether in poetry or sermon) served as a catharsis: by allowing the New Englanders to indulge in communal guilt for their sins, they enabled those same men and women to behave in ways that were natural for colonists in a new world—farming, trading, and amassing wealth.[18] The jeremiads may well have worked in the subtle manner that Miller suggests, helping New Englanders enter a more secular age. But they also reflect a desire to keep alive the dream of the holy commonwealth.

Many New Englanders took seriously the criticisms of the jeremiads and believed that without real reform there would be real punishments from God. And "punishments" there were: an increase in shipwrecks, smallpox, and fires. In 1676 Boston's North Church and forty houses went up in flames; three years later the business section of town burned down. During the years 1675–76 New Englanders were engaged in King Philip's War, the most destructive Indian war in colonial history. One tenth of all the adult white males of military age in New England were killed, and half of the ninety towns in Connecticut and Massachusetts were attacked—twelve were destroyed.

In 1679 Increase Mather and eighteen of his clerical colleagues petitioned the Massachusetts General Court to call a synod. They asked that two questions be addressed: "What are the evils that have provoked the Lord to bring his judgments on New England?" and "What is to be done so that those evils may be reformed?"[19] The Court called a meeting, known as the Reforming Synod, and it convened in September of 1679. In just ten days the delegates drew up a document listing New England's sins and proposing remedies.

The document, called "The Necessity of Reformation" begins with a compelling descriptions of the original Puritan mission in the wilderness.

The ways of God towards this his people, have in many respects been like unto his dealings with Israel of old: It was a great and high undertaking of our fathers, when they ventured themselves and their little ones upon the rude waves of the vast ocean, that so they might follow the Lord into this land....The Lord alone did lead them and there was no strange God with them. In the wilderness have we dwelt in safety alone, being made the subject of most peculiar mercies and privileges....The Lord hath (by turning a wilderness into a fruitful land) brought us into a wealthy place; he hath planted a vine, having cast out the heathen, prepared room for it, and caused it to take deep rooting, and fill the land, which hath sent out its boughs into the sea, and its branches to the river....If we look abroad over the face of the whole earth, where shall we see a place or people brought to such perfection and considerableness, in so short a time?

God was good to the first generation of New Englanders because they "neither sought for, nor thought of great things for themselves, but did seek first the kingdom of God, and his righteousness." Had the Congregationalists remained faithful to their "errand," the document claimed God would have continued his mercies. But the New Englanders had forgotten their divine mission and "God hath changed the tenor of his dispensations towards us, turning to do us hurt, and consuming us after that he hath done us good." Now it was "high time" for New Englanders to consider the reasons for God's displeasure. The document listed many transgressions. First it observed, "There is a great and visible decay of the power of godliness amongst many professors in these churches." Then it noted the presence of pride in many forms: servants, for example, wore clothing "above their estates and degrees" and dressed in apparel "not becoming serious Christians." Too many people disregarded the solemnity of divine worship: "It is a frequent thing for men...to sit in prayer time, and some with their heads almost covered, and to give way to their own sloth and sleepiness, when they should be serving God with attention."

The good Puritan was not only supposed to attend and be attentive in church, but also he or she should regard the whole Sabbath day as holy. On the Puritan Sabbath people were expected to do no work. They were even to eat their meals cold, and they could not take part in sports or even in conversations about worldly topics. Such was the ideal, but the ministers noted that many New Englanders were working and traveling on the Sabbath and engaging in "worldly, unsuitable discourses." And during the week "many families" were equally remiss, failing to "pray to God constantly morning and evening."

These New Englanders were charged with leading ungodly lives. They quarreled among themselves, exchanging "unrighteous censures, back-bitings, hearing and telling tales." They spent too much time in taverns. "There is much intemperance," the ministers said. "The heathenish and idolatrous practice of health-drinking is too frequent." Some people dressed in ways unworthy of their Christian calling: "laying out of hair, borders, naked necks and arms, or, which is more abominable, naked breasts." Their social lives were besotted with "mixed dancings, light behavior and expressions, sinful company-keeping with light and vain persons, unlawful gamings, an abundance of idleness."

In their business lives, the clergy continued, these New Englanders were equally corrupt. They lied to one another and sought to enrich themselves at the expense of their neighbors: "There are some traders who sell their goods at excessive rates," and "day laborers and mechanics are unreasonable in their demands." These descendents of men and women who came to New England for the sake of religion had fallen away from their sacred mission and now preferred wealth to salvation: "There hath been in many professors [of religion] an insatiable desire after land and other worldly accommodations, yea, so as to forsake churches and ordinances and to live like heathen, only that so they might have elbow-room enough in the world. Farms and merchandising have been preferred before the things of God...." In this mad rush for "elbow room" self-aggrandizement became the god of many: "A public spirit is wanting in most of men. All seek their own, not the things that are Jesus Christ's."

The founders of New England had sought to create a society that would be righteous in all things—every impulse of heart and mind would be directed to the service of God. In practice even the Thomas Shepards and John Winthrops of the holy commonwealth found that the felt presence of God was more a thing sought after than experienced. But their descendents exaggerated the holiness of the founders; so they were all the more discouraged by life in a society that seemed excessively worldly. And they were all the more eager to bring the real world closer to their ideal of the holy commonwealth. Having listed New England's sins, the ministers proposed a number of improvements: "We hope that the sunk and dying interest of religion will be revived and a world of sin prevented for the future." Heads of families were told to set good examples for their children and servants. The church was advised to maintain high standards of discipline, and the magistrates to see that those guardians of morality, the ministers, were properly paid. Congregations were urged to renew their church covenants, collectively and aloud, and to "declare our adherence unto the faith and order of the Gospel, according to what is from the Scripture expressed in the [Cambridge] Platform of Discipline."

After its fall session of 1679, the Reforming Synod reconvened in May of 1680 to consider a statement of faith. The members adopted the Savoy Declaration, which was already in use in whole or in part throughout New England. With this formal endorsement the declaration achieved a status it would maintain for more than two centuries as the touchstone of Congregational belief. The members of the synod hoped that by listing New England's faults, proposing remedies, and adopting a statement of faith they could turn the commonwealth back to its holy mission. Changes did occur in the ensuing months. Many Congregationalists took part in communal covenant renewals. And thousands of pious New Englanders preserved and passed on the spiritual and moral precepts of the founders. One was the author of the "The Legacy of a Dying Father," and there must have been thousands of other men and women like him, who practiced family prayer, honored the Sabbath, took notes in church, and sought to commune with the Lord.

But each decade brought new challenges to the ideal of creating a whole society of men and women like the "dying father." Congregationalism was certainly an important force throughout the colonial period of New England's history. But other forces were at work, increasing the worldliness of the Puritan colonies. Between 1697 and 1750 New England's imports from England increased by five hundred percent. In 1740 Benjamin Colman, minister of Brattle Street Church in Boston, described New England's metropolis as "a place of great trade and business, finery and dress."[20] Reformers had sought to close the taverns, but by the middle of the eighteenth century there were 150 in Boston alone.

Even churches and graveyards showed signs of secularization. The "Lord's barns" of the seventeenth century, which had been plain buildings, gave way to more elaborate structures. Typical of the new churches was the meeting house in Guilford, Connecticut, built in 1726, with a 120-foot steeple. Inside the churches pews were often assigned according to wealth. New England gravestones also reflected the changing attitudes. Most of the stones in the seventeenth century bore the images of skulls. But the stones in the middle eighteenth century were often carved with pictures of cherubs or even the portraits of the ladies and gentlemen buried beneath. The fact of death, which drove early New Englanders to seek refuge in God, seems to have been muted by these images.

In Massachusetts the government itself took on a new face with the demise of the original colonial charter in 1684. The British government made the province part of a "supercolony" consisting of the Puritan commonwealths plus New York and New Jersey and called the "Dominion of New England." At its head was an Anglican Royal Governor, Sir Edmund Andros. Suddenly the Puritans found their holy commonwealths ruled by a man who was hostile to their religion and their mission. He even demanded that adherents to the Church of England be allowed to worship freely in Boston, the Puritan citadel. Andros's regime came to an end with the Glorious Revolution of 1688–89, and a new charter was obtained in 1691. But royal supervision of Massachusetts continued: the governor was appointed by the crown, and the franchise was based on wealth rather than on church membership.

Thus royal edicts as well as worldly appetites widened the gap between the ideal and the real in New England. Shortly after the granting of the new charter, one of the great tragedies in American history, the Salem witchcraft trials, occurred. The trials can be viewed as yet another sign of the religious tensions of the period. In 1692 the daughter of a minister, Samuel Parris, and several of her friends accused some of the townspeople in Salem Village of bewitching them. A special court was convened and other citizens came forward with accusations against other "witches." Twenty people were executed during the next few months and ten times as many were accused. The witchcraft mania ended only after the net of accusations took in such prominent citizens as the Governor's wife.

Historians have identified many causes for the witchcraft trials. The preponderance of young girls among the accusers and of middle-aged women among the "witches" suggests generational tensions between young girls, closely confined in their homes, and their mothers. Public records indicate that earlier hostilities associated with land disputes helped determine who would accuse whom of covenanting with the devil. Tensions occasioned by the change in the government of Massachusetts and by the outbreak of an Indian war on the frontier may also have increased popular credulity.

The trials are also a window on the religious psyche of a people who had lost confidence in themselves. Unable to mold the society that they believed God demanded, they found it easy to believe that the devil was loose in New England. Seemingly he was perverting and twisting the very forms of religion. Like true Christians his followers were said to meet in assemblies, sign covenants, and take part in "communion." But they allegedly worshipped the devil rather than God.

Ministers and lay men and women alike found it easy to anthropomorphize the "corruption" around them into the form of the devil. But, curiously, the very purging of the devil lent support to the inexorable movement toward a more rational and more worldly New England. Very few people ever apologized for taking part in the witchcraft trials, but many came to doubt whether the devil had actually come to Salem. People had died who, upon reflection, seemed godly citizens. The most pious of New Englanders would continue to follow Puritan religious precepts, but the typical Congregationalists of the eighteenth century were less inclined to utopian expectations than the earliest Puritans. Less confident of their ability to create a perfect commonwealth, they were also less inclined to discover "witches" in their midst.

CONGREGATIONAL CLERICALISM

On October 28, 1724, a young man named Ebenezer Parkman was ordained in Westborough, Massachusetts. Parkman's ordination—an occasion that he referred to in his diary as "my solemn separation to the work of the gospel ministry"—was carried on with the dignity deemed appropriate to that ceremony in the early eighteenth century. Four ministers presided over his initiation into the clergy, and Parkman reported that it was "truly the greatest day I ever yet saw."[21] It was natural that Parkman should have been pleased. At that time the ministers were New England's most distinguished professional group.

But the formal preeminence of the clergy was deceptive. Parkman's "solemn separation," although marked by an impressive ceremony, reflected the troubled condition of the clergy in the early eighteenth century. Ordination had changed greatly since the first years of Puritan colonization. In the 1630s it called attention to the minister's position as a member and leader of a fellowship of Christian believers. Almost one hundred years later it had come to celebrate his admission into a different and narrower community, that of the professional clergy. The new ordinations reflected an obsession with the importance of the ministry—a kind of "Congregational clericalism." This development was clearly inconsistent with the ideals of the first New England pastors, and it suggests that in an increasingly secular society the ministers were no longer confident of their ability to command widespread public esteem.

Ordination in the early seventeenth century was a simple service in which a congregation formalized its appointment of a minister. It emphasized the minister's close attachment to his congregation rather than his special role as a clergyman. The best account of an ordination ceremony in the early years of settlement is found in the records of the First Church in Dedham. The members of this church, including its future minister, John Allin, considered the creation of their congregation far more important than the installation of its pastor. The church was formed on November 8, 1638, after nearly a year of preparation. It met during the following winter, admitted new members, and listened to Allin's preaching. Only after the winter was over did the congregation set about choosing and ordaining a minister. The formation of the religious community was of primary importance; the formal installation of a pastor, although desirable, was less significant.[22]

In 1639 the church elected Allin as its minister and after careful deliberation decided that since the members had the power to choose their minister, they also had the authority to ordain him, "ordination being but a declaration of the same and installing into that office." On April 24, 1639, the ordination ceremony was carried out. Members and ministers of other churches were invited to attend, but they had little to do in the proceedings. The essential steps were taken by members of the Dedham church. Allin preached the sermon; he and two laymen ordained John Hunting as ruling elder; finally, Hunting and two other church members ordained Allin as pastor. The visiting clergymen played no part in the laying on of hands whereby Allin was made minister of the church. Their participation was limited to a favorable testimony made by their representative, Samuel Whiting of Lynn, of "their love and approbation of the proceedings."

The service was typical of early New England ordination ceremonies. A church could be formed before its minister was chosen; the minister was selected by the congregation; and the ordination sermon was delivered by the new pastor himself. These procedures emphasized the minister's place within a brotherhood of Christian believers rather than his separation to a sacred priesthood of religious leaders.

Within a few years, however, this emphasis would change. By midcentury in most churches the new minister was ordained by other ministers rather than by laymen in the congregation. This development radically altered the character of the ceremony. By placing their hands on the minister's head, the people had symbolized the congregation's choice of one of its members to guide their religious lives. Ordination by other ministers, in contrast, emphasized the young man's initiation into a clerical order. The fact that by the late seventeen century laymen were generally excluded from the ordination service suggests that the ministers were no longer willing to base their legitimacy so exclusively on their relationship to the congregations they served.

During the early eighteenth century ministers began to claim that clerical status was bestowed by the ordination ceremony, rather than by the people's election. As the ceremony of consecration by the ministers came increasingly to be regarded as the most significant step in the creation of a minister, the clergy attempted to make the event more formal and sought to end the festivities that the service had sometimes occasioned. In his ordination sermon for William Gager in 1725, Eliphalet Adams noted, "I have so often seen such offensive disorders upon such occasions as these, people seeming to imagine that it was a time when they might allow themselves more liberty." He urged that there "be no rude, light or unseemly behavior in this assembly this day."[23]

As ordinations came to symbolize the solemn initiation of a novice into a formal profession, ministers no longer preached their own ordination sermons. When clerical power had been thought to flow from the congregation, it had been natural for the new pastor to address his people in his moment of consecration. Thus Allin and other ministers of his time had preached their own sermons. But in the early eighteenth century, with the ascendancy of the belief that authority passed from minister to minister, this practice became exceptional. In 1729 William Williams, pastor of Weston, Massachusetts, said, "The objections against the person to be ordained, his preaching his own ordination sermon, have prevailed very much against the late custom."[24]

Within a century of the settlement of New England, the ordination ceremony thus underwent a series of important changes. Ordination came to be performed by ministers rather than by laymen; the ordination ceremony rather than election by the people began to be regarded as "conveying" the ministerial office; ministers were occasionally ordained without having been chosen by the people of any particular congregation as their pastor; the ordination sermon was preached by older ministers rather than by the man being installed; and finally, in keeping with these other changes, the clergy began to insist that the ordination day should be regarded as a solemn occasion. These changes indicate that the ministers now regarded themselves as a self-perpetuating body of religious leaders.

The ministers' tendency to identify the religious life of the community with their own caste was made explicit in eighteenth century sermons about the clergy. With the growing emphasis on the professional significance of ordination and with the spread of the custom of having experienced ministers do the preaching, ordination sermons acquired new importance.

Characteristically these sermons were discourses on the ministry—its necessity, authority, and responsibility—and the tenor of the sermons was strongly sacerdotal, in contrast to the pastoral emphasis of Allin's ordination text of 1639 (1 Corinthians 3:9): "For we are laborers together with God: ye are God's husbandry, ye are God's building." His sermon does not survive, but we may reasonably suppose that Allin dwelt on the community of the faithful, himself included as co-laborer with his fellow saints, rather than on the sacred "separation" of the ministerial office. Although it is impossible to date the change precisely, most of the ordination sermons published a century later not only dealt primarily with the clergy, but stressed the peculiar importance of the ministers. At the same time clergymen also discussed their profession in pamphlets about their salaries, in funeral sermons, and in general discourses on the ministry. In these tracts they equated the prosperity of their professional class with the spiritual destiny of the whole community. Solomon Williams, for example, argued that not only a people's temporal benefits, but their chance for salvation as well, were dependent upon the well-being of their pastor. If you treat your minister kindly, said Williams, "You will not only be the means of brightening his reward and glory in the future world; but will also secure your share in a prophet's reward, when he shall shine as the brightness of the firmament, and as the stars for ever and ever."[25]

In keeping with the new view of ministerial importance, it became customary not to form a new congregation until a candidate could be ordained pastor at the same time. In the seventeenth century many churches had been formed and had held services for months or even years before a minister was ordained to serve them. But in the eighteenth century the formation of a new parish and the ordination of its pastor usually occurred on the same day, suggesting that without a minister there could be no church.

It is evident from these developments that the early Protestant ideal present in the founding of the Dedham church, of a "priesthood of all believers," had lost some of its power in the New England of the 1720s and 1730s. In the new ordinations the ministers tended to apply ideals to their own class that had once been associated with New England as a whole. No example of this change is more dramatic than an assertion that appeared in two ordination sermons in 1726. On January 19 at the ordination of John Lowell in Newburyport, Massachusetts, Thomas Foxcroft declared that "ministers are (as parents in the family) in a somewhat elevated and conspicuous station; they are as a city set on a hill which can't be hid." Eight months later on September 14 at the ordination of Nathaniel Morrill in Rye, New Hampshire, William Shurtleff echoed Foxcroft's words: "The ministers of Christ should remember that they are in a peculiar manner the *Lights of the World*; that they are as a city set upon a hill, which cannot be hid."[26]

When John Winthrop uttered his famous words about the "city upon a hill" almost a century before, he had intended to describe all of the residents of New England. But now an image that had once evoked the coherent destiny of a whole community was limited to the description of a single profession. In such sermons the preachers seemed to be saying that if New England as a whole would not be holy, then the ministers would separate themselves from the people and become the pure community themselves.

This new sense of identity encouraged ministers to consider ways to enlarge their spheres of action as clerics. Of course, Congregationalism had no hierarchy of priests and bishops that met separately from the people. But during the eighteenth century ministers became attracted to the idea of forming clerical associations, through which they could meet independently with fellow pastors and discuss religious matters. In Connecticut these associations were given legal standing; in Rhode Island, Massachusetts, and New Hampshire, their power was informal. But in all four colonies the formation of these organizations reflected the clerical aspiration for authority and independence.[27]

THE GREAT AWAKENING

During the early eighteenth century, Congregational clericalism, in its various forms, provided ministers with a sense of professional importance. The new ordinations were impressive ceremonies, and ministerial associations gave the appearance of increased authority and unity of the clergy. The ministers enjoyed the illusion of courtly authority that came to them as members of a sacred caste. But without the support of the laity, the ministers' exalted status was simply an illusion. And such support could not be taken for granted, for even in the midst of the secular tendencies of the eighteenth century, many lay men and women were deeply pious and highly interested in religious matters. They objected to the diminution of lay authority; they criticized ministers who apparently confused their own self-interest with the welfare of the church; and through their control of ministers' salaries, they could remind the ministers of their literal dependence on the people. Because inflation continually ate away at clerical incomes, ministers needed the good will of the people to maintain a decent standard of living.

Clericalism did not work. Far from solving the underlying problems of secularism that troubled eighteenth-century religious leaders, it contributed to those forces by encouraging ministers to become another faction simply contending for its own interests. Clericalism failed to reunite or spiritualize the community, and it failed to win respect for the ministers. The failure of clericalism contributed, however, to the strength of another movement that would have an important bearing on the ministers' position. This was revivalism, the effort to bring about the spiritual regeneration of the whole community.

During the eighteenth century, increasing numbers of ministers sought to awaken the piety of their congregations. Their longing for a revival drew its strength both from the pastors' self-interest as religious leaders and from their calling as pastoral guides. A religious awakening would deliver the clergy from the tensions and frustrations they experienced and would produce a godly society where pastors and people could dwell together in "mutual love."

New England Puritans believed that societies as well as individuals could be either sinful or regenerate. In the seventeenth century, many Puritans had come to America because they believed that England, as a society, was entering a period of religious decline. During the eighteenth century many people believed that the whole of New England had become degenerate. The essence of the problem was, they felt, that most people's hearts seemed set upon the selfish quest for worldly gain rather than upon the religious search for Christian grace.

The Congregational ministers had little difficulty in listing New England's deficiencies. But it was one thing to describe the problem, another to produce a solution. One means they had used to motivate their congregations was to describe natural disasters, such as epidemics, droughts, storms, or earthquakes, as chastisements from God; if people could be made to feel that their earthly well-being was dependent upon the favor of the Lord, they might be less obsessed with worldly goods and more eager for divine favor. When, for example, the colonists had difficulties in an Indian war on the northern frontier in 1724, William Waldron wrote his brother: "'Tis strange to me that the Indians should so escape us seeing we have so many men out after them....Heaven frowns and we may expect nothing of success while Heaven is angry with us."[28]

Such events could be regarded as judgments from God, but their impact was limited. Most of New England's afflictions either affected only individuals or small groups of people or else they were so general as to appear to be ordinary events. However, in the early eighteenth century one remarkable event did affect large numbers of New Englanders. This was the great earthquake of 1727, which shook much of eastern New England. In response there was a religious revival in many towns, which encouraged the ministers to believe that the regeneration and reunification of communities would lead also to renewed respect for their ministry.

The earthquake was followed by a period of heightened religious awareness. For a short time whole communities seemed to be regenerated and more attentive towards their ministers. But earthquakes and Indian raids could produce only local, temporary religious reformations. What was needed, seemingly, was a more direct outpouring of God's spirit upon the people of New England. In 1737, Jonathan Edwards, minister of Northampton, expressed the general sense of expectation. He wrote, "A dark cloud seems to hang over the land...and particularly a spirit of contention, disorder, and tumult, in our capital town and many other places. What seems to be for us to do, is to wait upon God in our straits and difficulties."[29] With the help of God's spirit, the ministers hoped, the people would be truly regenerate and the ministry would be properly respected.

Hopes for a general revival also were encouraged by local revivals that occurred from time to time in colonial New England. In Northampton Jonathan Edwards's grandfather Solomon Stoddard had presided over many "harvests" that brought large numbers of people into the church. Further south on the Connecticut River Timothy Edwards, Jonathan's father, led an impressive revival among his people in 1716. In 1735 Edwards himself nourished a revival that spread through the valley. His account, *Narrative of Surprising Conversions*, enjoyed wide circulation and encouraged Congregationalists throughout New England to hope for a revival.

Five years later the movement that would be known as the "Great Awakening" began. Its origins in New England can be traced to the preaching journey of George Whitefield during the fall of 1740. He was an Anglican minister who had preached revivalistic sermons in England to audiences of thousands. On Thursday evening, September 18, he came to Boston. The next afternoon he preached in the Brattle Street Church to a congregation that included between twenty and thirty ministers. Benjamin Colman reported that Whitefield's "holy fervor of devotion in prayers and of address to the souls of his hearers in preaching were such as we had never before seen or heard."[30]

After Whitefield's initial success in Boston, he visited other parts of New England, where he was continually encouraged by the settled ministers. George Whitefield spent only a few weeks in New England, but during the two years following his triumphant journey the revival affected almost all of the towns and villages of the region. After Whitefield's departure another itinerant preacher, a Presbyterian revivalist from New Jersey, Gilbert Tennent, arrived in Boston and made a more lengthy trip through New England, preaching in many places that his English predecessor had missed. Tennent was followed, in turn, by dozens of other preachers, who carried the gospel to all areas of New England.

Itinerant ministers like Whitefield and Tennent were important catalysts to revivalism in New England, but a far greater contribution to the Awakening came from local pastors. For many years they had tried to foster religious revivals. Many of them sought the help of itinerants to produce revivals in their parishes, but they alone nourished the revival from week to week after the itinerant preacher left. In its early stages, the Congregational ministers were the strongest supporters of the Awakening, for seemingly, they had everything to gain from the new enthusiasm for religion. The awakened people attended church in large numbers, listened attentively to the preachers' words, and respected the ministers' religious leadership.

In parish after parish the revival was fostered by the settled pastor. Many actually generated their own awakenings; so the movement had focal points in hundreds of communities throughout New England. For example, in June of 1741 Marston Cabot of Thompson, Connecticut, reported that there were signs of a revival in his town. "There seems to be a shaking of late among the dry bones. God increase it, and let those that have life already have it more abundantly." In August three candidates whom he examined for communion told him "they had been much enlightened and quickened by my late preaching."[31] Local ministers frequently helped one another produce revivals in their parishes. Eleazar Wheelock, who had preached successfully in his own Lebanon parish, was invited by other ministers in his region, including Jonathan Edwards, to assist them.

The events surrounding the most famous sermon of the revival provide a good example of the way that local pastors cooperated in fostering the Awakening. On July 7, 1741, Stephen Williams, Eleazar Williams, and a third minister conducted a religious service at the meeting house in Suffield, Connecticut. Stephen Williams reported that "the congregation [was] remarkably attentive and grave." That evening at a second service in Suffield "there was considerable crying among the people, in one part of the house or another, yea, and a screeching in the streets." The following morning the congregation was again "considerably affected and many cried out." At noon the three ministers dined with Rev. Peter Reynolds "and then went over to Enfield where we met dear Mr. Edwards of Northampton." The distance from Suffield to Enfield was only three miles. So it is quite possible that many of the Enfield townspeople had attended the recent Suffield meetings, and that the Suffield people, already wrought up to a high pitch of emotional intensity, accompanied the ministers to Enfield.

That afternoon Edwards preached what Williams called "a most awakening sermon." Williams reported the consternation caused by Edwards's preaching: "Before the sermon was done there was a great moaning and crying out throughout the whole house—'What shall I do to be saved. Oh, I am going to hell. Oh, what shall I do for a Christ.'" Edwards was "obliged" to stop preaching because of the "amazing" shrieks and cries. When the congregation finally became still, the ministers met separately with the people. Williams reported: "The power of God was seen and several souls were hopefully wrought upon that night and, Oh, the cheerfulness and pleasantness of their countenances....We sung an hymn, and prayed, and dispersed the assembly."[32] From Williams's account is it not clear whether Jonathan Edwards ever completed his Enfield sermon, which came to be known as "Sinners in the Hands of an Angry God." It is clear, however, that before Edwards even arrived in Enfield, the people of the region had been brought to a high pitch of religious excitement by the local ministers.

After the Enfield sermon there were revivals in other parishes in the region. Each of these revivals was directed by local ministers who assisted each other in conducting services. Similarly, the early revival in Boston and other towns was led by local pastors, who were assisted occasionally by itinerant ministers who were invited to preach. These were the halcyon days of the religious movement that came to be known as the Great Awakening. The community seemed reunited in piety and holiness. Men and women treated each other with charity. The ministers were able to offer dramatic religious leadership to their people, and the people, in turn, held their ministers in high esteem.

But the clerical euphoria of the early months of the Awakening was short-lived. An episode in Springfield after the Enfield sermon, and many other similar incidents throughout the colonies, indicated a disturbing course that the movement would soon take. After Stephen Williams had conducted his first revival meeting in Longmeadow—he was inspired by Edwards's example in Enfield to do so—he went to an evening service in nearby Springfield. At the end of the meeting he left the church and found his son, John, in the churchyard, "speaking freely, boldly, and earnestly to the people and warning of them against damnation and inviting them to Christ." Williams tried to interrupt his son, but the youth "seemed beyond himself and had great discoveries of the love of Christ and had a great concern for souls." Overwhelmed by the spirit within, the youth was determined to preach to others. This was Williams's first encounter with an aspect of the revival—a radical enthusiasm—that was soon to challenge all the settled pastors of New England.

NOTES

[1] "The Legacy of a Dying Father. Bequeathed to His Beloved Children," (Congregational Library, Boston, 1694), opening remarks.

[2] "Legacy," 1, 2, 9.

[3] "Legacy," 14, 14, 16, 15, 12.

[4] "Legacy," 19, 20, 21, 42, 54.

[5] "Legacy," 64, 97, 98.

[6] "Legacy," 87, 110.

[7] "Legacy," 31, 33, 86.

[8] "Legacy," 93-94.

[9] "A Disputation Concerning Church Members and their Children," in Walker, *Creeds and Platforms*, 296.

[10] Walker, *Creeds and Platforms*, 263-64, 313.

[11] "Preface to the Result of 1662," in Walker, *Creeds and Platforms*, 301, 302.

[12] "Preface to the Result of 1662," in Walker, *Creeds and Platforms*, 302-304.

[13] "Preface to the Result of 1662" in Walker, *Creeds and Platforms*, 304.

[14] Quotation from Miller, *Colony to Province*, 97.

[15] Quotation from Miller, *Colony to Province*, 98.

[16] Walker, *Creeds and Platforms*, 283.

[17] Michael Wigglesworth, "The Day of Doom," in Perry Miller and Thomas H. Johnson, eds., *The Puritans: A Sourcebook of Their Writings* (New York, 1967), vol. 2: 587-606.

[18] Miller, *Colony to Province*, 52.

[19] "The Necessity of Reformation," in Walker, *Creeds and Platforms*, 426, 433. The quotations that follow are from "Necessity," pages 423 to 434.

[20] Benjamin Colman to "Mr. Holden," January 6, 1734/35, Colman Papers, Massachusetts Historical Society, Boston.

[21] Francis G. Walett, ed., "The Diary of Ebenezer Parkman, 1719–1728," American Antiquarian Society, *Proceedings*, N.S., 71 (1961), 117-18. The material on the New England ministers in this chapter and chapter five is adapted from my essay, "Congregational Clericalism: New England Ordinations before the Great Awakening," *William and Mary Quarterly*, 3d ser., 31 (July 1974), 481-90, and my book *God's Messengers: Religious Leadership in Colonial New England, 1700–1750* (Baltimore, 1976).

[22] *The Early Records of the Town of Dedham* (Dedham, Massachusetts, 1888), vol. 2: 1-15, 17-18, 20.

[23] Eliphalet Adams, *The Work of Ministers, Rightly to Divine the Word of Truth* (Boston, 1725), 1-2.

[24] William Williams, *The Office and Work of Gospel Ministers* (Boston, 1729), 2.

[25] Solomon Williams, *The Glorious Reward of Wise and Faithful Teachers* (Boston, 1730), 22.

[26] Thomas Foxcroft, *Ministers, Spiritual Parents* (Boston, 1726), 26; William

Shurtleff, *The Labor That Attends the Gospel Ministry* (Boston, 1727), 30.

[27] Youngs, *God's Messengers*, 69-76. The separation of ministers and their people was attenuated by the reality of everyday life in New England's parishes. See Youngs, *God's Messengers*, 40-63.

[28] William Waldron to Richard Waldron, June 15, 1724, Library of Congress photostat at Massachusetts Historical Society, Boston.

[29] Jonathan Edwards to Benjamin Colman, May 19, 1737, Colman Papers, Massachusetts Historical Society, Boston.

[30] Benjamin Colman, notes on Whitefield's visit to Boston, in 1740 Colman Papers, Massachusetts Historical Society, Boston.

[31] Marston Cabot, Diary, June 7, 1741 and August 18, 1741, New England Historic Genealogical Society, Boston.

[32] Stephen Williams, Diary, July 7-9, 1741, Longmeadow Public Library, Longmeadow, Massachusetts.

5
REVIVALISM AND RATIONALISM

THE TURMOIL OF THE GREAT AWAKENING

During the early stages of the Great Awakening, roughly from 1740 to 1742, the ministers believed that the revival would issue in a new era of religious sincerity, brotherly love, and respect for the ministers. During the Awakening, however, men and women began increasingly to challenge religious institutions in the name of religious spirit. At first the ministers themselves had led the revival by preaching compelling sermons to their people. Then the people began to participate more actively in religious services by crying out, exhorting, and having visions. Next the radicals of the revival, lay people and clergy who believed they were directly inspired by God, began to disregard traditional religious practices. Uneducated men and women preached without formal preparation. Itinerant preachers invaded parishes and delivered sermons without the approval of regular pastors, and enthusiasts claimed that many clergymen were unconverted and hence unfit to lead their people. Thus, instead of improving the position of the ministerial profession, the Great Awakening actually undermined the position of the clergy. Ironically, the nourishing of the Great Awakening was one of the great achievements of the eighteenth-century clergy, and yet, its fruition posed the century's biggest challenge to their ideal of professional religious leadership.

The volatile quality of the Awakening is nowhere better described than in a famous passage from the spiritual autobiography of a Connecticut layman, Nathan Cole. Cole first heard that George Whitefield was preaching in Philadelphia, "like one of the old apostles, and many thousands flocking to hear him preach the Gospel." Word came of Whitefield's progress through New York and New Jersey, "which brought on my concern more and more, hoping soon to see him." Then suddenly one morning a messenger appeared saying that Whitefield would preach soon at nearby Middletown. Here is Cole's account of what happened:

I was in my field at work. I dropped my tool that I had in my hand and ran home to my wife, telling her to make ready quickly to go and hear Mr. Whitefield preach at Middletown, then I ran to my pasture for my horse with all my might, fearing that I should be too late. Having my horse, I with my wife soon mounted the horse and went forward as fast as I thought the horse could bear; and when my horse got much out of breath, I would get down and put my wife on the saddle and bid her ride as fast as she could and not stop or slack for me except I bade her, and so I would run until I was much out of breath and then mount my horse again, and so I did several times to favor my horse.

We improved every moment to get along as if we were fleeing for our lives, all the while fearing we should be too late to hear the sermon, for we had twelve miles to ride double in little more than an hour....And when we came within about half a mile or a mile of the road that comes down from Hartford, Wethersfield, and Stepney to Middletown, on high land I heard a noise of horses; feet coming down the road, and this cloud was a cloud of dust made by the horses' feet. It arose some rods into the air over the tops of hills and trees; and when I came within about 20 rods of the road, I could see men and horses slipping along in the cloud like shadows, and as I drew nearer it seemed like a steady stream of horses and their riders, scarcely a horse more than his length behind another, all of a lather and foam with sweat, their breath rolling out of their nostrils every jump. Every horse seemed to go with all his might to carry his rider to hear news from heaven for the saving of souls. It made me tremble to see the sight, how the world was in a struggle.

I found a vacancy between two horses to slip in mine and my wife said, "Law, our clothes will be all spoiled, see how they look," for they were so covered with dust that they looked almost all of a color, coats, hats, shirts, and horse. We went down in the stream, but heard no man speak a word all the way for 3 miles, but every one pressing forward in great haste; and when we got to Middletown old meeting house, there was a great multitude, it was said to be 3 or 4,000 of people, assembled together. We dismounted and shook off our dust, and the ministers were then coming to the meeting house. I turned and looked towards the Great River and saw the ferry boats running swift backward and forward bringing over loads of people, and the oars rowed nimble and quick. Everything, men, horses, and boats seemed to be struggling for life. The land and banks over the river looked black with people and horses; all along the 12 miles I saw no man at work in his field; but all seemed to be gone.

When I saw Mr. Whitefield come upon the scaffold, he looked almost angelical; a young, slim, slender youth, before some thousands of people with a bold undaunted countenance. And my hearing how God was with him everywhere as he came along, it solemnized my mind and put me into a trembling fear before he began to preach; for he looked as if he were clothed with authority from the Great God, and a sweet solemn solemnity sat upon his brow, and my hearing him preach gave me a heart wound. By God's blessing, my old foundation was broken up, and I saw that my righteousness would not save me.[1]

From the start, as suggested in this passage, the revival was accompanied by a sense of God's immediate presence in the world. Nathan Cole and the other farmers and artisans flocking towards Middletown seemed to be involved in a surrealistic drama. The God whom they had heard about all their lives seemed suddenly to be in their midst, and the world was in turmoil. At first this new spirituality was controlled by regular ministers. But some ministers began preaching in new ways, abandoning notes and speaking extemporaneously, apparently moved by the spirit of God. Sometimes it is difficult to know who was actually leading the revival in a particular parish. The ministers initiated the Awakening, but the "crying out" in the congregations may have been equally important in keeping emotions inflamed. Sometimes the revival came simultaneously upon minister and congregation, as if both were under the influence of forces beyond their control.

Such a revival occurred in Durham, New Hampshire, under the leadership of Rev. Nicholas Gilman. He reported that on November 17, 1741, in the evening, thirty or forty people came "from all quarters on the rumor that there was to be a meeting at my house." He prayed with them, read a religious tract, and "added a word of exhortation." Three days later he held another meeting in the evening at his home. Though the night was "dark and dirty" a large crowd gathered. Significantly, the work that Gilman chose to read them was Jonathan Edwards's *Narrative of Surprising Conversions*. Gilman said he "read part of it and made some remarks to the people." Quite possibly the news from other parishes where the revival was already in progress heightened expectations. At any rate, the town soon experienced an intense awakening.

Gilman reports that on January 29, 1742, he "had more joy than usual through the day." In the evening, when at the end of the service the people seemed in a great haste to leave the meeting house, Gilman said: "I was moved to tell them that if I could see them flocking to heaven as they were from meeting, it would make my heart leap within me." On hearing this the people "drew into the house again and were attentive." Gilman resumed preaching, and he and his audience "continued in religious exercises all night." He said that it seemed the Lord did "anoint me with that holy anointing...and as it were touched my eyes as with a coal from his altar." Gilman was not the only person affected that night. The whole congregation "had the presence of the Lord with us in a very wonderful manner." The people "held on through the night, blessing and praising, admiring and adoring God and the redeemer, sometimes praying, then singing, exhorting, advising and directing and rejoicing together in the Lord." Some members of the congregation even had visions. One "saw a white dove come down into the meeting house." Another "declared he saw two angels." A third "saw a bright light like an exceeding bright star about as big as a man's fist." Later Gilman recalled, "It seemed the shortest, and was, I think, the sweetest night that I have seen."

The religious intensity continued in Durham for the next few months. Gilman was passionately involved in the revival and his preaching seems to have inspired the town's awakening. But his ministerial voice was soon joined by the voices of lay persons who believed that the spirit moved them to participate. On March 4, Gilman encouraged a girl named Mary Reed to describe a vision to the whole church. After she spoke Gilman added a "word of exhortation" and then, he said, "It appeared to me that the Holy Ghost came down with power upon the people so that there was almost an universal outcry, some rejoicing and others lamenting, but few I believed were unmoved."

As time passed, the people were increasingly involved in the Awakening. A meeting on March 14 was built largely around their utterances. First Gilman preached a sermon; then he read "Mary Reed's Last Vision," which he had transcribed from her words the previous day. Then for a time the congregation appears to have led the service: "Two youths under good influences and of regular life, fell into visions and spake out, so that they were heard all over the congregation....People attended, some spake and exhorted, presently an outcry began which lasted til within night."[2]

Although Nicholas Gilman maintained a semblance of control over his parish, the spiritual powers that enabled him to initiate the revival were now shared with many other Christians. The Awakening began to undermine the unique position of the minister as God's representative. Claiming inner light as their authority, inspired—some would say "crazed"—ministers and lay people began to travel around New England preaching with or without the approval of local authorities. Some claimed that they had the power to condemn unconverted ministers.

A layman named Richard Woodbury, for example, wrote William Parsons, minister of South Hampton, New Hampshire, telling him that a great battle was coming. "We hear the sound of the trumpet and the alarm of war," he said. "Prepare to give account of your stewardship since you have had the care and charge of precious souls committed to you." He warned Parsons against being on the wrong side when the end came and identified opposition to the Awakening with opposition to Christ.[3] Implicit in Woodbury's warning was the idea that a person must be converted to be a successful minister. New England's pastors had always agreed that the clergy should be converted, but they were reluctant to make conversion a prerequisite for ordination and generally agreed that God's grace could be conveyed by the preaching of any minister, good or bad. People like Woodbury, however, often made spirituality the sole test of a minister's qualifications and made harsh judgments concerning the religious state of ministers.

The Great Awakening, which had at first inspired hopes for a new spiritual unity in New England, thus became the source of turmoil and divisions. By 1742 many Congregationalists identified themselves as supporters or opponents of the revival. The former were called "New Lights," indicating their support of the new light of the Gospel, which they perceived in the Awakening. Their opponents were called "Old Lights," and claimed to support the old faith of New England. These divisions inspired some men and women to quit the church to become Anglicans, Baptists, or Separates. The division also contributed to the creation of a distinctive New England Theology, built on the Old Calvinism, but characterized by distinctively American doctrines.

Whitefield himself occasioned the earliest division. In 1740 he told a congregation at Boston's Old South Church, "The generality of preachers talk of an unknown and unfelt Christ; and the reasons why congregations have been dead is, because they have had dead men preaching to them." While admiring Whitefield, even Jonathan Edwards thought this was going too far. When Whitefield visited Northampton that year, Edwards admonished him against accepting "impulses" as evidence of regeneration and "judging other persons to be unconverted."[4]

As the revival spirit coursed through New England in 1741 and 1742, an increasing number of ministers became annoyed at the pretensions and disruptiveness of its more fanatical leaders. In 1741 the Connecticut legislature called a synod, whose ministers declared their dislike of itinerant preachers. The next year the Connecticut legislature passed a law forbidding ministers to preach in parishes other than their own without the approval of the local pastor—upon pain of loss of salary. In 1743 the annual ministerial convention in Boston adopted a statement condemning "several errors in doctrine, and disorders in practice, which have of late obtained in various parts of the land." Thinking undoubtedly of meetings like those in Nicholas Gilman's New Hampshire parish, the ministers condemned "the disorderly tumults and indecent behaviors" that had accompanied many revival meetings.[5]

Charles Chauncy of Boston's First Church became the leader of the revival's opponents, and his *Seasonable Thoughts on the State of Religion in New England* (1743) became their bible. Chauncy's premise was simple: that most of the extravagant behavior occasioned by the Awakening had nothing to do with religion. An evangelist like Jonathan Parsons of Lyme could report with simple enthusiasm that during his sermon, "Several stout men fell as though a cannon had been discharged and a ball had made its way through their hearts."[6] And a New Light read such reports as evidence of the extraordinary working of God's spirit. But Chauncy, who once remarked that he hoped that his preaching would never be oratorical, looked on such behavior with disdain.

Chauncy questioned whether George Whitefield should even have come to New England. "I could never see, I own," wrote Chauncy, "upon what warrant, either from *scripture* or *reason*, he went about preaching from one province and parish to another, where the Gospel was already preached, and by persons as well qualified for the work, as he can pretend to be." Chauncy's account breathes contempt for Whitefield. The grand itinerant "pretends" to be a good preacher; he has "pompous" ideas of his own work.[7]

Although other New Englanders shared Chauncy's mistrust of religious radicalism, many sober Congregationalists continued to look upon the revival as God's work. Ninety of them met in 1743 in Boston, under the leadership of such men as Benjamin Colman of Brattle Street Church and Thomas Prince of Old South Church. They passed a resolution declaring "that there has been a happy and remarkable revival of religion in many parts of this land, through an uncommon divine influence." They admitted that there were "irregularities" in the movement, but they argued that these were not the essence of the Awakening. "Who can wonder," they asked, "if at such a time as this Satan should intermingle himself, to hinder and blemish a work so directly contrary to the interests of his own kingdom."[8] Sixty-four pastors added their names to the document, and statements of support were collected from forty-five others.

But despite the support of such ministers, the atmosphere in 1744, when George Whitefield made a second missionary trip to New England, had changed. Even the New Lights were wary of the extravagances that had followed the first journey. The faculties of Harvard and Yale issued statements criticizing Whitefield's methods, and throughout New England associations of ministers spoke against his being admitted to their pulpits. Relatively few converts came into the church in the wake of his second visit. But this fact, often cited as evidence of a diminution in revivalistic fervor, can be misleading. A parish of enthusiastic lay people may actually produce few new converts at a particular time, simply because most are already converted. Conversion tallies, in other words, are not necessarily an accurate measure of religious enthusiasm.

Throughout New England groups of men and women were attracted to the more radical elements of the revival—shouting, weeping, seeing visions. If they could not control their local church, they broke off and formed separate congregations. Known variously as Separates or Strict Congregationalists, they were often poor. They rejected the idea that a minister must be educated, and they also rejected the clerical associations through which ministers tried to control the revival. Believing that only true converts should be admitted to communion, they also rejected the Half-Way Covenant. Theirs was not an easy life. The Separate congregations were often disturbed by their own centrifugal tendencies—schisms tended to breed schisms—and they were persecuted by the state, which compelled them to pay taxes to the regular ministers. Some of these churches died out, many became Baptist.

THE MINISTER AS PASTORAL GUIDE

Most Congregationalists stayed within the church, but that fact owed less to clerical image ministers had created during the previous half century than to the clerical reality of their lives as pastors. Although the clergy were apparently determined to acquire an aura of special holiness, their work as ministers brought them close to the common men and women of their parishes. That proximity— rather than the claims of Congregational clericalism—was the basis for the enduring popularity of their church.

For every hour that the minister spent in the pulpit, he spent many more giving individual religious counsel to members of his parish. He did not simply pronounce doctrine on the Sabbath and then wait for the people to apply religion to their own lives. Instead he reinforced his sermons with four kinds of pastoral instruction: setting a good example, catechizing, giving counsel, and reprimanding. The pastor's handling of these duties was often the key to his success or failure as a minister.

The first of these tasks, setting a good example, was the sine qua non of the minister's work. If he failed in this and led a degenerate life, even the best of his sermons would be received as the teaching of a hypocrite. In the small towns of colonial New England, the pastor's moral life was a matter of public knowledge. If he were intemperate, committed adultery, or cheated his neighbor, the whole community would be aware of his transgression. Relatively few clergymen were actually involved in moral scandals, but those who were often ruined their ministerial careers. This was especially true of intemperance. In a study of four hundred Congregational ministers who settled in New England between 1680 and 1740, Clifford K. Shipton found that only 3 percent became involved in scandals. But of the six ministers who were charged with drunkenness, all were dismissed. A farmer or blacksmith might drink heavily and still perform his tasks, but a clergyman's private and public life could not be separated. If a man were intemperate, he could not be a minister.[9]

A second form of religious instruction was catechizing. During the eighteenth century the minister customarily conducted special meetings for children of the community to teach them religious principles. In addition, the ministers sometimes held meetings for the adults of their parishes. Israel Loring, minister of Sudbury, noted that at such times the pastor should adapt his instruction to the "capacities" of the audience and should not push his people "too hard."[10] In their pastoral labors the chief goal of the ministers was to speak to different kinds of people on their own level.

Sensitivity to an audience was even more essential in a third area of the pastoral ministry, counseling. By discussing the catechism the minister sought to make the people understand the principles of Christianity. By giving counsel to individual members of the parish, the minister helped men and women put those doctrines into practice. If the minister was diligent, this could be one of the most time-consuming parts of his work. Thomas Clap, for example, who later became president of Yale, kept careful notes on the spiritual condition of each of his seven hundred parishioners while he was minister at Windham, Connecticut. At the height of an early revival in Windsor, Connecticut, Timothy Edwards counseled as many as thirty people in a single day.

In pastoral visits the minister's object was to discuss with his people the condition of their souls. Such conferences acquired a particular urgency if a person was dying. Often the parishioners would send word to the minister when a member of the family was ill. During visits to the sick, ministers came into close contact with the miseries of their people. Ebenezer Parkman referred to such meetings as a time "wherein my Heart has often Trembled within me." Parkman liked to take his wife with him on these visits—perhaps to give additional encouragement to the afflicted.[11]

Undoubtedly, some of the most important pastoral visits were to men and women facing death. Such people were likely to be particularly concerned about the state of their souls. But pastoral counseling was intended to benefit the living as well as the dying. During visits the minister could clarify puzzling points of doctrine and help the parishioner know the state of his or her soul. Although the Congregationalists had no formal practice of confession that would allow the church member to unburden his soul in the presence of a clergyman, the pastoral visit served a similar purpose.

A fourth area of pastoral responsibility was particularly troublesome. Sometimes the minister had to discipline erring members of his church. If a sin was of a personal nature, such as a man's mistreating his wife, the pastor would first speak to him in private. If the offender did not immediately promise to cease doing wrong, or if his offence was public, he was admonished, and the elders and brethren of the church were informed of the offense. They and the minister could then cut the offender off from church privileges.

One problem that often troubled ministers was the vagueness of the moral law. There was, for example, no clear boundary between lawful entertainment and sinful revelry. Ebenezer Parkman has left a detailed account of his feelings on one such occasion. He had attended a barn raising and a supper that lasted until ten o'clock, which he considered a late hour. Parkman reported: "I manifested so much uneasiness that we were detain'd that I concluded everybody would retire home as Soon as they might." He went home, but then learned that "there were many yet behind and among them Some Heads of Family." So he arose and returned to the company. Having "acquainted" the host "with what Time of Night it was," he interrupted the revelers "and admonish'd them, and sent them home." Parkman reflected, "This Exerting my Authority gave me great uneasiness, but I was resolute to Show Impartiality and not be partaker of other Men's sins, as likewise to discharge my own Duty as Watchman in this Place and as having Care of their Souls."[12]

Being a faithful "watchman" and handling all of his pastoral duties well were probably the most difficult parts of a minister's work. He did not teach men and women to apply Christian doctrine to their own lives simply by making authoritative pronouncements about religion. Instead he sought to show the relevance of Puritan theology by applying it to the day-to-day circumstances of the human beings in his parish. In his secular life he sought to set a good example of Christian behavior. In catechizing he attempted to make his message comprehensible by adjusting it to the needs of his audience. During his pastoral visits he listened to people's religious thoughts and sought to help them confront their individual problems. Finally, in offering admonishments, he frequently acted with reluctance and in a spirit of humility.

The minister was further bound to the people by sharing in their common experiences. Most Congregational pastors were married and had children. Most also spent part of their time, like their parishioners, as farmers. At certain seasons, such as harvest, the minister might expect some help from his people. But part of his day was often devoted to menial labor. The clergy's commonplace books, which were primarily for religious notes, often contained extensive entries on agriculture. In one pastor's book, for example, one may read, "Mow grass that is full of polly-pod and brakey-stuff, the second week in July. Cut about this time cattle will eat it best and it will go furthest." Ministers even mingled pastoral and farm labors. Ebenezer Parkman reports that on one occasion he was raking in his fields when two members of his congregation, Mr. and Mrs. Jonas Brigham, came to report their religious experiences. He first recorded the husband's account. Then, he reported, "Mr. Brigham took my Rake whilst I wrote for his wife."[13]

The minister's association with the congregation was also apparent in his sermons. Their style and content were adjusted to the capacities and interests of average men and women, and they were relevant to the day-to-day problems of the parish. In the sermon, above all else the minister sought to make manifest God's presence in the world—in current events, in the passing of the seasons, and in the spiritual history of each person's soul. "A minister has nothing to say in the pulpit," declared one pastor, "but what concerns all the congregation, and he may if he will express it in words easy to be understood."[14]

Even while changing the ordination services to reflect their own importance, and while preaching sermons about the glory of the clergy, the ministers were in their daily lives bound close to their people by circumstance and vocation. During the Great Awakening, when their position was challenged by itinerant preachers, who claimed greater spiritual authority, their association with their people usually enabled them to continue as clerical leaders.

The ministers' status had been based in part upon their professional dignity and in part upon the effectiveness of their ministerial work. The Great Awakening forced them to place a new emphasis upon the more mundane, but more stable source of their power, their ability to work with lay men and women. Although the activities of religious enthusiasts were the most dramatic events of the revival period, it was usually the settled pastors who guided the revival in their parishes and counseled the people who had religious experiences. In this regard, a passage from Ebenezer Parkman's diary describing a barn-raising in 1750 is exemplary: "My neighbors raised my New frame and we sung part of Psalm 127...and Psalm 128....Sundry Neighbors sent and brought Cheese, Cake, Wheat Bread, etc. which with Some Apple Pyes which my wife provided made up our Entertainment."[15] From such communal events the ministry in hundreds of Congregational parishes derived strength during and after the Great Awakening.

OLD LIGHTS AND NEW LIGHTS

Most Congregationalists stayed within the church, but the Awakening sharpened lines of division on theological issues. Disparate tendencies in New England Calvinism had been apparent from the earliest years of colonization; in the 1740s they became more pronounced. The central problem was the question of people's role in their own salvation. Protestantism had begun with Martin Luther's assertion that men and women are saved by grace alone, not by their own good works. The Puritans embraced that idea as the central truth of their religion. But they were unwilling to view human beings as strictly passive in their own salvation. Men and women could not save themselves, the believed, but they could labor to make themselves *appropriate* vessels of saving grace. They could read the Bible, pray, and do good deeds, and so meet God halfway on the road to salvation. These activities were sometimes described as "preparation" for salvation. To some degree all the early Congregationalists were "preparationists." Certainly all encouraged godly behavior, whether or not a person had experienced conversion. But some put more emphasis on preparation than others, suggesting to critics that they believed good deeds were themselves efficient means of winning salvation.

The balance between works and grace was tenuous, and occasionally groups formed favoring greater emphasis on either human effort or God's dominion. By 1700 some Congregational ministers thought of themselves as belonging either to a "conservative" or a "liberal" wing of the church. Liberals identified themselves by their position on a number of ecclesiastical and social questions. They generally opposed making a formal statement of religious experience the criterion for full church membership. In their church creed they opposed rigid, dogmatic statements. They approved of reading the Scriptures in church without discussing their meaning—a practice the early Puritans had rejected. They might also enjoy a good meal, play cards, or even indulge in what some conservatives considered the depths of depravity—wearing a wig.

The most important point at issue between the liberals and conservatives was the question of proper admission standards for full church membership. The conservatives held to the traditional New England custom of requiring men and women to describe the work of God's grace on their souls before they could take communion. But, as we have seen, in the late seventeenth century a number of churches, particularly in the Connecticut valley, abandoned this rigorous test in favor of a simpler requirement that the prospective communicant be familiar with Christian principles and lead an outwardly moral life.

In this tolerant atmosphere some ministers began to read books that suggested a somewhat different view of religious truth than was embraced by the early Puritan divines. One of the most popular authors in New England in the eighteenth century was the Anglican Archbishop, John Tillotson. He was read avidly by New England college students and ministerial candidates, who admired his brilliant style and his clear thought. But Tillotson's God was hardly the all-powerful deity of the early Puritans. He was a God in whom it was *reasonable* to believe. This God, whom one could follow from "prudence," was different from the early Puritan God, whom people worshipped in awe. Although one could not hold explicit Arminian views—that men and women were saved by their own efforts—and remain a minister, many pastors tended to reject strict Calvinism and emphasize the role of men and women in their own conversion.

During the Great Awakening some ministers found "rationalism" all the more appealing as a counterbalance to what they regarded as the excesses of the revival. Sometimes they referred to themselves as Old Lights, while the supporters of the revival were known as New Lights. The terms are confusing because in doctrine both groups embraced traditional Calvinistic ideas, and both accepted eighteenth-century innovations.

The Old Lights stressed works and interpreted conversion as a gradual process requiring human effort. This view left little room for "fanatics" who saw visions and went from place to place preaching that grace was a sudden and blinding infusion of God's spirit. Charles Chauncy, the archenemy of the revival, was also one of the chief exponents of the new rationalism. But the opening gun of the post-Awakening battle between liberals and conservatives was fired by a man from the then-distant region of Martha's Vineyard. The latest in a distinguished line of Indian missionaries on the island, Experience Mayhew did not have the benefit of a Harvard degree. But he was regarded by many as a gifted minister, and the sons of Harvard agreed, without deliberate condescension, that had he but attended their university, he would have been one of the brightest men of his age.

In a treatise entitled *Grace Defended* (1744) Mayhew suggested that good works may lead to salvation. He put the case circumspectly, writing, "the best actions of the unregenerate are not properly called sins, nor uncapable of being conditions of the covenant of grace."[16] By cultivating the "means of grace" the unregenerate paid the price of their own salvation. In a similar vein Lemuel Briant, minister of Quincy, Massachusetts, wrote a sermon in 1749 with the suggestive title, *The Absurdity and Blasphemy of Depreciating Moral Virtue.*

The contrary position was suggested by the phrase in Isaiah, "All our righteousnesses are as filthy rags." Briant claimed that this passage was taken out of context by those who insisted that men and women were totally depraved in their natural state. Isaiah, he said, had not intended to condemn the righteousness of virtuous persons, only the puffed up self esteem of the wicked. He argued that "the great rule the scriptures lay down for men to go by in passing judgment on their spiritual state, is the sincere, upright, steady, and universal practice of virtue."[17] Such utterances led John Adams, who grew up in Briant's Quincy, to describe this liberal parson as the father of American Unitarianism.

Briant was conventional in crediting the moral virtues of the righteous to God; they were fruits of his spirit. But to his critics he seemed to be exalting personal over divine righteousness. Accused of making men and women vainglorious, he answered that it was a virtue to encourage people to have confidence in their own righteousness. This argument did not quite respond to the question, because orthodox Puritans were just as dedicated as Briant to nurturing a righteous community. What they opposed was making men and women *self*-righteous, so overconfident that they ignored their need for God.

Briant's discourse, delivered in Boston as well as Braintree, provoked a storm of protest from other ministers. John Porter, minister of North Bridgewater,

Massachusetts, published a sermon in 1750 whose title aptly summarizes its thesis: *The Absurdity and Blasphemy of Substituting the Personal Righteousness of Men in the Room of the Surety-Righteousness of Christ.* Porter reaffirmed a traditional Calvinistic position on salvation. He felt that people were totally depraved and must be led to see, "their universal guilt and pollution by nature, as descendants from Adam, their moral head, the first transgressor." In Porter's view the enemy was the modern teachings of certain "professed preachers of righteousness of the younger sort," who substituted the righteousness of man for the righteousness of Christ. Only Christ was perfectly righteous, he argued, and accordingly "the personal righteousness of the best men may be properly styled filthy rags."[18]

Scholar Alan Heimert has noted that at this stage in the growth of Arminianism, "Liberal utterance on controverted points of doctrine was an exercise, if not in pure obfuscation, then in avoiding what Calvinists took to be the issues."[19] Briant's reply to his critics is a good example of apparent "obfuscation." He challenged Porter to find "a single passage in my sermon where the doctrine of justification by the merit of man's personal righteousness is asserted." He did not claim that people won salvation through their own merit, only that the prophet Isaiah "did not design to brand the virtues of real good men with this odious character of filthy rags." As Briant continued this line of thought, he moved back and forth between assertions of divine sovereignty and claims of human merit. Stressing his orthodoxy he said, "Forgiveness of sin and final acceptance with the Father is through the merits of the Son." Then inclining to credit man with some merit of his own, he added, "But I always thought that so far as any man is pure (let it be in a greater or lesser degree) he is not filthy."[20]

In effect, Briant said that people are not without natural merit, *but* they need Divine grace for salvation, *but* they have some personal merit, *but* admittedly they need grace as well,...Was this obfuscation, the hiding of a belief in a radical position on human ability? Probably not. In these days when some Congregationalists were moving towards what would later be called Unitarianism, they had at least as much in common with the preparationists of the seventeenth century as with the Unitarians of the nineteenth.

Lemuel Briant died in 1754, but others continued to articulate what their opponents called the "Arminian or worse" position on salvation. In 1757 Rev. Samuel Webster, minister of Salisbury, Massachusetts, published an anonymous tract entitled, *A Winter Evening's Conversation on Original Sin.* Webster claimed that the idea "of our having sinned in Adam" and being thereby liable to eternal damnation was unscriptural, inhumane, and irrational: "Sin and guilt (so far as I can see) are personal things, as much as knowledge. And I can as easily conceive of one man's knowledge being imputed to another, as of his sins being so: no imputation, in either case, can make the thing to be mine, which is not mine, any more than one person may be made, in the like way, another person." Webster contended that only the body came from Adam; the soul came from God. Admittedly the body lays "the soul under some disadvantages, in respect to its rational exercises." But the notion that men were made sinners by Adam's sin was an "extreme absurdity."[21]

In reply Peter Clark, minister of Danvers, Massachusetts, published *A Summer Morning's Conversation* in 1758, blasting Webster for making "tragical exclamations" against the doctrine of original sin. Stating the traditional position, he declared, "The doctrine of universal apostacy of mankind, I am sure, is fundamental to the doctrine of redemption by Christ."[22] Clark's tract was embellished with endorsements from several of New England's leading ministers, including revivalists Thomas Foxcroft and Thomas Prince of Boston. In the process of criticizing Webster, Clark conceded a significant point to the opponents of strict Calvinism. Webster had claimed that one of the problems with the doctrine of original sin was that it implied that children dying as infants were damned. In response Clark did not reaffirm the idea of infant damnation, saying instead that the fate of infants was "among the secret things which belong to God alone," and suggesting that infants were most likely not liable to punishment.[23] The fact that even a defender of Calvinism would abandon one of the points of traditional belief, albeit a difficult doctrine, indicates the degree to which eighteenth-century theologians felt compelled to justify the ways of God to man—on man's terms.

The debates over Arminianism showed a tendency by some post-Awakening Congregationalists to apply human standards to an understanding of human nature. Another debate, this on the issue of the Trinity, exposed divisions among Congregationalists on the issue of God's nature. In each case there was a tendency to hold the deity to human standards of reasonableness. The leading Arian was Jonathan Mayhew, minister of Boston's West Church, where Lemuel Briant had preached his sermon against original sin. Like Briant and like his father, Experience Mayhew, the West Church pastor believed that good deeds lead towards salvation. He adopted the view on the nature of the Trinity, commonly known as Arianism, which placed Christ at a somewhat lower level than God. While not adopting the full-blown Unitarian position that Christ is human, he did consider him less than God. Other ministers followed Mayhew's lead, provoking Samuel Hopkins to remark in 1768 that "the Divinity of Christ was much neglected, if not disbelieved, by a number of ministers in Boston."[24]

Thus within two decades of the Great Awakening a number of New England ministers were embracing anti-Calvinistic positions on such issues as original sin and the Trinity. To some extent they were influenced by English theologians who advocated a "rational" approach to religious issues. And to some extent they were influenced by the atmosphere of the Enlightenment, which encouraged confidence in human ability. Additionally, they were reacting against the revival's disturbing manifestations of emotional religion. A God who acted in mysterious ways, paying little heed to human standards, seemed to encourage uneducated itinerant preachers, ecstatic disorders, and disregard for "civilized" rules of conduct.

The debate between liberals and conservatives after the Great Awakening might have left merely a footnote in the history of American theology, except for the presence among the disputants of one man who is generally regarded as the greatest intellect, as well as the best theologian, of colonial America. Jonathan Edwards delved far below the surface of the little debates that then divided Congregationalists and asked profound and enduring questions about the nature of the soul and of the world. George Bancroft said of Edwards, "He that would know the workings of the New England mind in the middle of the [eighteenth] century, and the throbbings of its heart, must give his days and nights to the study of Jonathan Edwards." Williston Walker called him "a man of more metaphysical genius than any other American."[25] In an age that celebrated human ability, Edwards reaffirmed the role of God in the universe, and did so in ways that still inspire debate and admiration.

JONATHAN EDWARDS, GOD, AND THE UNIVERSE

Jonathan Edwards admitted that some men misused the freedom of the Awakening to preach false religion. Some of them, he said, mistook superficial ecstasies for divine grace. But Edwards had stood before a congregation, preaching about sin and salvation, and had watched men and women overwhelmed with joy or sorrow, laughing, weeping, fainting. At such times he believed that he saw God moving among the people, speaking to their spirits. Such moments of contact with a living God were to him the essence of religion. He felt that it was absurd to suggest that salvation was a prosaic matter of the day's good deeds or that Christ was less than fully God—Christ was God, and salvation came through a deeply felt union with Christ. Edwards set forth his theology in treatises on original sin, the freedom of the will, and other theological topics, but his beliefs appear nowhere more clearly than in his personal narrative of his religious experience.

Edwards first took a personal interest in religion when, as a boy, he was affected by the preaching of his father, Timothy Edwards, who had nurtured a revival in his parish of Windsor, Connecticut. The boy was "much affected" and would pray five times a day in secret, and discuss religion with other children. With his schoolmates he built "a booth" in a remote swamp as a place for prayer. "My affections," he wrote, "seemed to be lively and easily moved, and I seemed to be in my element when engaged in religious duties." But in retrospect, he thought that his religious feelings had been superficial and self-serving. He had felt good about being good, and had mistaken that feeling for grace. He soon "returned like a dog to his vomit, and went on in the ways of sin."[26]

Years later, as a young man, Jonathan Edwards experienced a deeper, and to him genuine, conversion. While a student at Yale he suffered from a near-fatal case of pleurisy, and in his words, God "brought me nigh to the grave, and shook me over the pit of hell." When he recovered, Edwards resolved to break off "all ways of known outward sin." There followed in his life a classic

Puritan struggle through humiliation to grace. For a time his life was taken by "inward struggles and conflicts." He noticed a change in his inward self when he began to reconsider the doctrine of election: "From childhood up my mind had been full of objections against the doctrine of God's sovereignty, in choosing whom he would to eternal life, and rejecting whom he pleased, leaving them eternally to perish, and be everlastingly tormented in hell. It used to appear like a horrible doctrine to me."[27]

But now he "seemed to be convinced, and fully satisfied, as to this sovereignty of God, and his justice in thus eternally disposing of men, according to his sovereign pleasure." Edwards did not merely accept the doctrine of divine, arbitrary election, he embraced it. He was "fully satisfied;" his mind "rested in it;" there was a "wonderful alteration" in his mind; he achieved "not only a conviction, but a delightful conviction" of God's sovereignty. In the process of rejecting the most compelling argument against arbitrary election, that it was not fair to man, Edwards seemed to draw closer to God. Accepting God's "worst" characteristic opened the way for him to commune with God. "Absolute sovereignty," wrote Edwards, "is what I love to ascribe to God."[28]

Edwards now felt a "sweet delight in God and divine things." A particular biblical verse became for him the avenue of communication with the deity: 1 Timothy 1:17, "Now unto the King eternal, immortal, invisible, the only wise God, be honor and glory for ever and ever, Amen." The words were simple, the sort that one could read and dismiss as a commonplace expression of faith. But Edwards wrote, "There came into my soul, and was as it were diffused through it, a sense of the glory of the Divine Being; a new sense, quite different from any thing I ever experienced before. Never any words of scripture seemed to me as these words did." Edwards felt a heightened sense of spirituality. He thought about Christ, redemption, and salvation with "an inward, sweet sense" and his "soul was led away in pleasant views and contemplations of them." As he read the Bible, he now experienced, "an inward sweetness, that would carry me away, in my contemplations. This I know not how to express otherwise, than by a calm, sweet abstraction of soul from all the concerns of this world; and sometimes a kind of vision, or fixed ideas and imaginations, of being alone in the mountains, or some solitary wilderness, far from all mankind, sweetly conversing with Christ, and wrapt and swallowed up in God. The sense I had of divine things, would often of a sudden kindle up, as it were, a sweet burning in my heart; an ardor of soul, that I know not how to express."[29]

In such descriptions Edwards revealed the ecstatic experience that lay at the heart of his piety and theology. God was there to be sensed, adored, known. The whole world seemed changed by a new way of experiencing reality. "The appearance of every thing was altered; there seemed to be, as it were, a calm, sweet cast, or appearance of divine glory, in almost every thing. God's excellency, his wisdom, his purity and love, seemed to appear in every thing; in the sun, moon, and stars, in the clouds, and blue sky; in the grass, flowers, trees; in the water, and all nature." A century before it became fashionable to worship nature, Edwards was transfixed by the natural forces around him. He looked at the "clouds and the sky, to behold the sweet glory of God in these things; in the mean time, singing forth, with a low voice my contemplations of the Creator and Redeemer." He had formerly been terrified of thunder and lightning, but now he welcomed a storm for the chance to see God's handiwork in the heavens. "I felt God, so to speak, at the first appearance of a thunder storm; and used to take the opportunity, at such times, to fix myself in order to view the clouds, and see the lightnings play, and hear the majestic and awful voice of God's thunder, which oftentimes was exceedingly entertaining, leading me to sweet contemplations of my great and glorious God. While thus engaged, it always seemed natural to me to sing, or chant for my meditations; or, to speak my thoughts in soliloquies with a singing voice."[30]

In Edwards's description of his meeting with God, perhaps the most notable feature of all is his inclination to *sing* his feelings. Here is a man who was fully engaged in the life of the spirit, to the point of expressing himself in a language of song. Walking alone in the woods, thinking about God, he said, "It was always my manner, at such times, to sing forth my contemplations." Edwards's deep felt piety colored his whole life. He wept at times that he had come so "late" to religion, having wasted so many years of his young life. He delighted to think about heaven, where the saints could fully express their love for Christ and where friends would no longer be separated, as on earth. He longed to hear news of the progress of Christ's kingdom, and read the papers for reassuring reports.[31]

In Edwards's personal experience humiliation and sanctification went hand in hand, as it did for the early Puritans. He could say of himself, "When I look into my heart, and take a view of my wickedness, it looks like an abyss infinitely deeper than hell." Or, "My wickedness, as I am in myself, has long appeared to me perfectly ineffable, and swallowing up all thought and imagination; like an infinite deluge, or mountain over my head." At times during his ministry at Northampton he was so affected by a sense of his sinfulness that he shut himself up in a room for privacy and wept loudly. But out of sorrow grew hope. His sense of spiritual joy and calm came not from a contemplation of his own virtues, but from the thought of God's beauty and love. "I love to think of coming to Christ," he wrote, " and quite empty of self, humbly exalting him alone; cut off entirely from my own root, in order to grow into, and out of Christ; to have God in Christ to be all in all." I want "to lie in the dust," Edwards said, "and be full of Christ alone."[32]

The difference between Jonathan Edwards and an Arminian like Lemuel Briant was as much a matter of experience and sensibility as a question of doctrine. In his ecstatic sense of God's all-encompassing sufficiency, Edwards would say that all good deeds, including his own, were indeed but rags, because all that is good is from God. In Edwards's life the path to God had been through humiliation— through the recognition that God's sovereignty was so complete that he alone could determine who would be saved. That recognition had led Edwards to an acceptance of God, which in turn led to a closer relationship with God and a new way of seeing reality.

Edwards's religious experience colored his reaction to revivalism. Edwards felt that a person became aware of God when God revealed himself to a person. To him that process was not simply a message to the intellect; it was an enrapturing experience that changed heart, mind, and behavior. Edwards's *Narrative of Surprising Conversions* is full of passages such as this that describe the spirit of God moving through Northampton, as palpable as a summer breeze: "This work of God, as it was carried on, and the number of true saints multiplied, soon made a glorious alteration in the town; so that in the spring and summer following, Anno Domini 1735, the town seemed to be full of the presence of God. There were remarkable tokens of God's presence in almost every house."[33]

Edwards's God, then, was an all powerful deity who spoke through the stars and in thunderstorms and moved over the face of the land bestowing spiritual blessings on men and women. Believing that God was behind the Connecticut valley revival of 1734–35 and the Great Awakening of a few years later, Edwards ranked himself with the New Lights and devoted himself to describing in theological terms the character of the revivalist's God. Other ministers wrote treatises on various aspects of Puritan theology—original sin and the character of Christ, for example. Edwards did that and much more, going over the whole body of Puritan-Calvinistic theology and restating it in the light of modern ideas about humankind and the universe. He explored many of the deep philosophical questions: How do we know what we know? What is the nature of the universe? How do we make choices?

One of his first major works was a reply to Charles Chauncy. As we have seen, Chauncy was the leading opponent of the revival; he characterized the Awakening as a return to the Antinomian tendencies that had troubled early New England. In reply Edwards did not simply defend the revival; he asked just what is true religion? Edwards did not want to embrace the "errors" of the Awakening, the extravagances of passionate, but superficial "converts." But, in Williston Walker's words, he did seek "to foster a warm, emotional type of Christian character, touched and vivified by a sense of immediate communion between God and the human soul."[34] In *A Treatise Concerning Religious Affections* (1746) he argued that true religion consisted of "holy affections." Piety, he said, involved the light of the understanding as well as the heat of the passions; holy affections resulted in righteous acts as well as spiritual feelings. For Edwards the essence of true religion was a matter of the spirit. With this thought Edwards gave theological expression to the personal experience that had first brought him to a sense of God's presence—a feeling that even if God might condemn him arbitrarily to hell, he could love God for God's own sake.

A later generation of "Edwardseans" would corrupt this insight into the argument that a "willingness to be damned" was the essence of true religion. But that is not quite what Edwards meant, or how he experienced what he called holiness. At the moment when he accepted the idea of innate depravity and arbitrary grace, his feeling was not one of peril, but of acceptance. In the moment that he accepted God's sovereignty, he simply ceased "seeking himself" and sought God. The natural human yearning to achieve some kind of ultimate worth on one's own terms—without danger of arbitrary disparagement from a divine being—was part of the now-to-be-abandoned baggage of "seeking himself." But the underlying feeling was one of salvation, not damnation.

Shortly after the publication of *Religious Affections*, Edwards's ministry at Northampton came to an end. Edwards disliked the spiritual compromises of the Half-Way Covenant and the open communion embraced by his grandfather Solomon Stoddard. Many of his parishioners favored these practices. Others were annoyed when he proposed to punish young people who had circulated among themselves a manual for midwives—for them a form of pornography. Edwards incurred the hostility of some of Northampton's leading citizens, and with the approval of a council of ministers New England's foremost theologian was dismissed from his pulpit. Soon afterwards he found himself ministering to a small congregation, mainly Indians, at the frontier mission of Stockbridge, Massachusetts. There he went with his wife and seven children, and in those simple surroundings he composed some of the most profound religious works ever written by an American.

The question of man's freedom to work out his own salvation had vexed Congregationalists, and Edwards now turned to writing *Freedom of the Will* (1754). Sydney Ahlstrom rightly called this work "one of the literary sensations of eighteenth-century America."[35] Edwards argued that every event, moral as well as physical, must have a cause. The will chooses the highest good, as the mind perceives it. But in matters of personal salvation the human will was not free because the will could not even see God without God's help. Man cannot choose God until God reveals himself as the highest good. Again Edwards's own experience was fundamental: he came to know God only after God revealed himself. Because human nature is corrupted by sin, Edwards believed the unaided human mind cannot possibly know God and achieve salvation.

Edwards carried this argument further in *Original Sin Defended* (1758). He argued on several levels: a realistic view of the world showed sin to be everywhere; the Bible testifies to the curse of Adam on human nature. The most original and striking part of Edwards's argument was rooted in his understanding of being and the universe. All men and women partake of Adam's sin, he said, because all are one with Adam. All are one, because the creation has no existence whatsoever independent of God: God not only created the universe, he sustains it at every moment. "The existence of created *substance*, in each successive moment,...[is] wholly the effect of God's immediate power, in *that* moment, without any dependence on prior existence, as much as the first creation out of *nothing*."[36] Recognizing that this was a complex idea, Edwards offered a cluster of analogies: "The lucid color or brightness of the *moon*, as we look steadfastly upon it, seems to be a *permanent* thing, as though it were perfectly the same brightness continued. But indeed it is an effect produced every moment. It ceases, and is renewed, in each successive point of time; and so becomes altogether a *new* effect at each instant; and no one thing that belongs to it is numerically the same that existed in the preceding moment." So too the sound of the wind blowing now may be like the sound a moment ago, but it is not the same, "any more than the agitated air, that makes the sound,...or than the *water*, flowing in a river, that now passes by, is individually the same with that which passed a little before." Even substance itself must be recreated every moment: "If it be thus with the brightness or color of the moon, so it must be with its *solidity*, and every thing else belonging to its substance."

These images of moonlight, wind, and water are striking, but they were intended by Edwards simply to lead the readers beyond themselves to an understanding of the power of God. Just as moonlight is continually recreated by new beams of light, Edwards felt that all things in the universe must be constantly renewed by divine will and wisdom.

In this sense the continuance of the very being of the world and all its parts, as well as the manner of continued beings, depends entirely on an *arbitrary constitution*. For it does not at all necessarily follow, that because there was sound, or light, or color, or resistance, or gravity, or thought, or consciousness, or any other dependent thing the last moment, that therefore there shall be the like at the next. All dependent existence whatsoever is in a constant flux, ever passing and returning; renewed every moment, as the colors of bodies are every moment renewed by the light that shines upon them; and all is constantly proceeding from *God*, as light from the sun. *In him we live, and move, and have our being.*

Those who could follow Edwards's argument were brought to a conception of the universe not unlike that of the Puritan founders of New England or St. Augustine or the prophets of the Old Testament; each of those persons had come to an ecstatic sense of a universe where God was all in all. The question of original sin, which had occasioned these arguments, was now almost an afterthought. If God did indeed hold the world in the palm of his hand, as Edwards believed, why then of course he could so constitute being that all persons were one in Adam. And so said Edwards, "I am persuaded, no solid reason can be given, why God, who constitutes all other created union or oneness, according to his pleasure...may not establish a constitution whereby the natural posterity of Adam, proceeding from him, much as the buds and branches from the stock or root of a tree, should be treated as *one* with him."

No American argued more profoundly for the doctrine of original sin than Edwards, but again it should be remembered that in his mind that doctrine was not associated with cruelty or despair, but with his youthful conversion when he came to accept all aspects of Gods power, including arbitrary election of sinful persons. The experience in the moment of accepting original sin and arbitrary election had been for him, a feeling of love, not fear: "The appearance of every thing was altered; there seemed to be, as it were, a calm, sweet cast, or appearance of divine glory, in almost every thing."

While *Original Sin* was in press, Jonathan Edwards was invited to become president of Princeton. He accepted and moved to New Jersey. Shortly after his arrival, he was inoculated for smallpox, a relatively new and dangerous procedure. He caught the disease and died. He was then fifty-four and at the height of his mental powers. After Edwards's death his followers published several more of his works. *The Nature of True Virtue*, appearing in 1765, contained some of his most famous ideas, particularly the notion that true virtue is benevolence, or love, expressed towards "Being in general." This love binds man to God, according to Edwards, and also one Christian to another. Self-love, he said, the opposite of true virtue, is narrow and perverse, but Christian love looks beyond the self and brings with it a sense of spiritual beauty and joy.

In 1765 a second treatise appeared, entitled *Concerning the End for Which God Created the World*. In it Edwards completed the line of thought in *True Virtue*, arguing that the principle of universal benevolence applies also to the deity, who created the universe both as an expression of his love and in order to love himself more perfectly: "In the creature's knowing, esteeming, loving, rejoicing in, and praising God, the glory of God is both exhibited and acknowledged; his fullness is received and returned....The beams of glory come from God, and are something of God, and are refunded back again to their original. So that the whole is *of* God, and *in* God, and *to* God, and God is the beginning, middle and end in this affair."[37]

In passages like this the essential mysticism of Edwards, his ecstatic sense of communion with God, is apparent. The ardor underlying this and his other treatises was, arguably, Edwards's greatest legacy to his followers. Williston Walker noted that Edwards's influence rests as much in his conviction as in his ideas. "No small share of his power over those who have come in contact with him and with his writings is the feeling that he awakens that one is dealing not merely with an intellect of marvelous acuteness, but with a soul stirred by profound religious emotions, and a spirit that in a peculiar degree seemed to walk with God."[38]

That aspiration to "walk with God" had first brought Congregationalists to New England. It led to the ideal of visible sainthood and nourished the Great Awakening. In the writings of Jonathan Edwards, it was distilled into a theology that is as poetic as it is profound.

NOTES

[1] Nathan Cole, "Autobiography," in Alan Heimert and Perry Miller, eds., *The Great Awakening*, 184-86.

[2] Nicholas Gilman, Diary, November 17 and 20, 1741; January 29, Marcy 4 and 14, 1741/42, New Hampshire Historical Society, Concord.

[3] Richard Woodbury to William Parsons, May 23, 1744, in Gilman Notes, Massachusetts Historical Society, Boston.

[4] Quotations from Williston Walker, *A History of the Congregational Churches in the United States* (New York, 1894), 257-58.

[5] Quotations from Walker, *Congregational Churches*, 263.

[6] Quotation from Walker, *Congregational Churches*, 258-59.

[7] Charles Chauncy, *Seasonable Thoughts* (Boston, 1743), 36, 48.

[8] Quotation from Walker, *Congregational Churches*, 264.

[9] Clifford K. Shipton, "The New England Clergy of the Glacial Age," Colonial Society of Massachusetts, *Publications*, 32 (193-37), 51-52.

[10] Israel Loring, "Directions for Private Instruction and Catechizing," Loring Papers, Goodnow Library, Sudbury, Massachusetts.

[11] Francis G. Walett, ed., "The Diary of Ebenezer Parkman, 1719–1728," American Antiquarian Society, *Proceedings*, N.S., 71 (1961), 117-18.

[12] Wallet, ed., "Diary of Ebenezer Parkman," 72, 182.

[13] Ezra Carpenter, "Commonplace Book," Houghton Library, Harvard University; Wallet, ed., "Diary of Ebenezer Parkman," 73, 92.

[14] John Hancock, "Commonplace Book," Houghton Library, Harvard University, 93.

[15] Wallet, ed., "Diary of Ebenezer Parkman," 74, 174.

[16] Quotation from Walker, *Congregational Churches*, 270.

[17] Quotation from Walker, *Congregational Churches*, 271.

[18] John Porter, *The Absurdity and Blasphemy of Substituting the Personal Righteousness of Men in the Room of the Surety-Righteousness of Christ* (Boston, 1750), 2-5.

[19] Alan Heimert, *Religion and the American Mind from the Great Awakening to the Revolution* (Cambridge, Mass., 1966), 166.

[20] Quotation from Walker, *Congregational Churches*, 272.

[21] Samuel Webster, *A Winter Evening's Conversation* (Boston, 1757), 9, 16.

[22] Peter Clark, *A Summer Morning's Conversation* (Boston, 1758), 3.

[23] Quotation from Walker, *Congregational Churches*, 274.

[24] Quotation from Walker, *Congregational Churches*, 278.

[25] Quotation from Ahlstrom, *Religious History of the American People*, 298; Walker, *Congregational Churches*, 280.

[26] Jonathan Edwards, "Personal Narrative," in Clarence H. Faust and Thomas H. Johnson, *Jonathan Edwards: Representative Selections* (New York,1962), 57.

[27] Edwards, "Personal Narrative," 58.

[28] Edwards, "Personal Narrative," 57-59.

[29] Edwards, "Personal Narrative," 59-60.

[30] Edwards, "Personal Narrative," 60-61.

[31] Edwards, "Personal Narrative," 61-64.

[32] Edwards, "Personal Narrative," 68-70.

[33] Edwards, *Narrative of Surprising Conversions* (Exeter, N.H., 1805), 11.

[34] Walker, *Congregational Churches*, 282.

[35] Ahlstrom, *Religious History of the American People*, 305.

[36] Jonathan Edwards, "Original Sin" in Faust and Johnson, *Jonathan Edwards*, 335. The quotations from "Original Sin" which follow appear in Faust, 335-338.

[37] Quotation from Ahlstrom, *Religious History of the American People*, 310.

[38] Walker, *Congregational Churches*, 281.

6
NEW DIVINITY AND A NEW NATION

LAY PIETY: THE SPIRITUAL LIFE OF MARY FISH

Jonathan Edwards is the most important figure in the history of colonial American religious thought. But many New Englanders never heard Edwards preach and relatively few read his theological treatises. None the less, the religious culture that nourished a Jonathan Edwards also touched other men and women, many of whom never attended college or read theological treatises. A few of these lay persons left personal papers that allow us to explore their lives and thoughts. One of the most interesting accounts is that of a minister's daughter, Mary Fish. Her experiences while growing up during the Great Awakening and reaching maturity on the eve of the American Revolution suggest the ways that Puritanism entered the day-to- day lives of many colonists, and they provide the background against which we should understand the large events of the era: the fashioning of a new theology and the forging of American independence.

Mary Fish was born on May 30, 1736, in Stonington, Connecticut, the daughter of the Reverend Joseph Fish and Rebecca Fish. The family lived in a large parsonage on a hill overlooking Long Island Sound. The parish consisted of farms lying within three or four miles of Stonington. The Fishes were moderately well-to-do, in the way of most country parsons. Joseph Fish could afford one or two slaves, but his clerical salary was modest, and he often had to work in the fields beside his blacks. Rebecca Fish bore two more children, a second daughter, Rebecca or Becca, and a son, Joseph, who died the day he was born. The Fish girls were raised the way all good Congregational children were supposed to be, with frequent family prayers. Mary recalled in a memoir written many years later: "My father's practice was every day to take us into his study, immediately after family prayers in the morning, and hear us read, and he would give us advice for the day. He would also enjoin it upon us to read our Bibles by ourselves every day." The Fishes observed the Sabbath carefully, not even associating with anyone who "would talk of worldly matters on the Lord's day."

They reviewed each day at bedtime to "see wherein we had been culpable." And, the children were taught that sense of urgency that was so much a part of early Puritanism, and which Henry David Thoreau expressed so well in an aphorism: "As if you can waste time without injuring eternity." Mary expresses it this way: "They early taught us diligence—that we must always be doing something that would turn out to profit...and I feared that my father should at any time find me doing nothing, lest he should put the question, What? are you idle my child?"[1]

In 1741, when Mary was five, the Great Awakening arrived in Stonington in the person of one of its most radical supporters, James Davenport. Joseph Fish wrote a description of Davenport in the pulpit, revealing just how peculiar the enthusiasts must have seemed to moderate Christians: Davenport urged the congregation to cry out in joy or sorrow as he preached, and he led them with "the most violent agitations of body, even to the distorting of his features and marring his visage." He preached in "a strange, unnatural *singing tone*, which tended to *raise* or *keep* up the affections of weak and undiscerning people."[2] Davenport also encouraged the people to have visions of the spiritual world and relate their discoveries to others.

Joseph Fish believed that the spirit of God could touch people, and he had welcomed the Great Awakening. He even tried to see the best in Davenport, calling him "a wonderful, strange good man." But he was uncomfortable with this form of "worship." It seemed to him that Davenport was "frightening people out of their senses," rather than persuading them "as reasonable men, to make their escape unto Christ."[3] During the next decade Jonathan Edwards would develop his theology in response to just such considerations, arguing that true piety, or virtue, is present when both the mind and heart are touched by the Holy Spirit.

But during the Awakening Joseph Fish, and many other pious ministers like him, were not so much contemplating theological issues as fighting for their lives. Davenport was so powerful in eastern Connecticut for a time that ministers felt obliged to submit to his private examinations, hoping that he would approve their piety and not publicly condemn them. Fish noted that ministers trembled before Davenport, "as if [they] where going before the *judge of all the earth*."[4] Then came a hard blow to Fish: Davenport declared that he was not converted.

Fish's reaction is a testimony to the spiritual confusion that accompanied the Great Awakening. He might have joined Charles Chauncy and others in denouncing the revival and its crazed itinerant preachers. Instead, he regarded Davenport's condemnation as if it were a message from God. He ceased preaching for five Sabbaths and examined his soul. When he returned to his church in February 1742 he was more confident of his calling to the ministry. But the congregation was even more turbulent than before. As Fish tried to preach, shouts and cries broke out in the congregation so that he could hardly be heard.

Then Fish preached a sermon declaring that outcries, ecstasies, and trances were not sure signs of grace. In response members of the congregation shouted all the more that he was a false minister and an opposer of God's work. Dissidents broke up each of his services after that. Women sat in the aisle with their knitting, showing their contempt, and they and the men shouted insults at Fish. Soon the dissidents, about two thirds of Fish's congregation, split off into a Separate church. Fish attempted a reconciliation several times, but the Separatists wanted nothing to do with him, and he was left with a remnant of his former congregation. He stayed in his pulpit, but the disruption meant there were fewer people to pay his salary and seldom a new convert to the church.

Young Mary Fish must have been mystified by some of the events of the Awakening. But in other ways she led a normal Puritan childhood, even experiencing a few of the "remarkable providences" that made Puritans feel that God was watching over them. Her description of a family accident suggests something about the course of life in Stonington. Her parents had acquired a carriage, something of a novelty. In her memoir Mary recalls, "In those days we at Stonington knew but little about carriages, and we did not know but one horse was as good as another to go in a carriage." When their own horse was not available, they went to borrow a neighbor's. Although this horse worked in a cider mill and had never drawn a carriage, they assumed it would be able to pull them. Instead the horse bolted in fear, throwing Mary to the ground and breaking the carriage.[5] But, providentially, Mary was spared from serious injury.

Mary Fish grew into an attractive, intelligent young lady. In 1756 when she was twenty, she went to New Haven to attend Yale's commencement. Mary stayed with the Reverend Joseph Noyes and his wife, Abigail. There she met the minister's son, John Noyes. Their friendship grew, and they were married in the fall, two years later. John Noyes had hoped to become a minister, but he was sickly, and was only able to preach occasionally. Mary found him "a kind and affectionate husband." They had a child a year after their marriage, whom they named Rebecca after Mary's mother. The next spring Mary Noyes went to visit her parents in Stonington, taking their new granddaughter along. When Mary and her baby arrived Rebecca Fish was "in raptures." "This is just as I would have it," she exclaimed.

The reaction seems natural in a new grandmother, but Mary's sister was alarmed by her mother's behavior. "Take care my dear mother," she said, "this is all uncertain bliss and may change." In this reaction we can see the Puritan assumption that all things in the world are from God, and that God can take them away as quickly as he gives them—especially if one becomes obsessed with the object and forgets the maker. Thomasine Winthrop had found comfort in that belief in 1616 when she lay on her deathbed. Generations of Puritans had embraced the idea of God's sustaining providence. Jonathan Edwards created a new scientific way of describing that providence, speaking of rays of light and divine imminence. The reaction of Mary's sister to her mother's simple comfort in a new child indicates the degree to which the idea of God's providence was imbedded in New England culture.

That night Mary Noyes had difficulty sleeping, now anxious about the child. At midnight she went to the baby and found her burning with fever. The child languished four days and then died. Grandmother Fish later lamented that she had been "so stupid" in not once thinking that "the babe was mortal." The family waited for three days, hoping that news would reach New Haven in time to summon John Noyes to the funeral. When they could wait no longer, they went to the cemetery without the father. On the way Joseph Fish made a typically Puritan remark, drawing together suffering, loss, and redemption: "These are melancholy steps, but the path of glory leads through the grave, and it is well worth while to undergo the pains of bearing and of parting with children if thereby we people the redeemer's kingdom."

When the family returned from the cemetery, they found that John Noyes had just arrived. He must have embraced his wife and shared her sorrow, but he was in a "resigned frame" of mind. In other words, he accepted the loss as being ordained by God, which "shewed us that the Lord was with him and supporting him." Mary, however, could not make that adjustment. The world did not seem right to her; she could not accept her child's death as the act of a benevolent God. "Having never before lost any near relative," she said, "I was like a bullock, unaccustomed to the yoke." Just as Jonathan Edwards had at first rejected the "yoke" of arbitrary election, Mary at first rejected the yoke of divine providence.

There is a poetry in the way that Puritans like Mary, even without the benefit of a college degree and advanced theological training, wrestled with the meaning of religion in the face of life's tragedies and dilemmas. Mary returned to New Haven. "I went out full and returned empty," she remarked. But God could give as well as take away, and "God graciously gave me another babe." She regarded this child as a Puritan was supposed to, as a gift from God, dependent upon God for its continued life. "With different eyes did I look on him," she wrote. "I always viewed him as mortal and mine no longer than God was pleased to lend him." Such attitudes might have made men and women uncaring. But in Mary, as in other Puritans, this "loving the world with weaned affections," as they called it, did not diminish the world of flesh and blood. Mary remarked, "Every night I felt thankful that he was alive."

During a five-year period in the 1760s, Mary gave birth to four children, three boys and a girl. The children were healthy, but their father was not. John Noyes suffered from epilepsy and consumption. A doctor told Mary that he could not live long, and once more she faced death. "This was a dagger to my heart," she wrote. "I had been manufacturing some linen for him with which he had been pleased, and in the evening I went to bring it in from out of doors, but how sad did everything look; it seemed as if the glory was departed from this world." Her "other self" was dying, and with his death, she thought, "will expire my happiness."

This was a natural response, but it was a retreat to her feelings of earlier years, when she was not accustomed "to the yoke." This time, however, she caught herself, and confronted the news of her husband's vulnerability with the reassurance of Puritan doctrine. She considered that if her children were angry because "I thought it best to take away something they valued among their playthings," and in reaction they threw away the rest of their toys, she would consider them "undutiful children" who "needed the rod." Thereafter she was determined to enjoy her husband's company with "thankfulness" while he lived. Every night she felt glad that he had been "loaned" to her for another day.

The Puritans were students of the soul, as alert to fluctuations of the human spirit in relationship to God, as Eskimos are said to be attuned to the variety of snowflakes. The perspective Mary described, where one would consider a beloved spouse as loaned to her, was the ideal Puritan relationship to life. God was so real and so present to the Puritans that, ideally, they were aware of—and comfortable with—the surrounding ocean of God's spirit, even while living among the islands of temporal friendships.

And yet Mary found hard to accept the impending loss of her husband. Mary recounts that one day John was "more ill than common." "I was overcome," she wrote, "and hid my face behind the curtain to conceal my tears." John knew she was crying and said, "Don't weep, my dear. I do not doubt your affection for me, but if my friends look sorrowful, I shall go the sooner, as it will grieve me and sink my spirits." She then asked him if he "could leave me and our dear children with God." John replied, "Yes, he will be a husband and a father."

In this conversation we can hear echoes of the talks between John and Thomasine Winthrop 150 years before; one feels that the Noyeses and Winthrops could have been neighbors in seventeenth century England. John Noyes lingered on for a few more months, attended by watchers when Mary had to sleep. On the day that he died, "His breath grew shorter and shorter." He told Mary that "death had no terrors for him, and that he left us with him who would be a husband and father." A minister came to pray with him and asked "if his hope stood firm." He answered yes and said no more. Soon afterwards, "He threw himself back and expired as one falling into a calm sleep." Mary adds, "Thus died that dear good man."

Mary Noyes was able to provide for herself with the rent from land she had inherited and by taking in boarders in New Haven. During the next few years she faced death again and again. Her mother-in-law died, and Becca, her only sister. Then in May of 1770 her only daughter was "taken ill of canker and worms." She was a little over four, but was patient in taking whatever medicine her mother gave her. She might first taste it and say, "It is not good, Mama." Then Mary would explain that she had to take it to get well, and "she would open her little mouth and take anything." After ten days of illness she died. Mary wrote, "I closed her eyes myself, and felt in some measure resigned, knowing that God could give a good reason why he had thus afflicted me."

After losing so many dear relations, and "accepting" each loss as the will of God, it would seem that Mary Noyes would have no trouble accepting other events in her life as providential. But self-mortification was as complex as life itself. Mary was proud of her own spiritual qualities, and rightly so. She lived a moral life, raised Christian children, and loved God despite her misfortunes. But her pride was itself a flaw that a Puritan "physician of the spirit" could recognize, and it brought on a great spiritual crisis.

The immediate reason for the crisis is not entirely clear. Mary refers to it in veiled terms in her memoir and journal. But it appears that during the months after her daughter's death she was pursued by a suitor and "led him on." She must have welcomed some diversion at this time in her life, and she probably gave the man reason to think that she cared for him more than she did. When she refused to marry him, she was criticized by some in New Haven for having been fickle. She retreated to her parent's home in Stonington, and for months she was tormented with distressing thoughts. She was upset that people in New Haven disparaged her character. It was unfair, she told herself. She felt unwilling to have her character "roughly handled." She was so upset that she had difficulty sleeping and even began "to suspect my stability of mind."[6]

The threat to Mary's reputation was bad enough, but it mingled with an even more serious problem in Mary's mind—she began to feel estranged from God. "I mourn that I had no more communion with God," she confided in her journal, "O this dreadful deadness of heart." Her obsession with her reputation had set up a barrier between herself and God. Her father told her "that perhaps my character had been my idol, and that I ought to be willing to give up even that." But sometimes the advice we get is not the advice we want, and one can imagine Mary glaring at her father, angry that he would accept these unjust attacks on her character.

Then slowly she began to agree with him, and "wean" herself away from an obsession with her character. She wrote, "my pride wanted mortifying," and she acknowledged that she was "distressed with my stubborn will and proud heart." She came to see that her estrangement from God was a far greater problem than her apparent loss of reputation. Her preoccupation with that loss was itself a cause of the estrangement. With such thoughts, reported in her journal, came moments, even days, of calm. As she grew to be thankful for such periods of spiritual contentment, even though her reputation might still be tarnished, she felt closer to God. "Oh may this calm frame continue," she wrote, "and I never more dishonor God by distrusting his goodness."

Mary's life did not change all at once. She was "sometimes calm and trusting" and "sometimes ready to sink." In May 1771, six months after she fled from New Haven Mary could still be distressed "by hearing reports to my disadvantage." Preoccupied again with her reputation, she asked herself, "When shall I get above the frowns and flatteries of the world." And, predictably, she felt estranged from God again, writing the next day, "I mourn that I had no more communion with God. Oh this dreadful deadness of heart." But the months passed, and Mary worried less and less about the events of the previous year. In August 1771 she noted the anniversary of her daughter's death, expressing gratitude that the Lord "has not since made any farther breaches upon my little family."

This sense of gratitude for her blessings was Mary's path to salvation, temporal as well as heavenly. Mary felt spiritually calm. "How good it is to feel awake and alive!" she could write. During the winter of 1772, she noted how differently she felt from the previous winter. "A strange creature I am!" she wrote. "For I every day this winter experience in my mind what I would have given the world to obtain last winter—that is, resignation to God's will....It seems to me as if last winter Satan had desired me that he might sift me as wheat, for I was tempted and was ever ready to give up every thing and to question every thing as I thought I had been entertaining false hope [of salvation]."

But despite her new found calm, Mary Noyes still experienced what we would consider normal feelings about her worldly losses. One night in March 1772 she wrote, "My sorrows came afresh into my mind, the last wound bleeding again, even the death of my dear little Mary." But her faith reassured her: "I have reason to think that my dear ones that are gone now occupy the place prepared for them by their redeemer, and [I] ought not to have wished to detain them a moment after Christ had prepared" to receive them. Mary's growth in Puritan piety, like Jonathan Edwards's, came with an acceptance of human limitations and divine omnipotence. Of course she did not, like Edwards, found a theological school, but her grace influenced several generations of her descendents.

Many challenges lay ahead of Mary. She would remarry during the Revolution, lose her husband to Tory kidnappers, get him back, face bankruptcy, raise children and grandchildren, and see some of her descendants settle in Ohio. During the next four decades she would become a Puritan matriarch, an example to several generations of her family. In lives like hers the essential fiber of Puritan piety was passed on to the new republic. Mary Fish once remarked that she was grateful "that we have so many in our land who preach the plain truths of the gospel, and do not puzzle their hearers with metaphysical matters hard to be understood and perhaps erroneous. Our dear savior was plain and easy in his teaching—witness his sermon on the mount." "Metaphysical" issues would occupy much attention among the Congregationalists during the era of the American Revolution, as theologians debated the nature of sin and salvation. But the religious experiences of Mary Noyes are reminders that the "plain truths of the gospel" continued to influence many New Englanders in the era of the American Revolution, just as they had a century and a half before.

THE NEW DIVINITY

The "metaphysical matters" that seemed to Mary Noyes to be troubling too many New Englanders involved a cluster of issues growing out of the post-Awakening debates about free will, salvation, and other matters. With the death of Jonathan Edwards in 1758, other ministers carried on the task of reworking Calvinist ideas in the idiom of the eighteenth century. Sydney Ahlstrom has remarked that none of Edwards's disciples "was true to his essential genius."[7] None was as brilliant a theologian, none compared with Edwards in the ability to convert feelings into words, and each modified Edwards's ideas in ways he might not have liked. But the "New Divinity" forged by Edwards's followers dominated Congregational thinking until well into the nineteenth century, and was in many respects inspired by his work.

Joseph Bellamy was the oldest of Edwards's immediate disciples. A gifted preacher, he might easily have exchanged his pulpit in the small Connecticut town of Bethlem for one in a major city, but like many Puritan ministers before him, he enjoyed life away from the metropolitan centers. In a sermon published in 1758 entitled *The Wisdom of God, in the Permission of Sin*, Bellamy argued that sin, awful though it is, was permitted by God because it contributed to the good of the universe as a whole. He defended the Trinity from attacks by Jonathan Mayhew, and in tracts published in 1769 and 1770 he followed Edwards in attacking the Half-Way Covenant, leading the way to its abandonment in many churches. Bellamy's most important book indicates his ability go beyond his mentor, even while remaining allied to the Edwardsean tradition. In *True Religion Delineated* (1750), Bellamy described salvation and Christian life in Edwardsean terms, but argued for general atonement, whereas Edwards had favored the theory of limited atonement. Many works of Edwardsean theology were written after the death of the master, but *True Religion* was published in Edwards's lifetime and endorsed by him, indicating that Edwards was open to seeing his disciples develop their own ideas. Bellamy in turn influenced many followers. His home in tiny Bethlem was crowded with ministerial candidates; sixty came during his lifetime.

Samuel Hopkins was a younger disciple of Edwards, and according to some accounts was Edwards's closest friend. He was not the preacher that Bellamy was, but he was a powerful controversialist. He is sometimes referred to as an "ultra-Edwardsean," and his followers were known as "Hopkinsians." Hopkins studied theology while living with Edwards and then became minister of Great Barrington, Massachusetts, in 1743 and Newport, Rhode Island, in 1770. He followed Edwards in associating true virtue with benevolence. And he argued that God rules the world in such a way as to create the greatest possible good. But in the process God permits a certain amount of sin for the benefit of the universe. Despite God's control over sin, he said, sinners are no less responsible for their acts. These doctrines are suggested in the long title of one of Hopkins's most important works, *Sin, through Divine Interposition, an Advantage to the Universe, and yet This No Excuse for Sin or Encouragement to It* (1759). According to Hopkins, true benevolence in the individual consists in preferring the glory of God, even the doctrine of arbitrary election, over personal gain. And the true test of a Christian, he said, is in the complete acceptance of God's will—even a willingness to be damned.

This concept of "unconditional resignation" was just the sort of proposition that Mary Noyes would undoubtedly characterize as metaphysical. But in Edwards, a similar thought had opened his heart to an ecstatic sense of God's majesty. And for that matter, Mary herself found that the way to a closer relationship to God was to mortify her own self: "my pride wanted mortifying." The willingness-to-be-damned doctrine may have seemed to many plain New Englanders a somewhat perverse notion, but it was a metaphor, none the less, for the idea of humility that had been the bread and butter of Puritan preaching for almost two centuries.

In fact the idea may have come to Hopkins as much from Mrs. Edwards— Sarah—as from her husband. While Hopkins was living with the Edwardses in Northampton in 1742, Sarah Edwards underwent a profound religious experience, focusing on a feeling of absolute submission. Williston Walker wrote, "One wonders whether the impressionable young theological student, then an inmate of the Northampton home, may not have received something of his inclination toward this test of Christian character from the mystical, exalted, winsome wife of his instructor."[8]

Hopkins was also known for his argument that moral qualities are manifested in the choices or "exercises" of the will. Those choices, he said, were determined by the "bias" of the heart: in unconverted men and women the bias will be towards evil and through regeneration the bias is directed toward good. Since sin was a matter of exercises of the will, men and women were not guilty of sin simply because Adam had sinned. None the less, Hopkins held that personal sin was an effect of Adam's original sin, and it begins as soon as a child acts. Walker noted: "The divine efficiency is the ultimate cause of all acts, good and bad; but since sin is in the act or exercise and not in its cause, sin belongs to man and not to God."[9] Through Hopkins and other disciples, Hopkinsianism became one of the important threads of Congregationalism.

But the New Divinity did not dominate all Congregational churches. Its opponents were equally vocal, and during the two decades before the American Revolution a number of brushfire wars erupted in the New England presses, pitting New Divinity theologians against their opponents. Some of the opposition were liberals developing a theology that gave more credit to human aspiration than traditional Puritanism. Others were "Old Calvinists," who adhered closely to traditional views of sin and salvation but mistrusted the theological speculations of the New Divinity supporters. The basic argument involved how to regard the efforts of unredeemed men and women. Hopkins argued that although they ought to seek salvation, without grace they grew worse and worse no matter how hard they pursued salvation. His opponents admitted that someone who read the Bible, attended church, and prayed might still not be regenerate, but they said that anyone who used these "means" to work for salvation was growing better, not worse.

In 1761 Jonathan Mayhew published a typical liberal tract, *Striving to Enter in the Strait Gate*, in which he argued that regeneration required human effort.

The book drew on the preparationist tradition, but in suggesting that work was necessary to salvation, Mayhew seemed to be crossing the boundary that separated works from grace as the road to salvation. "By 'striving' to enter in at the strait gate," wrote Mayhew, "is meant in general, exerting ourselves with vigor, or using our earnest endeavors to that end; to obtain the salvation of our souls, or finally to gain admission into the kingdom of heaven. It is opposed to indifference, negligence and sloth; and implies an intense application of the mind and faculties, in order to effect what we have in view." In order to be able to strive effectively, Mayhew said, a person must be "at least a speculative believer of the Gospel." He or she must "earnestly" desire salvation, must strive against sin, and must obey God's commandments. Such passages suggest that Mayhew was pure Arminian, placing salvation in human hands, and ruling out the need for divine grace. But in other passages Mayhew argued that a man must be "awakened" to a sense of sin, and must pray to God, "for the illumination of his holy spirit."[10] In thus mixing human and divine effort, Mayhew is as much a representative of the preparationist strain, which had been in Puritanism from the start, as a precursor of nineteenth-century religious liberalism.

None the less, Congregationalists in post-Awakening America were highly attuned to matters of nuance, and some felt that Mayhew's opinions were heretical. Hopkins replied to Mayhew's Striving in 1765, after Mayhew's death, with *An Enquiry Concerning the Promises of the Gospel, Whether Any of Them are Made to the Exercises and Doings of Persons in an Unregenerate State.* Hopkins answered no to the question implied in the title. The activities of the unconverted were of no spiritual value, even in seeking after Christ. The ways of salvation, he said, were "clothed with holiness," and the "unholy" were "set at the greatest distance from these things, and men never will desire and choose them until they have a heart friendly to holiness, which is the new heart given in regeneration." The unconverted person might go through the motions of striving for Christ, but only those who knew Christ could yearn after him, and only those who were regenerate knew him: into this circle of knowing and desiring only the converted gained admission. Although they might appear to desire Christ, the unconverted, said Hopkins, "are enemies to the just God and Savior, and neglect and refuse the salvation offered."[11]

Hopkins, in turn, was answered by other pastors, including Jedidiah Mills of Huntington, Connecticut, who published *An Inquiry Concerning the State of the Unregenerate under the Gospel* (1767). Mills tried to stigmatize Hopkins by claiming that his views were "agreeable to other enthusiastic visionaries." He argued that "the divinity here exhibited appears to me strange and new, never before advanced in the Christian world by any divine of tolerable sense and reputation."[12] The pamphlet warfare continued through 1773, when Hopkins published his most important and controversial work, *An Inquiry into the Nature of True Holiness*. Following Edwards, Hopkins defined the love of God as "universal, disinterested good will." That goodwill, including the love of one's neighbors and all other good works, Hopkins said, was possible only in a person who loved God. The love of God came, in turn, from God himself, not from the sort of moral exercises encouraged by such writers as Mills. "God's universal, disinterested good will," wrote Hopkins, "supposes our hearts to be in the exercise of the same, for benevolence is implied in taking pleasure in benevolence....This therefore supposes that good will is implied in that love to God, which leads us to the love of good will to our neighbor."[13]

THE AMERICAN REVOLUTION

Many generations later Americans looking back at the 1760s and 1770s would be particularly aware of another conflict, the growing struggle between England and the colonies. But for many Congregationalists the debate over the nature of regeneration was easily as important as the imperial dispute. While the Stamp Act was being debated and tea was being thrown into Boston Harbor, theologians were engaged in the greatest doctrinal conflict to occupy Americans to that time.

Historians have filled many a page arguing just how the spirit of Puritanism entered the passions of Revolution. The liberal theologians tended to emphasize human effort, and the conservatives or Calvinists focused on God's role in life. Some historians argue that liberal pastors, more trusting in the value of human effort, were more effective in encouraging human attempts to fight the British. Others argue that the Calvinists, confident of God's favor, were the more effective. All in all, the difference between the two religious persuasions in their commitment to the Revolution has been exaggerated. Pastors on both sides of the theological issues delivered similarly patriotic discourses. Most agreed on these points, which entered their sermons in various ways:

1. America, and particularly New England, was especially favored by God.

2. England's threat to the American government was also a threat to American religion.

3. God's favor to New England could not be taken for granted; the colonists had to keep God's favor by living righteous lives.

4. If Americans repented and followed the ways of the Lord, he would favor them in war as well as peace.

The third point was perhaps the ministers' favorite. They were ordained to lead people to repentance and salvation—the war and the possibility of defeat was a new stick with which to beat sinners. Sometimes it is hard to tell whether the ministers' fondest hope was to lead the people to victory or to lead them to reform. But, then, the question would not have occurred to them: they were doing both. The result was a "heady brew" of Puritanism and libertarianism—the secular doctrine, inherited particularly from John Locke, that governments are formed for the welfare of the governed.

A good example of the patriotic sermon was preached by Joseph Fish, father of Mary Fish, in 1755 during the French and Indian War. The sermon illustrates a strain of thought, both religious and nationalistic, that was recurred in the conflict with Britain:

> The armies of France, with their savage allies, have entered into our inheritance, and begun their hostilities upon us. Our possessions, our lives, liberties, and all that is sacred or worth living for, lie at stake; so that we cannot long enjoy the good land that our God has given us, nor the holy religion that he has taught us, unless we make a vigorous defence, and push the enemy from our borders....To arms then, my brethren! To arms, ye friends of liberty! Go and take the field, and fight the battles of the Lord....Only trust in the Lord, and go against your enemies in his name, and he will send you a million of angels, if need be, to encamp about you, to cover your heads in battle, and make your arms victorious.

These words of encouragement were reassuring, but Fish would have been unorthodox if he had left his audience beaming with self-satisfaction. God's angels would protect only his own people, those whom had experienced regeneration: "Our God is a holy God of purer eyes than to behold evil, or look upon iniquity. He loveth righteousness and hateth wickedness."[14]

As relations between Britain and America worsened following the French and Indian War, many Congregational ministers preached sermons against the British government similar in tone to the sermons preached by Fish and others during the French and Indian War. A sermon preached by William Gordon, minister of Roxbury, on December 15, 1774, on the eve of the Revolution, provides a good example. It is valuable for its familiarity rather than its uniqueness. Hundreds of sermons, perhaps thousands, contained almost exactly the same ideas. Gordon himself comments on the "surprising agreement in opinion" that was apparent in patriots throughout the colonies. It was "as though the inspiration of the most high gave them the like understanding."[15]

We tend to assume that radio and television have homogenized American society. But long ago, ministers, the provincial press, word of mouth, Committees of Correspondence, and the Continental Congresses shared ideas continually. One patriot's speech frequently sounds like another's simply because it's author borrowed from another, or both borrowed from a common source. Sometimes the ministers varied the proportions and applied more or less heat. Gordon preached a few months after the Coercive Acts (1774) had closed the Port of Boston and altered the government of Massachusetts. He was certain that Britain intended to reduce the colonies to "a state of slavery"—a good libertarian perspective.

Some of Gordon's remarks were secular in orientation. For example, he noted with pride that the colonists were good shots. But the point he emphasized was that the colonists would prevail if they made peace with God. Puritans ministers had been making this point for 150 years in New England, and they were good at it. In the tradition of the jeremiad, they made two seemingly contradictory statements: (1) New Englanders were peculiarly holy, and (2) New Englanders were peculiarly depraved.

The preachers made the two ideas work in tandem: because New Englanders were uniquely holy they had a special responsibility to be righteous; so their failings were especially lamentable. But because they were uniquely righteous, they could overcome their failings. The spiritual energy generated by this combination of favor and guilt gave Puritanism some of its vitality. For example, Gordon reminded his audience of the unique Puritan heritage: "Through the original blessing of Heaven upon them [the Puritans], which, perhaps, never displayed itself and wrought more effectually, except in the instance of the Jews, they are become a considerable nation." At the same time he castigated the people for their sins: "Is not this people strangely degenerated, so as to possess but a faint resemblance of that godliness for which their forefathers were eminent?" He urged his people to experience true holiness: a "sense of the beauty of holiness" and "soul-sanctifying love to God." The enemy was strong, but through the exercise of Puritan virtue, he said, the colonists could prevail: "We are warranted to expect that at length, in the exercise of prudence, fortitude, and piety, we shall get well through our difficulties."

Most Congregational ministers came to believe that God was on the side of the American Revolution. They preached patriotic sermons on the Sabbath and at special occasions, such as militia musters. Ministers hosted day-long spinning bees in their parsonages, where women spun clothes for the soldiers. Many ministers went to war as chaplains, and a few actually bore arms in times of particular danger. Many educated their people on constitutional issues and even drew up public papers. Jonas Clark, of Lexington, Massachusetts, wrote practically every public paper for the town during the Revolutionary era, and even drafted instructions to the Lexington representatives in the General Court.[16] The Congregational pastors were so consistent in their patriotism that they acquired the name the Black Regiment from the British.

There were several reasons for their support of the Revolution. To some degree they simply followed their people—as pastors they sought to preach doctrines relevant to the current needs of the parish. As the idea that Britain was attempting to tyrannize the colonists gained support, the ministers naturally sided with their people. But in many cases the ministers were in the vanguard of the patriot movement. Jonathan Mayhew, for example, preached an early revolutionary sermon, *The Danger of Unlimited Submission*. The Congregationalists had come to America fleeing religious tyranny; so they were accustomed to thinking of themselves as the righteous remnant of a corrupt English nation.

Events preceding the Revolution reinforced this impression. Not only did England appear to threaten the colonists by imposing taxation without the approval of colonial representatives, but on the eve of the Revolution the British also discussed the possibility of another innovation, the creation of Anglican bishops for America. During the decade before the Revolution the controversy over the meaning of such a policy agitated the Congregational clergy. A case could be made that as a practical measure the Anglican church in America—well established in the south, embryonic in New England—needed local bishops.

For example, a Congregational minister could be born, educated, and ordained in America. But a native born Anglican had to go to England for ordination, and a substantial number died while abroad of smallpox, which was a constant danger to the American visitor to Britain. By and large, however, the Congregational clergy did not see the practical side of this issue. They were the descendents of Puritan pastors who had been harried from the land of England by Anglican bishops and archbishops. Who could guarantee that they would not be oppressed again if Anglican bishops were established in America?

In such ways religion and revolution were intermingled. But it would be a mistake to assume that Puritanism in either its more liberal or more conservative form was interchangeable with patriotism during the Revolution. Religion was not simply the handmaiden of politics, and many ministers were disturbed by the tumult of the Revolution, questioned whether God approved of mob action, and considered that their people were paying too much attention to politics and not enough to God. Some became patriots almost as an afterthought, as the changing politics of their parish and colony created an independent America where once there had been British provinces.

STEPHEN WILLIAMS: RELUCTANT PATRIOT

Stephen Williams, minister of Longmeadow, Massachusetts, in the Connecticut River Valley, is a good example of the minister who was a Puritan first, a patriot second. During the crises leading up to the Revolution, Williams was not sure which side was right and which wrong. When a Boston mob, protesting the Stamp Act, pillaged the house of Lieutenant Governor Thomas Hutchinson, he referred to the act as a "horrid" event. "Oh what will the spirit of licentiousness do?" he wrote in his diary. "The Lord have mercy upon us, reform and restrain the rage of the people that are mad upon their lusts. O that the land may be humbled, for these our crying abominations, that are so offensive to God and dishonorable to our holy religion."[17]

A few weeks later, when the Stamp Act was about to go into effect, Williams noted that business would probably be interrupted by the activities of the patriots. His response was critical: "O that this people may be kept from further tumults and be still and know that God is God." When the Stamp Act was repealed in 1766 Williams prayed that the news would "make us an *obedient thankful people*." Williams's reaction to the Stamp Act was typical of his attitude towards the revolutionary crisis as a whole. In 1769 he traveled to Boston and was bothered by what he saw: "I had on my journey opportunity to observe the temper of the people. They cry out for *liberty* and are in a special danger of *licentiousness*. Great complaining, but yet few among us (I fear) enquiring, what have I done, etc.[to offend God]....Oh Lord, be pleased to restrain and curb the haughty spirit of people."[18]

Again and again Williams's diary reflects the traditional Puritan view that misfortunes are punishments from God and can be warded off only by repentance. Thus, when a misfortune such as the Boston Massacre occurred, he was more attuned to the spiritual message that the people must reform themselves than to the political message that Britain was a tyrant. His diary entry on March 9, 1770, four days after the Massacre asked God to "pity, pardon, spare, and reform us." Williams's view of providence was apparent a few weeks later when he mended the lightning rod on his house. Somewhat apologetically he noted in his diary, "Although I think it is a proper thing to put up the rod, since such discoveries have been made as to the nature of electricity, yet I desire to have my eyes to the God of glory who thunders, for protection."[19]

From crisis to crisis the Revolutionary movement built, creating in New England an atmosphere that Stephen Williams deplored. "A dark, cloudy, rainy day," he wrote on October 7, 1772, "and things appear to me *dark* as to our civil and religious privileges—a spirit of discontent, uneasiness, and even of licentiousness prevails in this land." Apparently archpatriot John Hancock appreciated the power of the pulpit and was eager to secure the support of country pastors to the cause of freedom. In the fall of 1772 he sent Stephen Williams a "canister with a pound of green tea"—most likely smuggled Dutch tea, because the colonists were boycotting British tea to avoid paying a duty. A year later tea entered Williams's diary for another reason. He wrote, "We hear that the *multitude* have risen, and have taken all the tea (belonging to the East India Company) that was on the ships in Boston Harbor, broke the boxes in pieces, and flung it into the sea. A strange affair indeed. The Lord mercifully regard this poor people, that are for doing every one what is good in his own eyes, not regarding we have yet a king in our Israel."[20]

The next year the British passed the Coercive Acts, closing the Port of Boston and dissolving the Massachusetts Legislature. Williams noted with alarm that a neighboring minister was "a warm man among the sons of liberty" and was in danger of "running into wild measures." In contrast Williams favored "calmness and moderation....Without deep repentance and reformation we can expect nothing but destruction. The Lord be pleased to pour out his spirit upon us." He noted that there was "a mighty cry for liberty—which seems to be a desire to do as each one likes." Williams believed that the people should direct their efforts to discovering the *sins* that brought about the *punishment* of the royal edicts. In sermons he told his congregation that "repentance and reformation" was the "only proper course to be taken in this day of distress." Rather than bringing liberty to the colonies, the patriots seemed to Williams to "have a tendency to fling us into confusion and to bring us to lose those very privileges that they pretend to be so very fond of."[21]

During the fall of 1774 and the winter of 1775 as the patriots gathered munitions and drilled for battle, Williams continued to counsel moderation and repentance. On April 16, 1775, a young ministerial candidate, Emerson Foster preached to Williams's congregation. The sermon was political, "a discourse," wrote Williams, "I was sorry to hear on the Sabbath." Four days later rumors reached Longmeadow that a battle had been fought in Lexington and Concord.

The next day Williams prayed with a company of minutemen bound for Boston, and on April 22 he confided to his diary, "A war is begun."[22]

But Williams still continued to be cool to the revolutionary movement. Patriot Emerson Foster preached for him again in May and "was very popular and doubtless greatly pleased our warm people." Williams was pleased that Foster at least said, "We had no reason to expect help and relief without repentance and reformation." The news in May that the patriots had taken the British fort at Ticonderoga only left Williams worried that "we shall feel the horrors of a Civil War in a little time." A few days later on the Sabbath he prayed that the King would do what was right in the sight of the Lord and not be "led astray by flatterers." This seems innocuous enough, but in those heady times Williams was beginning to run into the danger of seeming to oppose the Revolution. One of his congregation accosted him after the service and criticized him for praying for the king—whose head should be "cut off."[23]

With feelings running so high, Williams might have suffered the fate of people considered to be Tories, opponents of the Revolution. One had been ridden out of a neighboring town backwards on a horse and told never to return. Another lost the windows of his house to an angry mob. Williams noted "a coldness among my own people toward me because they apprehend I don't think with them as to the present times and measures." Shortly after the beginning of the Revolution, the parish decided to hire an assistant for Williams, who was now eighty-two years old. He was not certain whether they were acting out of sympathy for his weakness or in hostility to his views.

During the early months of the war, Williams was worried by the confusion that accompanied the Revolution; he thought Americans might divide into those supporting and those opposing the Revolution. And as his diary indicates, he continued to lament the patriot's impiety.

June 5: "How little is God in our thoughts."

June 10: "Keep us from trusting to ourselves, to our sword and bow, but help us to put our trust in the Lord."

June 30: "Things very dark: tumults, and various reports from one place and another—the drought very great, the very trees wither, the leaves dry, the fruit falls—oh Lord, be pleased to eye thy land and awaken us to repentance."

July 1: "How stupid and senseless are we as a people."

Williams was pleased to report on September 5 that a council of five churches had unanimously adopted a testimony against "the God provoking evils prevailing in the land," and advised reform. In such ways Williams continued to emphasize spiritual reform.

But after the war entered its fifth month, a new priority entered Williams's thoughts. Almost unconsciously he began to sympathize with the revolutionary movement, even though he continued to worry about the spiritual values of his people. So, for example, when he learned on September 9 that an American army was marching towards Canada, he did not criticize the soldiers for vanity, as he might have in the past. Instead he wrote simply, "Oh that God would be with them." His orientation was beginning to shift, and almost unconsciously he was becoming part of a new community. On September 19 he noted that his son-in-law Gideon had left for the army. God "give him to behave as a good Christian and a good soldier," Williams wrote. On November 4 he recorded a prayer for "my own dear native land"—meaning America. And on November 21, he prayed that the Lord would "mercifully preserve and direct" the American forces in Canada.[24]

The Revolution was now half-a-year old, but it still seemed strange to Williams. "The year past has been the most remarkable year that I ever saw," he wrote. Williams still found much to lament about the new age. When a servant deserted him to enlist in the army, he wrote, "It appears to me very dark that apprentices may be taken away from masters....What confusion is like to follow such measures. Are we not fighting for liberty?" He was unhappy that children and apprentices could engage in military service without parental approval. And yet religion and revolution began to combine in his mind. He believed that the Americans had suffered because of their evil ways, and at the same time he could write that England was guilty of "arbitrary and tyrannical measures." He could still chastise his revolutionary people for lack of piety, but somehow the Revolution itself had become a given, rather than a sign of impiety. When a mob in Berkshire County, Massachusetts, attacked the local court, he regretted that their behavior "reflected" badly on the Continental Congress and the army. The news of American naval successes filled him with pleasure at his nation's victories—and occasioned the standard reservations about pride. The victories, he wrote, "seem to be smiles of providence on the American cause and call for our thanks, but the Lord grant we may rejoice with humbling."[25]

In 1776 Williams attended "a religious exercise" commemorating the anniversary of Lexington and Concord. That June he reported with pleasure that the colonists had won a victory over "the enemy." Still, it was hard for him to think of America as a separate nation. Like many other Americans, Williams hoped at first that the Revolution would lead to reformation rather than separation. On July 6, two days after the official adoption of a declaration of independence at Philadelphia, Williams offered a prayer for "this flock, and town; this land, and the English nation."[26]

"And the English nation..." America became a new nation on July 4, 1776, but the nation would be at war for another seven years before Britain would officially recognize that fact. And even among Americans the news of independence spread slowly and entered the popular consciousness even more slowly. It was not until August 11, 1776, that Williams read a copy of the Declaration of Independence to his congregation. And as in so many other matters, the document led him to a spiritual moral: "This day I read publicly (being required thereto by the provincial council) the declaration (of the continental congress) for independency—the Lord grant that we may have our dependence upon God—when we cease from man."

That summer and fall George Washington faced the worst hardships of the war, being defeated again and again by the British in battles in and around New York City. During this time, Thomas Paine wrote his most famous lines: "These are the times that try men's souls. The summer soldier and the sunshine patriot will in this crisis shrink from the service of his country, but he who stands it now deserves the love and praise of man and woman." In these months Stephen Williams came to embrace the patriot's cause. He felt that his people still needed to be chastised for their sins, but they were his people, and he was their minister. England was seeking to destroy them, and he knew whose side he was on. On October 20, 1776, he wrote this passage in his diary, reflecting his complete metamorphosis into a patriot: "Oh, that the Lord of hosts and God of armies would be with us—shield and protect our military men—prepare for what is before us. Give us to acknowledge God in all our ways. Oh Lord, don't give us up as a reproach to our oppressors. Wilt thou be pleased to restrain them and spare thy people in much mercy....Oh that God himself would arise in this very critical day—arise, oh Lord, I do beseech thee for our help."

Five years later victory was near. George Washington had surrounded a British army at Yorktown. Stephen Williams was in his eighty-ninth year. As so often in the past, he still found his people wanting in spirituality. On October 17, the anniversary of Burgoyne's surrender at Saratoga, the people celebrated in a way that hardly seemed appropriate to Williams: "This day the great guns were fired at the town and in the evening sky rockets were set off and other fireworks—this in remembrance of Gen. Burgoyne's surrender. I am sorry such measures were gone into. I had rather it had been observed in a religious manner and praise given to God for his mercies. The Lord be pleased to enable us to put our trust in him." A few days later news arrived that the British had surrendered at Yorktown. "Not unto us, oh Lord," wrote Williams, "not unto us, but to thy name be the praise and glory."[27]

The new world was in certain ways more secular than the world in which Williams was born almost ninety years before. Some idea of the change can be seen in Williams's account of his visit to a sick old man in his parish on the eve of the Revolution. Williams told him that "I feared the youth in the place played cards." Williams noted, "This account affected him with grief and caused him even to weep." One imagines that Williams also wept over such matters. We see his sense of a beleaguered Puritan tradition in need of support in his report a few years earlier of this dream: "I had a dream last night of seeing some venerable ancient divines, particularly the Rev. Dr. Increase and Cotton Mather—a comfortable interview with them. I don't know that there is anything special in this...but I desire to make this improvement of it: to follow their faith."[28]

Stephen Williams' career as a patriot hardly makes a case for the Congregational clergy as the chief instigators of the Revolution in New England. Some, like Ebenezer Gay in Hingham, were much cooler to the movement than Williams and were branded Tories. Others, like Boston's

Charles Chauncy, were avid patriots. The foremost leaders of the Revolution in New England were lay people like Samuel Adams and John Hancock. But Williams's patriotism is instructive, exemplifying as it does the blending of Puritanism and revolutionary ardor in a man whose attitude toward the Revolution was midway between that of the most loyal and most patriotic clergy. In men like Williams, the Puritan ethos worked in its essential form: in the belief that men and women must subordinate worldly ambitions to spiritual values.

The world was turned upside down during Williams's long ministry. Some of his colleagues led in that upheaval; others resisted longer than he did. Some styled themselves New Divinity Men, others Old Calvinists, and others liberals. But most, like Williams, discovered what so many other Congregational ministers had learned in the past, that they must stand with one foot squarely in parishes they served and the other in the world of religious ideals. Sometimes the ministers led society; sometimes they had to hurry to catch up with public affairs. But in the pull and tug between the spirit and the world, most managed to preserve much of traditional Puritanism in a changing world. Through their efforts Congregationalism would enter the life of the new nation.

NOTES

[1] Quotation from Joy Day Buel and Richard Buel, Jr., *The Way of Duty* (New York, 1984), 7, 8.

[2] Quotation from Buel and Buel, *Way of Duty*, 11.

[3] Quotation from Buel and Buel, *Way of Duty*, 10-11.

[4] Quotation from Buel and Buel, *Way of Duty*, 12.

[5] Mary Fish's Reminiscences, Silliman Family Papers, Beinecke Library, Yale University. The quotations that follow until otherwise indicated are from these reminiscences.

[6] Mary Fish's Journal, Silliman Family Papers, Beinecke Library, Yale University. The quotations that follow until otherwise indicated are from the journal.

[7] Sydney Ahlstrom, *Religious History of the American People*, 311.

[8] Williston Walker, *Congregational Churches*, 289.

[9] Williston Walker, *Congregational Churches*, 290.

[10] Jonathan Mayhew, *Striving to Enter in at the Strait Gate* (Boston, 1761), 8, 11-20.

[11] Samuel Hopkins, *An Enquiry Concerning the Promises of the Gospel* (Boston, 1765), 27-29.

[12] Jedidiah Mills, *An Inquiry Concerning the State of the Unregenerate Under the Gospel* (New Haven, 1767), 5.

[13] Samuel Hopkins, *An Enquiry into the Nature of True Holiness* (Newport, 1773), 38-39.

[14] Joseph Fish, *Angels Ministering to the People of God, for their Safety and Comfort in Times of Danger and Distress* (Newport, R.I., 1755), 27-28.

[15] William Gordon, *A Discourse Preached December 15th, 1774*, in John Wingate Thornton, ed., *The Pulpit of the American Revolution* (Boston, 1860), 211.

The following quotations from Gordon's Discourse, appear on pages 219, 221, 212, and 222.

[16] Alice Baldwin, *The New England Clergy and the American Revolution* (Durham, N.C., 1928), 161-66, 94-95.

[17] Stephen Williams, Diary, August 31, 1765, Longmeadow Public Library, Massachusetts.

[18] Williams, Diary, November 2, 1765; July 24, 1766; June 8, 1769.

[19] Williams, Diary, March 9 and 29, 1770.

[20] Williams, Diary, October 7, 1772; December 10, 1773.

[21] Williams, Diary, June 6 and 29, 1774; July 10 and 28, 1774.

[22] Williams, Diary, April 16, 22, 1775.

[23] Williams, Diary, May 11, 16, and 21, 1775.

[24] Williams, Diary, June 5, 10, and 30, 1775; July 1, 1775; September 19, 1775; November 21, 1775.

[25] Williams, Diary, January 6, 1776; November 29, 1775; February 20, 1776; January 6, 1775; March 5, 1776; December 9, 1775.

[26] Williams, Diary, April 19, 1776; June 11, 1776; July 6, 1776.

[27] Williams, Diary, August 11, 1776; October 20, 1776; October 17, 1781; October 29, 1781.

[28] Williams, Diary, October 14, 1775, December 13, 1771.

7
EXPANSION AND REFORM

CONGREGATIONALISM AND DENOMINATIONALISM: THE PLAN OF UNION

With the formation of the United States, Congregationalism was one church among many in the new nation. It was the dominant church in New Hampshire, Massachusetts, and Connecticut. But in various other parts of the country Presbyterians, Methodists, Quakers, Baptists, and Episcopalians were predominant. With the opening of the west, Congregationalists would compete with other denominations for converts. This would be difficult because for roughly the first fifty years of independence the Congregationalists did not even think of themselves as a denomination.

We are so accustomed to thinking of religious denominations today that it is difficult to imagine a time when Congregationalists were not a self-conscious denomination. The term suggests an acceptance of the fact that there will be many different organizations of Christians in the nation. But the Puritans had come to America with the expectation that the church and the commonwealth would be one. Congregationalists had been forced to live with the fact of some diversity, but in 1783 at the end of the revolutionary war, Congregationalism was still the established church in most of New England.

Ironically one of the events that encouraged Congregationalists to think of themselves as a denomination was a temporary alliance with Presbyterians. In 1801 the two churches adopted a Plan of Union for evangelizing the west. Sympathetic to each other in doctrine, they agreed to set aside differences in polity for the sake of creating churches in regions where there were not enough men and women to support ministers of both groups. The pastor could belong to either denomination, and the church could belong to either the local general association (of Congregationalists) or the local presbytery (of Presbyterians). Within each church, discipline was to be administered by committees composed of members of both denominations. In the case of disputes, the churches could appeal to a council consisting of both Presbyterians and Congregationalists. The churches were sometimes referred to as "presbygationalist."

The plan worked well in evangelizing the west, and with the assistance of both churches several "Plan of Union colleges" were formed: Hamilton (New York, 1812); Western Reserve (Ohio, 1826), Knox (Illinois, 1837), and Illinois (1829). But Presbyterianism benefited more than Congregationalism. The Presbyterian emphasis on strong organization gave the denomination an advantage over the independent-minded Congregationalists. Between 1800 and 1850 roughly two thousand churches in New York, Ohio, Illinois, and Michigan that began as predominantly Congregationalist evolved into Presbyterian churches.[1]

The two denominations also ran into difficulty on points of doctrine. Each had to deal with liberal and conservative wings in its own group. Sometimes it was easier to take out those frustrations on the other denomination than to reconcile internal differences. In 1827, for example, controversy over new revivalist techniques pitted liberal-minded Presbyterians against conservative Congregationalists. The center of the conflict was a Presbyterian frontier evangelist, Charles Grandison Finney. He offended the orthodox by claiming that men and women could assist in their own conversion and that they could attain a state of perfection on earth. Both of these positions were contrary to the traditional Puritan view of the great distance between people and God.

Finney's success was sensational. He encouraged men and women to be saved immediately, as he preached, and many achieved an ecstatic sense of spiritual rebirth under his tutelage. He was the George Whitefield of his era, and just as Whitefield had encountered opposition, so did Finney. If, however, Whitefield had been too much a Calvinist for some of the orthodox, Finney's problem was exactly the opposite. In encouraging men and women to have confidence in their own powers, he seemed to have embraced Arminianism. Lyman Beecher, then minister of Hanover Street Congregational Church in Boston, met with Finney in New Lebanon, New York, in July of 1827 to try to persuade him to be more moderate. Beecher failed, and many Congregationalists wondered about the wisdom of an alliance with a church that included Finney.

A few years later Beecher himself was the center of a controversy that chilled relations between the denominations. He had moved west and had become president of Lane Seminary in Cincinnati. A series of heresy trials took place within Presbyterianism during the 1830s, and in 1835 the church indicted Beecher, on the claim that he placed too much emphasis on the value of human effort in salvation. He was tried before a presbytery in Cincinnati and acquitted, but Presbyterian suspicion of Congregational liberalism continued. In 1837 conservatives gained control over the Presbyterian general assembly. They expelled three synods in New York and Ohio from the church, severed relations with societies consisting of Congregational and Presbyterian representatives, and dissolved the Plan of Union.

Some Presbyterians continued to associate with the Congregationalists, but the union had been severely damaged. Other matters further divided the two denominations. During the 1830s and 1840s many Congregationalists embraced the abolitionist cause. Because almost all of the denomination's members lived in the North, this did not threaten Congregational unity. But Presbyterianism stretched deep into the South, making the denomination reluctant to embrace an issue that could cause a North-South rift. In 1852 the Congregationalists had a national convention at Albany, New York, the first synod of their church since the seventeenth century. The delegates voted unanimously to accept the inevitable and abandon the Plan of Union.

Two other developments at this time facilitated the growth of denominational self-consciousness among the Congregationalists. At the Albany convention the church created the Congregational Library Association to facilitate the collecting of books on church history. The next year the American Congregational Union was formed to promote the denomination's growth, particularly through helping to build new meeting houses.

THEOLOGICAL DISPUTES AND THE UNITARIAN SCHISM

The abortive union with the Presbyterians is one thread in the story of Congregational denominationalism in the nineteenth century. Developments in theology and voluntary organizations also influenced the change. Following in the path of Jonathan Edwards and Samuel Hopkins, other ministers took up the cause of religious orthodoxy among the Congregationalists. Stephen West succeeded Edwards at Stockbridge in 1758 and became a New Divinity theologian through the influence of a neighboring pastor—Samuel Hopkins. In 1772 West published *Essay on Moral Agency*, defending Edwards's *Freedom of the Will*. He was also known for *Scripture Doctrine of the Atonement* (1785), which contains the novel argument that the atonement was meant to show God's character, particularly his disposition towards men for breaking the law. West said that the atonement involved no obligation whatsoever upon God to save sinners.

Another second-generation Edwardsean, Jonathan Edwards, Jr., was for many years pastor of North Church in New Haven. His career followed that of his father to a remarkable degree in that he was eventually dismissed from his pulpit in a doctrinal conflict, served for a time in an obscure parish, was appointed president of a college, Union, and died shortly after taking office. Like his father he was an astute theologian, but in the words of Williston Walker, "He lacked the poetic nature and the warm mystical feeling which made the temperament of the father so rare a combination of the intellect and of the heart."[2]

The younger Edwards was best known for his effort to put down yet another outbreak of liberal sentiment, this time on the question of universal, as opposed to limited, salvation. In 1770 John Murray, an English Universalist, arrived in America. In 1779 after preaching extensively through the colonies, he settled in Gloucester, Massachusetts, as pastor of a Universalist congregation. Murray had been raised a Calvinist and was tormented as a youth by the doctrine of limited atonement. He came to believe that all men and women are saved through

Christ's death. Another innovator, Charles Chauncy, the one-time scourge of the revivalists, had been attracted to universalism for years, and during the 1780s he published three anonymous tracts, including *The Mystery Hid from Ages...or, the Salvation of All Men* (1784). Chauncy believed that sinners were punished in the afterlife, but held that there were limits to their torment, and that eventually all would be saved.

Jonathan Edwards, Jr. attacked these views in *The Necessity of Atonement* (1785) and *The Salvation of All Men Strictly Examined* (1790). Like Stephen West, Edwards argued that Christ's death placed no obligation on God to save sinners. God forgives the sinner freely, Edwards said, not because of the atonement: "This atonement constitutes no part of the personal character of the sinner: but his personal character is essentially the same, as it would have been, if Christ had made no atonement." The atonement served another purpose entirely, demonstrating God's justice, which requires the punishment of sinners. With the crucifixion "an exhibition" is "made in the death and sufferings of Christ, of the punishment to which the sinner is justly liable."[3] This was often referred to as the "governmental" or "New England" theory of atonement, and it dominated Congregational thought for a century.

During the late eighteenth century the New Divinity began to divide into different schools, the more conservative following Hopkins and his protege Nathaniel Emmons, the more moderate led by Timothy Dwight. Emmons was born in 1745 and graduated from Yale in 1767. He was minister of Franklin, Massachusetts, from 1773 until 1827. Emmons was particularly noted for developing Hopkins's idea that holiness and sin are "exercises" of the will. Like Hopkins he held that the essence of sin is selfishness and the essence of holiness is disinterested love. Man's spiritual nature is a chain of exercises, he said, each good or bad; the will is free, but God is the "efficient cause" of all actions. Emmons stressed people's active roles in their own salvation, and he described sin and salvation as voluntary acts; human guilt is not simply inherited from Adam "for moral depravity consists in the free, voluntary exercises of a moral agent; and of consequence cannot be transmitted by one person to another." But, he said, "in consequence of Adam's first transgression, God now brings his posterity into the world in a state of moral depravity."[4] Later critics would say that Emmons was "having it both ways," arguing for divine causality and human volition.

These ideas, couched in the metaphysical language of the New Divinity, grew out of a religious conviction that followed the classic Puritan pattern. We can get a better understanding of Emmons's ideas if we look at his career. As a youth he had occasional thoughts of God, particularly when his sister died of consumption. Then, he said, "I had some lively apprehensions of the state of the damned, especially of the lake that burneth with fire and brimstone." But he soon lost these feelings and was not troubled again until he began to study divinity and decided upon "the great importance of becoming truly religious." Then he began reading the Bible daily and praying in secret. Like the Puritans of old, Emmons felt that the final change of conversion came to him from God: "One night there came up a terrible thunderstorm, which gave me such an awful sense of God's displeasure and of my going into a miserable eternity, as I never had before. I durst not close my eyes in sleep during the whole night, but lay crying for mercy with anxiety and distress. This impression continued day after day, and week after week, and put me upon the serious and diligent use of what I supposed to be the appointed means of grace."

Emmons went to study theology under New Divinity preacher John Smalley. The "plain" preaching he now heard helped persuade him of "the plague of my own heart, and of my real opposition to the way of salvation revealed in the Gospel." In a statement reminiscent of Jonathan Edwards's mood on the eve of his conversion, Emmons wrote: "My heart rose against the doctrine of Divine sovereignty, and I felt greatly embarrassed with respect to the use of means." Emmons found himself overawed by God's sovereignty and desperate in his own helplessness. "But one afternoon," he wrote, "when my hopes were gone, I had a peculiar discovery of the Divine perfections, and of the way of salvation by Jesus Christ, which filled my mind with a joy and serenity to which I had ever before been a perfect stranger. This was followed by a peculiar spirit of benevolence to my fellow men, whether friends or foes. And I was transported with the thought of the unspeakable blessedness of the day, when universal benevolence should prevail among all mankind."

Few passages embody as clearly as this the sentiments connecting Calvinism, Edwardseanism, and Hopkinsianism. Emmons came to "the way of salvation by Jesus Christ" by recognizing the absolute sovereignty of God and his own utter helplessness, just as Calvin demanded. His sense of "joy and serenity" in his new relationship to Christ was accompanied by "a peculiar spirit of benevolence to my fellow men," as Edwards could have predicted. And he came to regard his best efforts to win salvation as useless, for even "the best desires and prayers of sinners were altogether selfish, criminal, and displeasing to God"— just as Hopkins claimed.[5]

Emmons was famed for his systematic approach to theology—and to life as a whole. He spent much of his life in his study, even eating his meals there. "There was a place on the right side of the fire for the tongs, and on the left side for the shovel. Precisely so, must the wood be laid on the fire, and the ready hearth-brush must almost instinctively do its duty in keeping dust and ashes in their places." Working sixteen hours a day (and living until he was ninety-five) Emmons wrote some six thousand sermons during his lifetime, and many tracts. He once refused to replace a fallen board from his fence, fearing that it would lead him to other worldly activities. His subjects included Sunday schools, church polity, church music, and the propriety of closing a prayer with the word *Amen*. But he was best known for his writing on the fall, atonement, sin, the will, and regeneration. His ideas could be summarized in a single sentence, "Strict Calvinism brings God near to us: all opposing systems keep him at a distance."[6]   Emmons is generally regarded as filling in the details in the model of New England Theology that came to him from others. Emmons trained roughly a hundred ministerial candidates, creating an army of converts to strict Calvinism.

Timothy Dwight developed that theology in another direction. He was born in Northampton shortly after Jonathan Edwards's departure and was, through his mother, a grandson of Edwards. He attended Yale, served as a chaplain during the revolutionary war, and became a minister in Fairfield, Connecticut. In 1795 he was chosen president of Yale, where he is credited with making Edwardseanism the ruling doctrine. As president he preached every Sunday, developing ideas that were published as *Theology Explained and Defended* (1818, 1823). Dwight led in the formation of a moderate party among Edwards's followers by arguing that ministers should exhort sinners to use the "means of grace." Dwight believed that certainly a person remained sinful as long as he or she was unregenerate, but he gave more credit to the sinner who sought redemption than did Hopkins or Emmons. "Supposing the man's disposition substantially the same in both cases," Dwight argued, "he is less sinful when he performs the act, than when he neglects or refuses to perform it." Consequently Dwight felt that the minister should urge the sinner not only to await divine grace, but also to follow the path to salvation, in the confidence that his or her own efforts through such acts as praying and reading the Bible could lead in the right direction. "In his preaching and advice," wrote Dwight, "a minister is not to confine himself to the mere enjoining of Faith and Repentance; but is to extend them to any other conduct in itself proper to be pursued."[7]

Timothy Dwight was honored at Yale by the creation of a professorship of didactic theology bearing his name. Its most famous holder was Nathaniel William Taylor, who carried even further Dwight's confidence in human nature. As Dwight Professor from 1822 to 1857, he formulated a doctrinal position that came to be known as the New Haven Theology. Taylor's basic claim was that men and women had the ability to reject sin and choose God.

Opponents claimed that Taylor was embracing Arminianism. The foremost among these critics was Bennet Tyler, pastor of the Second Congregational Church of Portland, Maine. He formed a pastoral union in 1833 to oppose the spread of the New Haven Theology. And he and his supporters founded Hartford Theological Seminary in 1834 to uphold a more conservative position on sin and salvation.

The conflict within Congregationalism over the role men and women played in their salvation was set against the background of a far more serious doctrinal division. Since the seventeenth-century Congregationalists had essentially "agreed to disagree" about the role of man and God in the process of salvation. Orthodoxy had been less a single absolute position than a continuing dialogue, sometimes friendly and sometimes acrimonious, between ministers who placed relatively more or less emphasis on man or God. At times the debate was passionate, as between Charles Chauncy and Jonathan Edwards or Nathaniel Taylor and Bennet Tyler. But those and other adversaries had continued to call themselves Congregationalists and had remained within the same church.

During the early 1800s, however, a liberal faction within the church was pushed and pulled into forming an entirely new denomination, the Unitarian church, carved out of the body of Congregationalism. The Unitarians would trace their past to such Congregational liberals as Charles Chauncy and Jonathan Mayhew. But eighteenth-century Congregationalism had managed to accommodate these theological liberals. A more serious breach occurred in 1805 with the appointment of liberal Henry Ware to the Hollis Professorship of Divinity at Harvard. In reaction, conservative Jedidiah Morse protested that Ware was not an orthodox Calvinist and was therefore ineligible to hold the post. A situation that many Congregationalists had been willing to ignore became the subject of public dispute. Frustrated by the apparent "loss" of Harvard, conservatives created Andover Theological Seminary. Most of Boston's churches were of the Unitarian persuasion; so conservatives formed the Park Street Church in Boston in 1809. Morse added fuel to the flames of disagreement in 1815 with the publication of *Review of American Unitarianism,* in which he identified the liberals with infidelity. In Baltimore in 1819 William Ellery Channing delivered a stirring defense of liberalism, "Unitarian Christianity." During the next few years the schism became more and more pronounced. The majority of Boston's Congregational churches and many others throughout New England became Unitarian. Finally in 1825 the liberals created the American Unitarian Association, embracing for themselves a separate denominational identity.

The Unitarian separation, like the abortive union with the Presbyterians, heightened denominational awareness among the Congregationalists. Part of the acrimony of Tyler Bennet against Nathaniel Taylor was based on the fear that the New Haven liberals would go the way of the Unitarians into separation. But this fear also encouraged cooperation, even while raising the specter of division. By 1825 many Congregationalists felt that it was better to tolerate a certain diversity within their denomination than to raise barricades that could create another schism, and another, and another.

VOLUNTARY ASSOCIATIONS

One activity that united Congregationalists was the formation of associations for spreading Christianity. The roots of the nineteenth-century societies can be found in the formation of local groups in the eighteenth century. In 1774, for example, the Congregationalist General Association of Connecticut raised funds to send missionaries to scattered congregations in frontier New York and Vermont. In 1798 the Missionary Society of Connecticut was founded and in 1799, the Massachusetts Missionary Society. During the first decade of the nineteenth century, Congregationalists created dozens of voluntary associations to promote education, Bible reading, and moral reform. Some were molded into national organizations—including the American Education Society (1815), the

American Bible Society (1816), the American Colonization Society (1817), and the American Temperance Society (1826). Some of these associations were joint efforts with the Presbyterians, but they tended to come under Congregational control after the Plan of Union was abandoned.

Through voluntary associations, the Congregationalists tried to accomplish two things that had once been the province of the local parishes in the Puritan commonwealth. The societies tried to bring about reform, leading men and women to the "suburbs of heaven." And they tried to work these reforms on a national scale. Local events in New England encouraged this new orientation. In 1800 the Congregational church was still established in Connecticut, Massachusetts, and New Hampshire—that is, the church was supported by taxes. Communicants in a few other denominations were allowed to "sign off," a procedure that allowed their proportion of taxes to go to their own churches. But all in all, the system served the Congregationalists well. In 1818, however, a new state constitution in Connecticut provided for disestablishment. And in 1819, New Hampshire passed the Toleration Act, taking away tax support.

Congregationalists in Massachusetts, seeing the handwriting on the wall, waited anxiously for their own churches to be cut loose from public support. Ironically, the Unitarian schism lessened their apprehensions. In 1820 the Massachusetts Supreme Court was asked to consider who owned the parish property of churches divided between Congregationalists and Unitarians. In cases where a majority had adopted Unitarianism, the Congregationalists formed new parishes, but sought to retain the property of the dissident church. In the "Dedham decision" Chief Justice Isaac Parker, who happened to be a Unitarian, ruled that a separating church lost its claim to church property—and even its claim to be an established church. Since congregations were defecting to Unitarianism with alarming regularity, especially in Boston, some Congregationalists felt they had nothing to gain by continuing the system of religious establishment. In 1833 a constitutional amendment passed in Massachusetts, eliminating the church tax provision. By then some clergymen actually welcomed the change as an inducement to win converts by a strong ministry.

Ministers faced other professional challenges in the new republic. In some respects their prestige declined with the growth of other professional classes, such as doctors and lawyers. Their career patterns also tended to change as it became common for ministers to serve several parishes during a lifetime—a rarity in colonial America. This increased their sense of separateness as members of a mobile community of clergy. Some of the larger voluntary organizations also encouraged this separate status, creating positions for ministers in organizations other than local parishes. The texture of religious life changed, in addition, with an increasing number of female church members. By 1835 twice as many women as men were Congregationalists. Although no women had yet been received into the ministry, some joined with men in supporting and undertaking foreign missions.

THE MISSIONARY IMPULSE

The institutional embodiment of the missionary impulse—and one of the most important of Congregational voluntary societies—was the American Board of Commissioners for Foreign Missions. The board had its beginnings in the most unlikely of settings—a New England haystack. In 1806 Samuel Mills, a student at Williams, and several of his classmates met regularly in the woods to discuss religion. One day they were caught in a thunderstorm and burrowed into a haystack for shelter. As they continued their meeting, Mills was suddenly struck with a revelation: if the religious spirit of New England was languishing—as he thought it was—then it was because Congregationalists had become too parochial and forgotten their mission in the world. Beyond the borders of New England were millions of men and women who were born in sin and would die in sin because they had never been shown the way to Christ. Their fate and that of the American Congregationalists were linked: by setting out to convert the heathen, Mills thought, New Englanders would spread the faith and rekindle their own dwindling piety.

Mills carried this conviction with him to Andover Theological Seminary, where he made friends with other young men who shared his vision. On June 27, 1810, they met with the General Association of Massachusetts—the clerical organization for the state—and told the assembled ministers that they felt "the duty and importance of personally attempting a mission to the heathen." The delegates were impressed with the sincerity of the young seminarians. One praised the "devout consecration of this missionary band" and said, "They were unpretending, modest, of a tender and childlike spirit." Samuel Worcester, pastor of the Tabernacle Church in Salem, said of their spokesman, Adoniram Judson, "If his faith is proportioned to his voice, he will drive the devil from all India."[8]

Some of the delegates objected that such an enterprise was impractical. India and the other remote quarters of the globe were as far away as six months by sea from New England. How could they raise funds for such an enterprise? Who would travel so far to preach the gospel? What would they find when they arrived at their destination? Despite such doubts the Massachusetts association decided to experiment with the idea. On June 29, 1810, the American Board of Commissioners for Foreign Missions was formed with the backing of the association. Connecticut Congregationalists were invited to join, and having accepted, they hosted the first meeting of what came to be known as the American Board. Then there was a delay of a year before further action.

Samuel Mills, needing to complete his studies at Andover, could accept the delay, but his friend, Adoniram Judson, was impatient to begin his mission. So he went to England, and received the backing of the London Missionary Society, which had been formed a few years before. Eager to retain Judson, the

American Board met in 1811 and commissioned him and four other young men as missionaries to India. They were ordained at Salem Tabernacle in 1812 and set sail for Asia.

From the start their mission was plagued with difficulties. Upon arriving in Calcutta the missionaries learned that war had broken out between England and the United States. The English authorities refused to allow them to land. One missionary went on to Madagascar, Judson and a friend sailed to Burma, and the other two eluded the authorities and made their way to Bombay. Soon other troubles arose. Two of the missionaries died of disease, and the eloquent Judson, while converting the natives to Christianity, became a convert himself—to the Baptist faith.

Despite these setbacks, the American Board succeeded in raising funds to support missions. Congregationalists in New England filled collection plates and rewrote wills to encourage the glorious enterprise. Soon the church was supporting scores of missionaries in India, Ceylon, South Africa, Turkey, the Sandwich Islands, and on the American frontier. The board established its first Indian mission in 1818 among the Cherokee at Brainerd, Tennessee. During the next decade the board established missions in the South among the Creek, Choctaw, and Chickasaw.

An American Board missionary, Samuel A. Worcester, was a leader in the effort to use the courts to prevent the federal government from removing the Cherokees from their homeland to Tennessee. The Supreme Court decided in his and the Indians' favor in *Worcester v. Georgia*, but Andrew Jackson refused to enforce the decision, and most of the Cherokee were sent to Oklahoma. American Board missionaries followed them there, and worked among other tribes throughout the United States.

One of the largest American Board missions was among the Sioux, where Congregational ministers preached and established schools. During the 1880s the Santee Normal School in Sioux country enrolled more than 200 students at a time. Other missionaries worked among the Tetons, Blackfeet, Winnebagos, and many other tribes.

As Congregational lay men and women moved West they seldom traveled in communities with their ministers, as had the first settlers of New England. Frontier missionaries, sponsored by eastern societies, often served as preachers first to Indian, then to white congregations. Griffith Griffiths, for example, was a Welsh clergyman who immigrated to America and served as Congregational missionary at Alturas, California, among the Modoc Indians during the 1880s. He organized the local temperance movement, wrote for the newspaper, and was eventually called to another frontier outpost, a white congregation in Eureka, California.

Why were Congregationalists so willing to give their money, and in some cases their lives, to missions? In part, the American Board and other missionary organizations drew on unique sources of energy within the Congregational experience. The Puritans had come to New England to create "a city upon a hill"—a holy commonwealth others would admire and emulate. To a degree they were successful. During the seventeenth-century churches consisted of visible saints, and those saints ruled the state. Most New Englanders worshipped in Congregational churches, and many followed Puritan precepts in their daily lives. But the world of the nineteenth century was a different world. In the new nation Congregationalism was but one denomination among many. So the original ideal of a holy commonwealth could never be realized in the form envisioned by John Winthrop and other Puritans. But some of the grandeur of the Puritan "errand into the wilderness" was recaptured in the mission movement. Many Congregationalists felt in supporting the missions a sense of religious purpose not unlike that experienced by the early Puritans. Like the founders of their denomination, they felt they were involved in an enterprise that would enlighten the world.

THE VOYAGE OF THE *THAMES*

America changed greatly during the first two centuries following the arrival of the *Mayflower*, and so did Congregationalism. But these changes should not be exaggerated. When we look closely at the piety of a single clergyman, we discover a faith not unlike that of the early Puritans. The following story takes place on a voyage as hazardous as any undertaken by the Pilgrims.

On November 20, 1822, the merchant ship *Thames* set sail on Long Island sound, bound for the Sandwich Islands. On board were several Congregational ministers, including a young man named Charles S. Stewart, who would write an account of this voyage and of his subsequent life in Hawaii. Published in 1828 under the title *Journal of a Residence in the Sandwich Islands*, Stewart's report provides a window on nineteenth-century Congregationalism and suggests links between Stewart's faith and the Congregationalism of the Puritan founders of New England.

In some respects Stewart's voyage was a different sort of mission from that of the first New Englanders. The missionaries aboard the *Thames* were going to Hawaii to convert the natives to Christianity. The Puritans, too, had preached to non-Christian natives, but only after they had first established communities of English settlers and ministered to them. Only slowly did a few of these ministers come to devote some of their time to missionary work. Stewart and his companions, on the other hand, would minister almost entirely to the natives. As we follow Stewart's journey, however, from "Puritan" New England to the mid-Pacific frontier of Hawaii, we are struck with the similarity between his religious sensibilities and those of the early Congregationalists.

The *Thames* sailed slowly along the smooth waters of the sound past the bright and cheerful landscapes along the shores of Connecticut and Long Island. Then it cruised past Montauk Point and Block Island into the open ocean. At first the sea was calm, but within two days the ship was hit by a fierce storm. Stewart, like the Puritan colonists of two centuries before, faced the possibility of shipwreck.[9]

The cabin was dark; torrents of water drove over the ship and down the companionway; loose boxes and furniture slid from side to side; the terrified passengers clung to their berths and waited. "The wind howls dismally through the spars and rigging," wrote Stewart, "and every wave that rushes along the sides of the vessel, or breaks above the bulwarks and thunders over our heads seems to threaten destruction." Stewart finally went on deck to view the storm and was astonished. "Imagine for a moment," he wrote, "the mountains...to be rolling in every direction, with high and broken swells over the lake and valley. Just so monstrous are the billows that rage around us."[10] As the vessel struggled up these walls of water the timbers groaned, and the ship seemed about to founder.

Then a huge wave swept over the bow, burying several crewmen. A moment later Stewart saw their hats "sweeping topmast-high on the passing wave." He feared that they too had been carried overboard, but as the water flowed off the deck, he saw them clinging to the bow. Like the Puritans before him, Charles Stewart saw the hand of God in the storm. "Never before was I so deeply impressed, as in this conflict of the elements, with my insignificance as a creature, in the sight of Him who 'commandeth the winds and the waves, and they obey him.'" And like the Puritans, Stewart saw God protecting his ship in the storm. "How happy for us is the assurance that every hair of our heads is numbered," he wrote, "and that without Him not even a sparrow falleth to the ground."[11]

The storm finally let up, and the ship sailed on towards Tierra del Fuego. Each day Stewart faced life in ways that echoed the Puritan experience. The Puritans, sorrowing at the loss of their homes in Old England, reminded themselves that life is but a pilgrimage to a heavenly country and told themselves that the spirit might thrive even when life on earth was painful. Similarly Stewart consoled himself, "only by hurrying my thought to that world of gladness, where there will be no more separation." The Puritans often spoke of coming to New England with a "suffering mind." In the same spirit Stewart contrasted life in New England with the life he would live in the Sandwich Islands. If "self enjoyment" were the main object of life, he said, then "the elegant sufficiency" of an American home would have satisfied his needs. But he and his fellow missionaries aboard the *Thames* sought to achieve "these great ends of existence": the salvation of souls, the glory of God, and the good of man. Stewart continued, "We most willingly bid farewell to all the charms of civilized life, and welcome the simplicity and rudeness of a missionary hut." In their "huts" they would "count for joy" the trials ahead.[12]

Although the journey took five months, the work of the missionaries began as soon as the ship was on the high seas. The ministers did their best to turn the *Thames* itself into a kind of holy commonwealth. They worshipped twice on the Sabbath and met for prayers each morning and evening. In good weather they met on the quarterdeck, and as the ship slipped through the night, they praised their God, repeating in the dark from memory familiar biblical texts and hymns. "It is sweet, indeed," wrote Stewart, "to hear our hymns of praise floating on the breeze, and to listen to the voice of prayer addressed from the midst of these mighty waters to Him who protects, and who only can defend and bless us."[13]

As the ship sailed from a New England winter, through an equatorial summer, and back into the cold of Cape Horn, a change came over the crew. Stewart noted, "The blessing of God is upon us." The sailors were more attentive at worship, during the Sabbath quiet reigned throughout the ship, and the crewmen read the Bible and "other appropriate books." On the morning of January 25, 1823, the ship labored through a gale under a single storm sail. The storm had begun in the night and, Stewart reports, "The howling of the tempest—plunging of the vessel—and trampling and hallooing of the sailors, effectually prevented our taking any rest." Stewart made his way on deck and watched as seamen labored in the rigging seventy feet above, trying to remove the upper masts and yards for the ship's safety. Clinging to the rigging, they were whipped through an arc of ninety feet with each roll of the ship. Stewart writes: "The unnatural sound of their voices, as they screamed to make themselves heard below, were caught by the wind, and borne away on the tempest, came to the ear like the shrieks of the dying; and I dared scarce look up, for a moment, lest I should see some one, in despite of every effort, thrown into the raging sea, where no power of man could have secured him rescue." The storm raged until dusk, then the wind lessened, and Stewart knew they would survive the day.

At nightfall he stood alone on the quarterdeck, looking at the empty ocean. He felt, he said, something of the desolation of the scene. Suddenly a hand reached out and touched him. He turned and saw a crewman, whom he identifies only as "R-, one of the hardiest of our crew." R's face was troubled, and he asked Stewart simply, "What must I do to be saved?"

Seven generations of Congregational ministers had encouraged men and women to ask exactly this question. But surely no conversion experience in Congregational history began more dramatically than this confrontation on the quarterdeck of the storm-tossed *Thames*. R had attended the Bible class on the previous Sunday and discussed religion with Stewart immediately afterwards. He now told Stewart that the discussion had so affected him that he had "scarcely eaten or slept during the whole week." Stewart hoped that "the spirit of God" had begun to work on his soul.[14]

Like the early Puritans Stewart believed in the "priesthood of all believers," the capacity of one regenerate lay man or woman to influence others. During the days that followed he and the other missionaries saw further signs of religiosity among the sailors. R reported that a foul-mouthed seaman named "C-" had "knocked off swearing" and was "constantly overhauling his Bible." The two had worked high on a mast during a storm, and although they could not move an obstinate sail, C "never swore a word."[15]

Another sailor, "G-," met frequently with Stewart. Observing him during his watch, Stewart noted that his "countenance and manner" showed him "under the influence of thoughts and feelings bordering on agony." A few days later G came to him during night watch, so full of emotion that he could hardly speak. Finally he managed to say that in his soul "old things had passed away, and all things become new." Stewart spoke with him for a time, then left him "rejoicing in the fullness of hope."[16]

As the *Thames* rounded Cape Horn, after battering against wind and wave in Drake Strait, and sailed into the Pacific, the ship became more and more like a holy commonwealth. Other men came to Stewart to discuss their souls, and the sailors talked to one another about salvation. Everywhere there were signs of heightened religiosity. Looking down into the steerage one evening, Stewart saw a sailor on his knees reading the Bible: "His attitude, countenance, and whole appearance, gave strong testimony that he was searching the Scriptures for 'the words of eternal life.'"[17]

"There is a seriousness from the quarter-deck to the forecastle," wrote Stewart, "that forces itself on the observation of every one." Among the religious-minded seamen, R, the man who first came to Stewart, was an exemplar of the Puritan spirit. He realized fully that good deeds alone would not save him. "I know now what I am to do!" he told Stewart. "I have read my bible, and have prayed; I have tried for weeks, and for months, to be religious, but I cannot; I have no true repentance, no real faith, and God will not hear my prayers; what can I do? I feel that my soul will live forever; and without the grace of God, I know it must eternally perish."

Here was the dilemma of the Puritan sinner, yearning to do good, but unable to fulfill the demands of God's law. Here was the classic problem of the serious-minded from the time of Luther and Calvin, through the Congregational fathers and the revivalists of the Great Awakening. And here too was the classic solution to the dilemma of salvation: one night R came to the missionary and said, "Oh, Mr. Stewart, I have found the right way *to believe*; it was the righteousness of Jesus Christ I needed. Now the whole Bible is not *against me*, as it used to be, but every word is *for me*; because I see and feel how God can be just, and yet justify an ungodly sinner."[18]

A few days later R had the opportunity to counsel C, the man Stewart had seen reading the Bible in steerage. C told R that he believed in the Bible, but did not know how to get the faith that the Bible demanded of the sinner. R told him, "I can tell you what it [faith] is not: it is not *knocking off swearing, and drinking, and such like*; and it is *not reading the Bible, nor praying, nor being good*; it is none of these; for, even if they would answer for the time to come, there is *the old score* still, and how are you to get clear of that? It is not any thing you have done or can do; it is only believing, and trusting to what *Christ has done*; it is forsaking your sins, and looking for their pardon and the salvation of your soul, because he died and shed his blood for sin; and it is nothing else."[19]

On the Hawaii-bound *Thames*, as in the early days of Congregational New

England, simple people discovered the central message of Puritanism, that salvation comes through faith in Christ's sacrifice. "A doctor of divinity might have given C a more technical and polished answer," wrote Stewart, "but not one more simple or probably satisfactory." As the ship neared Hawaii, Stewart and his fellow missionaries felt that the spirit of God was already with them, helping them to bring converts to the faith. On Sunday, March 30, Stewart felt the spirit of piety throughout the ship. The sky was "of a purity" he had never seen before. "About the ship," wrote Stewart, "scarce a sound was heard from the opening of the morning till the close of the day, but the rippling of the water as we sailed through the deep, or the voice of worship as we bowed before our God." On the faces of the sailors, "these rough but interesting men," Stewart saw expressions of concern—sorrow in some, joy in others. A sense of order and quiet prevailed throughout the ship, and under the bright Pacific sky Stewart wrote, "I could not but fancy that I saw 'HOLINESS TO THE LORD' inscribed on the cloud of canvass spread to the breeze."[20] Three weeks later the *Thames* reached Hawaii.

FIGHTING SLAVERY

During the first half of the nineteenth century, Congregationalism followed the frontier across the United States to the Midwest, Oregon, and California. Missionaries built Congregational churches in Hawaii and would soon win converts in China and Japan. The toughened denomination that survived disestablishment in the East and abandoned its dependence on Presbyterians in the West, was also in the forefront of the crusade to end slavery. Congregationalists were leaders in many of the antislavery societies that sprung up in the North during the 1830s and 1840s.

Best known among the Congregational abolitionists was Harriet Beecher Stowe, who was born in Litchfield, Connecticut, in 1811. Her early life as daughter of a minister shows the prevalence of Puritan values in nineteenth century New England. Memories of a Puritan childhood permeate her book, *Oldtown Folks.* Stowe says of a grandmother: "With all her soul, which was a very large one, she was an earnest Puritan Calvinist. She had been nourished in the sayings and traditions of the Mathers and the Eliots, and all the first generation of the saints who had possessed Massachusetts. To these she added the earnest study of the writings of Edwards and Bellamy, and others of those brave old thinkers who had broken up the crust of formalism and mechanical piety that was rapidly forming over the New England mind."[21]

Stowe's monumental contribution to abolitionism, *Uncle Tom's Cabin*, draws its strength from her spiritual values. Even without its religious overtones, the account of decent slaves and a cruel master would have created indelible images of the evil of slavery. But the account gained power with the contrast between the spiritual characters of master Simon Legree and slave Uncle Tom. Legree drinks and swears; Tom reads the Bible. Legree tells Tom that he must beat a fellow slave. Tom refuses, saying that is something he will never do. Legree tells Tom he must obey because he owns him body and soul. In an answer that must have sent shivers of sympathy through millions of Christian spirits, Tom answers that no one owns his soul—no one but Christ.

A few years later Congregationalists, along with other Americans, fought a war over the issue of slavery. During the Civil War the religious spirit of early Congregationalism was reflected in the holiday of Thanksgiving. The holiday was a local and occasional event until Abraham Lincoln issued a proclamation in 1863 calling for a national day of Thanksgiving for Union successes in the Civil War. We have no detailed account of the first Pilgrim festival, but the *New York Times* carried this report on Thanksgiving in 1863:

From Maine to California, a day of National Thanksgiving was celebrated yesterday. Thousands of clergymen held forth from their pulpits, and hundreds of thousands of men, women and children united in ascriptions of praise to Heaven. In New-England, in the Middle States, in the Valley of the Mississippi, in the Far West, and on the coast of the Pacific the people were of one mind. In our Armies, stationed on the Potomac, on the Tennessee, on the Upper and Lower Mississippi, and on the headwaters of the Arkansas—in our Navy, stationed all along the Atlantic and Gulf coasts, and on all the rivers of the South—our soldiers and our sailors kept holiday, and acknowledged that not alone their own valor and endurance, but a higher Power had led them on the victory. In the City of San Francisco, as we learn by telegraph, there were national salutes and ringing of bells morning, noon, and night, and in the evening there was a grand assemblage of the people, and a general illumination of the City; and from the farthest East, we have reports of a like character. In New York we have seldom known a holiday to be so generally kept.[22]

The next year the North went one step further in celebrating Thanksgiving and raised thousands of dollars to provide turkeys for the soldiers and sailors fighting for the Union. The nineteenth century saw many changes in Congregationalism and also saw areas of continuity. The national Thanksgivings of the Civil War era contained elements of both. A Pilgrim festival had become a national holiday—fitting token of Congregationalism's place in the larger community of the nation as a whole.

NOTES

[1] Mary K. Cayton, "Congregationalism from Independence to the Present," in Charles H. Lippy and Peter W. Williams, eds., *The Encyclopedia of The American Religious Experience* (New York, 1988), 486.

[2] Walker, *Congregational Churches*, 294.

[3] Quotations from Walker, *Congregational Churches*, 298, 299.

[4] Quotations from Walker, *Congregational Churches*, 301.

[5] Quotations from William B. Sprague, ed., *Annals of the American Pulpit* (New

York, 1857–69; 1969), vol. 1: 653-60.

[6] Quotations from Sprague, *Annals*, I, 704-5.

[7] Quotation from Walker, *Congregational Churches*, 302.

[8] Quotations from Marion L. Starkey, *The Congregational Way* (Garden City, N.Y., 1966), 186, 187.

[9] C. S. Stewart, *Journal of a Residence in the Sandwich Islands* (Honolulu, Hawaii, 1970—facsimile reproduction of 1830 edition), 38.

[10] Stewart, *Sandwich Islands*, 39.

[11] Stewart, *Sandwich Islands*, 40.

[12] Stewart, *Sandwich Islands*, 41, 46.

[13] Stewart, *Sandwich Islands*, 67, 47.

[14] Stewart, *Sandwich Islands*, 64-67.

[15] Stewart, *Sandwich Islands*, 76-77.

[16] Stewart, *Sandwich Islands*, 77-78.

[17] Stewart, *Sandwich Islands*, 78-79.

[18] Stewart, *Sandwich Islands*, 78.

[19] Stewart, *Sandwich Islands*, 82-83.

[20] Stewart, *Sandwich Islands*, 81-83.

[21] Harriet Beecher Stowe, *Oldtown Folks* (Cambridge, Mass., 1966), 70-71.

[22] *New York Times*, August 7, 1863, 4.

8

PROGRESSIVE ORTHODOXY

INDUSTRIAL AMERICA

As so often happens after a great moral crusade, the United States turned to more secular interests after the Civil War. The change did not come immediately, however, and it was not universally accepted. The idealism that carried many Americans into the war to end slavery continued among the thousands of men and women who went south after the war to work for Reconstruction. A few of the visitors were carpetbaggers, eager to enrich themselves on the spoils of war. But many more went to help the freed men and women in their new lives. Samuel Chapman Armstrong, for example, was a Union general who moved to Virginia after the war and founded Hampton Institute, a college for blacks. Agencies such the Freedman's Bureau established schools for exslaves.

But within a few years the movement to assure that blacks were equal as well as free had lost its momentum. In 1877 the government withdrew the last federal troops from the South, allowing the southern states to govern themselves. State legislatures which had, for a short time, included many blacks soon passed Jim Crow laws segregating and disfranchising the freed men and women. Blacks traveled on Jim Crow railway cars and slept in Jim Crow hotels. And in court they were even required to swear on Jim Crow Bibles, as if the Lord favored segregation.

Some Americans objected to the new arrangements that left the work of freeing the slaves half finished, but the majority were willing to let the South develop its own institutions. Besides, segregation existed in the North as well, particularly in schools. In fact, a philosophy of racism was gaining new adherents and a "scientific" base. Scholars promulgated a racial theory of history—some races were said to be particularly well-suited to governing because they had particularly good genes.

Such theories were especially welcomed by upper middle class persons, usually of Northern European origin, who worried about blacks and also about the southern and eastern Europeans. These "new immigrants" were passing through Ellis Island by the millions annually during the 1890s. Prejudiced Americans were often willing enough to employ the immigrants as domestic servants, mill workers, or miners. But they were comforted by the knowledge that race as well as economics separated the teeming masses from themselves.

The upper class was made comfortable too by the growth of American industry. This was the age of the "Captains of Industry"—or the "Robber Barons"—depending on your perspective. Andrew Carnegie was both. He immigrated from Scotland with his parents in 1848, when he was eleven. He worked as a telegraph boy, a railroad superintendent, and an iron manufacturer. By buying out his competitors, purchasing modern machinery, and paying low wages, he built a steel empire and accumulated almost half a billion dollars—in an age when four thousand dollars would buy a good house. One of Carnegie's admirers said he was "born with two sets of teeth and holes drilled for more."[1]

People like Carnegie appreciated the new theories of evolution developed by Charles Darwin and Herbert Spencer. Darwin's *Origin of Species* was published in 1859 and soon enjoyed a wide audience in America. Spencer's writings on social Darwinism followed soon afterwards. Spencer's ideas were wonderfully congenial to the age of industry, combining respect for the status quo with a faith in progress. He believed that those who were on top were there because they deserved to be there—"survival of the fittest." Through competition the fittest would continue to prevail and carry the world to new heights of prosperity.[2]

In the heady atmosphere of the age, it was easy to believe that humans were omniscient. Their minds could probe the mystery of life and explain the evolution of species and societies. They could tear iron ore from the earth and transform it into girders for tall buildings. The Bessemer converters, huge blast furnaces at Andrew Carnegie's steel plants, provide a symbol of the age. An acquaintance described Carnegie's reaction the first time he saw one: "Nothing that he had ever seen was so picturesque, so fascinating, so miraculous in its easily controlled force and fury. It was half a furnace and half a cyclone, yet it was obedient to the touch of a boy's hand. Give it thirty thousand pounds of common pig iron, and presto! the whole mass was blown into steel."[3]

Here was a world in which humanity was in control, and it brought unprecedented challenges to the church. Congregationalism confronted the new age and was enlivened by it.

DENOMINATIONAL UNITY

An eighteenth-century New Englander, explaining his earlier beliefs once remarked that he had sucked in a belief in witchcraft with his mother's milk. That belief had been so prevalent until the time of the Salem trials, that no one thought to question it. In the same way a sense of the importance of caste, whether race or class, pervaded life after the Civil War. One of the most famous statements of this philosophy came from a Congregational minister in Cincinnati, Josiah Strong. He became a national celebrity with the publication of his book, *Our Country* (1885), in which he argued that the Anglo-Saxon was superior to all other people in both religion and politics.

A more important development for the history of Congregationalism was a growing awareness of another kind of caste, that of religious identity. Just as men and women were asking themselves "who are we?" in racial terms, they also tended to become more conscious of their religious identity. Having abandoned their efforts to unite with the Presbyterians, Congregationalists were free to celebrate the uniqueness of their own religious heritage. At a time when genealogists were writing family histories in response to the new consciousness of genetics, church historians began writing the history of denominations. Two scholars, Leonard Bacon and Williston Walker led the way for the Congregationalists.

Bacon was the son of a Congregational missionary in the old Northwest. He attended Andover Seminary and Yale and was pastor of the First Congregational Church in New Haven for more than half a century, from 1824 to 1881. His best known book, *The Genesis of the New England Churches* (1874) celebrates the history of his denomination.

Williston Walker is the best known of the Congregational historians and taught at Hartford Seminary and Yale. Toward the end of the century he published *The Creeds and Platforms of Congregationalism* (1893) and *A History of the Congregational Churches of the United States* (1894). In the preface to his compilation of creeds and platforms he anticipates that the volume will "illustrate the essential unity as well as the healthful growth which has marked the development of creed and practice from the founders of Congregationalism to our own day."[4]

The new denominational consciousness was reflected in these histories and also in efforts to organize a national meeting of the Congregational churches. In 1864 the Convention of the Congregational Churches of the Northwest declared that the crisis of the Civil War demanded "consultation, cooperation, and concert among our churches."[5] The Illinois General Association approved of the idea and invited other state organizations to unite in promoting the meeting. A few months later, in November of 1864, delegates met at the Broadway Tabernacle Church in New York to make plans for a larger convention. They appointed committees to prepare preliminary statements on such matters as doctrine and polity. Representatives to the national council were chosen by the various churches gathered in local conferences or associations, with two delegates for each ten churches. As in seventeenth-century synods, lay people as well as ministers attended. They met in Boston, "the primitive and historical home of their faith."[6]

On June 14, 1865, a few months after Lee's surrender at Appomattox, 502 delegates and 16 representatives from Congregational bodies in other countries gathered at Old South Church. One of their first challenges was to consider a declaration of faith. Being Congregationalists and wary of authoritative creeds, they approached the matter with caution. The committee appointed by the preliminary council began its report with the statement that "they could not regard it as their function to prepare a Confession of Faith to be imposed by act of this, or of any other body, upon the churches of the Congregational order." They quoted the Saybrook Platform: "It was the glory of our fathers, that they heartily professed the only rule of their religion, from the very first, to be the Holy Scriptures." And they cited Cotton Mather in *Magnalia Christi Americana*: particular churches have always retained their liberty in "confessions drawn up in their own forms."[7]

The committee was reluctant to disrupt the doctrinal equilibrium of the churches. Their report declared, "It has not appeared to the committee expedient to recommend that this Council should disturb this 'variety in unity'—as Cotton Mather happily describes it—by an attempted uniformity of statement in a Confession formulating each doctrine in more recent terms of metaphysical theology." They chose to "characterize" Congregational doctrine in general rather than to reduce it to a "theological formula."[8] Accordingly they declared their adherence to the great seventeenth century statements of creed—the Westminster Confession of Faith and the Savoy Declaration. Then, finally, the committee members declared that they saw some purpose in summarizing the values that united Congregationalists. They did this, in part, "to promote a closer fellowship of all Christian denominations in the faith and work of the gospel." In addition, they noted that "certain destructive forms of unbelief" threatened the faith.

Reminiscent of the catalogue of evils compiled by the Reforming Synod of 1680, the new catalogue of "destructive" ideas provides a crisp survey, almost Puritan in its tone, of current forms of "unbelief." The delegates complained of ideas that "assail the foundations of all religion, both natural and revealed; which know no God but nature; no Depravity but physical malformation, immaturity of powers, or some incident of outward condition; no Providence but the working of material causes and of statistical laws; no Revelation but that of consciousness; no Redemption but the elimination of evil by a natural sequence of suffering; no Regeneration but the natural evolution of a higher type of existence; no Retribution but the necessary consequences of physical and psychological laws."[9]

As was so often true in the reforming synods of the seventeenth century, Congregational laments provide a good index of what people at the time were thinking: the Congregationalists were living in a world in which it was increasingly possible to think that all things that mattered could be measured, explained, and ultimately controlled by people. The sense of threat from a secular America encouraged the committee members to overcome their scruples about creeds, and so, despite their reservations, they suggested that the convention adopt a testimony of their common faith.

They proposed a testimony that states simply:

There is one personal God, who created all things; who controls the physical universe, the laws whereof he has established; and who, holding all events within his knowledge, rules over men by his wise and good providence and by his perfect moral law.

God, whose being, perfections, and government are partially made known to us through the testimony of his works and of conscience, has made a further revelation of himself in the Scriptures of the Old and New Testaments,—a revelation attested at the first by supernatural signs, and confirmed through all ages since by its moral effects upon the individual soul, and upon human society; a revelation authoritative and final. In this revelation, God has declared himself to be the Father, the Son, and the Holy Ghost; and he has manifested his love for the world through the incarnation of the Eternal Word for man's redemption, in the sinless life, the expiatory sufferings and death, and the resurrection of Jesus Christ, our Lord and Saviour, and also in the mission of the Holy Ghost, the Comforter, for the regeneration and sanctification of the souls of men.

The Scriptures, confirming the testimony of conscience and of history, declare that mankind are universally sinners, and are under the righteous condemnation of the law of God; that from this state there is no deliverance, save through "repentance toward God, and faith in the Lord Jesus Christ;" and that there is a day appointed in which God will raise the dead, and will judge the world, and in which the issues of his moral government over men shall be made manifest in the awards of eternal life and eternal death, according to the deeds done in the body.[10]

This statement had the virtue of reaffirming many traditional Congregational beliefs without endorsing strict Calvinism, particularly in regard of predestination. A second committee was appointed to appraise the work of the first and to determine whether the council should issue a declaration of faith. On June 21, five days after the first report, the new committee offered a more rigorous creed including a statement accepting "the system of truths which is commonly known among us as Calvinism." That system exalted "the sovereignty of God" and exhibited "the exceeding sinfulness of sin."[11]

A sharp debate followed this report, some synod members favoring and others opposing the reference to Calvin. Some wanted to leave out the reference, arguing that it was a "party name" and would be divisive. Others asserted that no decent Congregationalist could fail to be a Calvinist. One delegate claimed, "The man who, having pursued a three year's course of study,...is not a Calvinist, is not a respectable man." These were hardly conciliatory words, and for a time it seemed that the convention might be seriously divided. The hour was late, and the meeting adjourned without reaching a decision.[12]

The synod leaders reasoned that a majority of the delegates wanted to include the name of Calvin, but that a substantial minority opposed the inclusion either because of Arminian leanings or hostility to any sort of "party shibboleth." Fortunately the convention was due to meet at Burial Hill in Plymouth the next day, a spot hallowed in Congregational life by the memory of William Bradford and the Pilgrims. In Williston Walker's words, "A reunion on so memorable a spot, under circumstances so provocative of generous sentiment, seemed to some of the cooler leaders of the Council an opportunity to secure the united declaration of faith which the previous day's session had failed to bring."[13] They set to work on a new statement, which was completed by one of the members as the trainload of delegates rattled toward Plymouth.

At Burial Hill the delegates heard the declaration, and after a short debate they approved it with only two dissenting votes. The Burial Hill Declaration begins with a paean to the historical saga of Congregationalism: "Standing by the rock where the Pilgrims set foot upon these shores, upon the spot where they worshipped God, and among the graves of the early generations, we, Elders and Messengers of the congregational churches of the United States in National Council assembled,—like them acknowledging no rule of faith but the word of God,—do now declare our adherence to the faith and order of the apostolic and primitive churches held by our fathers...." It continued, "We declare that the experience of the nearly two and a half centuries which have elapsed since the memorable day when our sires founded here a Christian Commonwealth,...has only deepened our confidence in the faith and polity of these fathers." The declaration reiterates briefly and simply the doctrines associated with Congregationalism: "the common sinfulness and ruin of our race," "the expiatory death of Christ," "the organized and visible church."[14]

The declaration reflects a resurgence of Congregationalists' pride in their particular denomination, but the Burial Hill Declaration, reducing doctrine to the most fundamental common denominator, also suggested the fellowship of Congregationalists with other Christians. There is even an ecumenical spirit in the declaration. The council declared, "Knowing that we are but one branch of Christ's people, while adhering to our own peculiar faith and order, we extend to all believers the hand of Christian fellowship, upon the basis of those great fundamental truths in which all Christians should agree." In particular, the declaration suggests that in small towns Congregationalists should join with other Christians to form united churches.

Additionally the Burial Hill Declaration describes the social role of the church: "It was the grand peculiarity of our Puritan Fathers, that they held this gospel, not merely as the ground of their personal salvation, but as declaring the worth of man by the incarnation and sacrifice of the Son of God; and therefore applied its principles to elevate society, to regulate education, to civilize humanity, to purify law, to reform the Church and the State, and to assert and defend liberty; in short, to mold and redeem, by its all-transforming energy, everything that belongs to man in his individual and social relations."[15] This reference to the social role of Congregationalism looks backward to Puritan New England, but also reveals values that would feed the Social Gospel movement a few years later.

The Burial Hill Declaration was the only declaration of faith that an assembly representing American Congregationalism as a whole had adopted since agreeing upon the Cambridge Platform of 1648. But it was not generally used as the creed of particular churches; they tended to continue using their own local creeds. In explanation Williston Walker noted that the declaration was "hardly consonant with the judicial precision usually looked for in a statement of intellectual conviction."[16] It was useful, however, as a reference point for Congregationalists in an age of change. And it suggests the willingness of the church to accept many different points of view for the sake of denominational unity.

A platform on polity adopted by the assembly played a similar role in the history of the church. The convention adopted a "Statement of Congregational Principles," which Walker describes as "an admirable epitome of the principles of modern Congregationalism." It summarizes the polity of the church in three concise statements:

First, The principle that the local or Congregational church derives its power and authority directly from Christ, and is not subject to any ecclesiastical government exterior or superior to itself.

Second, That every local or congregational church is bound to observe the duties of mutual respect and charity which are included in the communion of churches one with another; and that every church which refuses to give an account of its proceedings, when kindly and orderly desired to do so by neighboring churches, violates the law of Christ.

Third, the ministry of the gospel by members of the churches who have been duly called and set apart to that work implies in itself no power of government, and that ministers of the gospel not elected to office in any church are not a hierarchy, nor are they invested with any official power in or over the churches.

The statement of principles is a good example of the continuing Congregational effort to balance opposing values: local autonomy and mutual association, clerical leadership and lay authority. Like the Burial Hill Declaration, it tended to remain in the literature rather than be read by congregations or emblazoned over altars. One can almost hear Williston Walker sigh as he wrote almost four decades later, "The days of elaborate platforms, like that of Cambridge, are as fully past as those of lengthy confessions."[17]

But although Congregationalists were reluctant to adopt as authoritative even such broad statements of their faith as the Burial Hill Declaration and the Statement of Congregational Principles, their meeting of 1865 established a precedent for regular national assemblies. Congregationalists were unwilling to declare exactly who they were, but they enjoyed the sense of their membership in a historic faith. Congregationalism was their denomination, their religious caste.

Soon afterwards delegates at the Pilgrim Memorial Convention met in New York and issued a statement recommending that the Congregational state conferences and associations "unite in measures for instituting on the principle of fellowship, excluding ecclesiastical authority, a permanent National Conference."[18] Grumbling about the need to preserve independence was heard in some of the state associations, notably those of New York and New Jersey, but "fellowship" without "ecclesiastical authority" was a formula that all would eventually accept.

In 1871 delegates met in Oberlin, Ohio, for a national conference and adopted a constitution for a triennial national council. Their pronouncements, like the Burial Hill Declaration, stressed the common beliefs of all Congregationalists. They approved of "the great doctrines of the Christian faith, commonly called evangelical, held in our churches from the early times, and sufficiently set forth by former General Councils." The delegates again emphasized their willingness to cooperate with other churches. In a "Declaration on the Unity of the Church" they stated that they made no "pretension to be the only churches of Christ." In the "common work" of evangelizing in America and abroad they desired to "work in friendly cooperation with all those who love and serve our common Lord." "It is our prayer and endeavor," their declaration concluded, "that the unity of the church may be more and more apparent."[19]

The statements adopted at Oberlin, according to Williston Walker, illustrate "the catholicity of spirit which has accompanied this growth of denominational consciousness." Walker continued, "Though nowhere expressly stated, the understanding at Oberlin at its adoption, and the interpretation since usually put upon it, is that it holds out the olive branch of denominational fellowship to brethren of Arminian sympathies, and is but a further illustration of that desire not to limit Congregational brotherhood to those who hold exclusively the system known as 'Calvinism.'"[20]

Many Congregationalists were satisfied to leave it at that, but some in that age of denominational consciousness wanted a clearer declaration of just what they were expected to believe. Meeting in 1880 the Ohio association addressed the national council, asking it to consider drawing up a "formula that shall not be mainly a reaffirmation of former confessions, but that shall state in precise terms in our living tongue the doctrines which we hold today."[21] The next year the national council appointed a committee of twenty-five commissioners to draw up a creed, not as an authoritative statement, but as a reference point for the Congregational churches. In 1883 the committee completed a statement of faith that came to be known as "The Commission Creed." It reads:

I. We believe in one God, the father Almighty, Maker of heaven and earth, and of all things visible and invisible;

And in Jesus Christ, His only Son, our Lord, who is of one substance with the Father; by whom all things were made;

And in the Holy Spirit, the Lord and Giver of life, who is sent from the Father and Son, and who together with the Father and Son is worshiped and glorified.

II. We believe that the providence of God, by which he executes his eternal purposes in the government of the world, is in and over all events; yet so that the freedom and responsibility of man are not impaired, and sin is the act of the creature alone.

III. We believe that man was made in the image of God, that he might know, love, and obey God, and enjoy him forever; that our first parents by disobedience fell under the righteous condemnation of God; and that all men are so alienated from God that there is no salvation from the guilt and power of sin except through God's redeeming grace.

IV. We believe that God would have all men return to him; that to this end he has made himself known, not only through the works of nature, the course of his providence, and the consciences of men, but also through supernatural revelations made especially to a chosen people, and above all, when the fullness of time was come, through Jesus Christ his Son.

V. We believe that the Scriptures of the Old and New Testaments are the records of God's revelation of himself in the work of redemption; that they were written by men under the special guidance of the Holy Spirit; that they are able to make wise unto salvation; and that they constitute the authoritative standard by which religious teaching and human conduct are to be regulated and judged.

VI. We believe that the love of God to sinful men has found its highest expression in the redemptive work of his Son; who became man, uniting his divine nature with our human nature in one person; who was tempted like other men, yet without sin; who by his humiliation, his holy obedience, his sufferings, his death on the cross, and his resurrection, became a perfect Redeemer; whose sacrifice of himself for the sins of the world declares the righteousness of God, and is the sole and sufficient ground of forgiveness and of reconciliation with him.

VII. We believe that Jesus Christ, after he had risen from the dead, ascended into heaven, where, as the one mediator between God and man, he carries forward his work of saving men; that he sends the Holy Spirit to convict them of sin, and to lead them to repentance and faith....

VIII. We believe that those who are thus regenerated and justified, grow in sanctified character through fellowship with Christ, the indwelling of the Holy Spirit, and obedience to the truth; that a holy life is the fruit and evidence of saving faith; and that the believer's hope of continuance in such a life is in the preserving grace of God.

IX. We believe that Jesus Christ came to establish among men the kingdom of God, the reign of truth and love, righteousness and peace; that to Jesus Christ, the Head of his kingdom, Christians are directly responsible in faith and conduct; and that to him all have immediate access without mediatorial or priestly intervention.

X. We believe that the Church of Christ, invisible and spiritual, comprises all true believers, whose duty it is to associate themselves in churches, for the maintenance of worship, for promotion of spiritual growth and fellowship, and for the conversion of men; that these churches, under the guidance of the Holy Scriptures and in fellowship with one another, may determine—each for itself—their organization, statements of belief, and forms of worship, may appoint and set apart their own ministers and should co-operate in the work which Christ has committed to them for the furtherance of the gospel throughout the world.

XI. We believe in the observance of the Lord's Day, as a day of holy rest and worship; in the ministry of the word; and in the two sacraments, which Christ has appointed for his church: Baptism, to be administered to believers and their children, as a sign of cleansing from sin, of union to Christ, and of the impartation of the Holy Spirit; and the Lord's Supper, as a symbol of his atoning death, a seal of its efficacy, and a means whereby he confirms and strengthens the spiritual union and communion between believers and himself.

XII. We believe in the ultimate prevalence of the kingdom of Christ over all the earth; in the glorious appearing of the great God and our Saviour Jesus Christ; in the resurrection of the dead; and in a final judgment, the issues of which are everlasting punishment and everlasting life.[22]

The Commission Creed fulfilled the desire for more precision in the statement of Congregational beliefs, and most of it would have been acceptable to the first Puritans—scripture is divinely inspired, man is inherently sinful, salvation is by Christ's grace alone. Yet the creed avoids the issues that might have divided the church. It does not attempt to state exactly how Christ's mediation takes place or what role men and women play in their own salvation. On the issues of free will, original sin, and predestination, the creed reiterates the formula worked out by Nathaniel William Taylor and embodied in the New Haven Theology: there is no salvation from sin "except through God's redeeming grace" and God's providence is "in and over all events," and yet "the freedom and responsibility of man are not impaired, and sin is in the act of the creature alone."

The creed was soon adopted by many local congregations. "Its merits are obvious," wrote Walker, "It is simple, clear, and modern. It represents a fair consensus of the actual present faith of the Congregational churches."[23] In an age of consolidation the Congregationalists managed, almost miraculously, to establish a national council and produce several statements of faith and practice, without alienating substantial segments of the church. Their self-consciousness also grew with the creation of a national periodical, the *Congregational Quarterly* (1859) and with the founding of two new Congregational seminaries: Chicago Theological Seminary (1855) and Pacific Theological Seminary (1866). These efforts towards cooperation were particularly useful because in the new industrial era the Congregationalists would soon face unprecedented challenges from secular thought and social unrest. Their success in uniting their denomination and entering the new age owes much to one of the most attractive figures in the entire history of the Congregational churches, Horace Bushnell.

HORACE BUSHNELL AND PROGRESSIVE ORTHODOXY

For more than a century, ever since the ideas of the Enlightenment had reached America, Congregationalists had faced the challenge of justifying their faith in a world that appeared to work effectively without divine intervention. During the eighteenth century the challenge came from Newton and Locke. Jonathan Edwards and his followers offered a way of preserving orthodoxy while comprehending the Enlightenment, but many Congregationalists decided that Unitarianism offered a more sensible blend of Christianity and reason. Within a century of Edwards's death, science was offering other challenges—new explanations for the origin of species and the forces of geology. Under the "new criticism" the Bible itself was subjected to scientific study.

The successes of secular thought were undeniable, not only in new theories about nature and society, but in new inventions, such as the Bessemer converters in Andrew Carnegie's steel mills, which gave tangible proof of man's capacity to comprehend and control the natural world. The challenge facing all Christian denominations was to preserve traditional beliefs while recognizing the importance of the new sciences. During the later part of the nineteenth century, no denomination was more successful than the Congregationalists in forging a theology that synthesized traditional Christianity and modern thought.

The leading figure in liberal Christianity was Horace Bushnell, a Connecticut clergyman who gained a national following in 1847 with the publication of *A Discourse on Christian Nurture*. While not denying the reality of sin, Bushnell claimed that human effort and divine grace were so closely related that parents could *nurture* a child's growth into the world of spirit. "The Christian life and spirit of the parents, which are in and by the spirit of God," wrote Bushnell, "shall flow into the mind of the child."[24] In a brief autobiographical fragment, found among his papers, Bushnell described how the mingled love of God and mother had nurtured him to maturity from "the merely mollusk and pulpy state" of infancy: "When I broke into this little, confused consciousness, it was with a cry,...perhaps it was something prophetic, without inspiration, a foreshadow, dim and terrible, of the great battle of woe and sin I was sent hither to fight. But my God and my good mother both heard the cry and went to the task of strengthening and comforting me together."[25]

As a text on child-rearing, *Christian Nurture* enjoyed an influence comparable to that of Benjamin Spock's *Baby and Child Care* in the twentieth century. Bushnell impressed Victorian parents with a sense of their ability—and responsibility—to lead their children to salvation. In 1892, for example, a friend recommended the book to Anna Roosevelt, mother of Eleanor Roosevelt, then eight, and of two younger boys. Anna read the "blessed book" late into the night and determined to raise her children to respect "the Right." She told her friend, the book "has helped me to better resolutions, which only God will know how I keep."[26]

In the history of religious thought, *Christian Nurture* is less important for its suggestions on child-rearing than for the new approach it offers to understanding how nature and grace interact. The course of Bushnell's thought was implicit in *Christian Nurture*. He came to believe that the natural and supernatural worlds were "consubstantial" rather than separate. Christ's death did not so much satisfy God's demand for payment for sin as it enabled men and women to live a spiritual life. This idea came to be known as the "moral influence" theory of atonement, and like the idea of Christian nurture it encouraged optimism about the capacity of human beings to achieve salvation. Bushnell felt that just as a parent could be trusted to work with Christ in imparting grace to a child, so could any Christian trust his or her own experience to impart religious truth. At a time when scientists and sociologists were demanding an empirical basis for assertions about the world, Bushnell argued that religious feelings were themselves empirical phenomena. In the words of Mary K. Cayton, Bushnell developed "experience-based explanations of the implications of Christian theology for evangelical action."[27]

The emphasis on studying personal feelings in religion found classic expression a few decades later in William James's *Varieties of Religious Experience* (1902). But James, a psychologist, made no claim for the connection between personal experience and divine influence, while Bushnell regarded religious feelings as the datum of supernatural grace. Sometimes referred to as "Progressive Orthodoxy," Bushnell's approach to experience led him to develop a distinctive theory of religious language. He admired Samuel Taylor Coleridge's *Aids to Reflection* (1825), which offered an alternative to the dry rationalism of much contemporary theology. Bushnell argued that Christians should emphasize the truths underlying creedal statements. Accordingly, theologians should worry less about the doctrines dividing them and more about the spiritual truths that all sides acknowledged—and experienced. Religious statements, Bushnell felt, should be regarded as metaphors evoking truth, not as the truth itself. In a sermon preached in 1853 on the twentieth anniversary of his ordination as pastor of North Church in Hartford, Bushnell declared, "My preaching never was to overthrow one school and set up another, neither was it to find a position of neutrality midway between them, but as far as theology is concerned, it was to comprehend, if possible, the truth contended for in both."[28]

Bushnell advocated "Christian comprehensiveness" as the goal of religious thought. "Let Calvinism," he wrote, "take in Arminianism, Arminianism Calvinism; let decrees take in contingency, contingency decrees; faith take in works, and works faith; the old take in the new, and the new the old—not doubting that we shall be as much wiser as we are more comprehensive, as much closer to unity as we have more of the truth."[29]

Consistent with his philosophy, Bushnell attempted to preach and write in a language close to human experience. He would, he said, "invert the relations of dogma and spirit."[30] A biographer wrote, "He reasoned, not with his intellect merely, but with his whole nature, and his solid thought moved steadily forward with a mastery of energetic words, a majesty of statement, a glow of spiritual passion which have given his sermons what appears to be a permanent place in the literature of the Church."[31]

Bushnell rejected Calvinistic ideas about innate depravity and the burdensome distance between God and humanity. So he seems to have gone a long way from the traditional Congregational beliefs of John Cotton, Cotton Mather, and Jonathan Edwards. And yet as he himself suggested in his writings, language may obscure underlying spiritual realities. Just as Edwards's conversion experience helps us understand his theology, Bushnell's spiritual life helps us under-stand his ideas—and suggests that he was not so fundamentally at odds with the Puritans as his theology suggests. In fact, his conversion experience followed a pattern that would have been recognizable to Calvin, Luther, and the early Puritans. At two points in his life revelatory experiences jostled him away from a course that nature had apparently set for him. In 1831 he was attending Yale Law School, intending to become an attorney, when a religious revival swept through the college, and he decided to become a minister. But he still hoped for fuller communion with God. The death of his "beloved little boy" in 1843, according to his wife, may have driven him "through mental struggles, trials, and practical endeavor, to achieve a deeper spirituality."[32]

Shortly afterwards, when he was a minister in Hartford, he had a mystical ex-perience of communion with God. His daughter describes the episode: "On an early morning in February his wife awoke to hear that the light they had waited for, more than they that watch for the morning, had risen indeed. She asked 'what have you seen?' He replied, 'The Gospel.' It came to him at last, after all his thought and study, not as something reasoned out, but as an inspiration—a revelation of the mind of God himself." This was the most profound religious experience in Bushnell's life. In his later years he wrote, "I seemed to pass a boundary...from...partial seeing, glimpses and doubts, into a clearer knowledge of God and into his inspirations, which I have never wholly lost. The change was into faith—a sense of the freeness of God and the ease of approach to him."[33]

Bushnell incorporated his experience into a book published that year, *God in Christ* (1849). The work became the cornerstone of his reputation in American religious thought, allowing him to exercise an influence that is often compared to that of Jonathan Edwards and Reinhold Niebuhr. H. Shelton Smith declared, "With the exception of Edwards, Bushnell was probably the most creative Protestant theologian that America produced before the twentieth century."[34] He was an innovator, and yet as is so often the case in the history of Christianity, his originality consisted mainly in applying an old insight to new circumstances. Martin Luther had "discovered" salvation by faith as a correc-tive to the contemporary emphasis in the Catholic church on salvation by works. But the idea itself was not new; it came to Luther from Paul. Similarly Jonathan Edwards emphasized old ideas about religious experience and "true conversion" in an atmosphere in which human effort was gaining favor as the road to salvation. Now Bushnell, growing up in an age of intense doctrinal controversy, had "discovered" that something fundamental in religion comes from outside society and the human mind.

"Christian faith," he wrote, "is the faith of a transaction. It is not the com-mitting of one's thought in assent to any proposition, but the trusting of one's being to *a being*, there to be rested, kept, guided, molded, governed, and pos-sessed forever....It gives you God, fills you with God in immediate experimen-tal knowledge."[35] Bushnell told his congregation that salvation must come from God. "It moves from him and not from you," he said, "it is no vague struggle to ascend some height you cannot see, no wearisome, legal drill of duty and self-cultivating discipline. It is simply and only to have your whole being filled and occupied and transformed by Christ."[36]

Bushnell is sometimes credited with originality in stressing a sense of the "freeness" of God and the "ease" of approach to him. The Puritans, in apparent contrast, struggled for a sense of grace; so Bushnell's idea of "ease" in the presence of the divine may seem radical. But like the Puritans he sought grace for years before feeling he had come into communion with God. He once remarked that his spiritual life "required *many* turns of loss and recovery to ripen it."[37] Bushnell was like the Puritans in needing to struggle for grace, and they were like him in feeling that once grace was attained it could be proximate, familiar, easy—at least sometimes. John Cotton, for example, wrote of "swimming in grace." "There is such a measure of grace," he wrote, "in which a man may swim as fish in the water, with all readiness and dexterity." Such a man, he said, "is every way drenched in grace."[38]

The Puritans had stressed companionship with God as well as alienation from God. In Bushnell, then, the idea of God's companionableness is not new. But in a society radically different than the New England of two centuries before, the idea acquired new significance. Bushnell's emphasis on Christian nurture suited the needs of an age of social and industrial engineering; but, at the same time, his love of spiritual experience kept religion alive as a deeply felt emotional force. In his emphasis on both nurturing and grace, he reflected the optimism of the age—God was proximate in man and nature. The world, a good place, would grow better and better.

Bushnell's optimism was especially apparent in his *Nature and the Supernatural* (1866) in which he argued that heaven and earth together constitute "one system of God." The book's charm and power lie in its examples of the mingling of nature and spirit in daily life. In a famous anecdote Bushnell told of an exslave coming to visit him one afternoon. Bushnell was out when the man known as "Old Law" arrived, saying he brought "a message from the Lord." Bushnell's wife and his daughter, Mary, invited the man in and listened to him while they waited for the minister's return. He told them about his dreams and revelations. He had seen the ark of the Lord and "a trail of glory kep a-windin' out of it, an' a band ob angels was all about, an' de angels kep' a-comin' up an' a kethchin' hole ob de trail."[39]

Mary was ready to dismiss the man as a fanatic, but then her father arrived. "There was a moment," Mary wrote, "for observing the contrast between the two men, placed by nature so widely apart in the scale of being. The old African, at his lean height of dilapidation, with his narrow skull and visionary aspect, had yet a dignity of bearing which expressed his sense of the importance of his errand. On the other hand, my father's clear-cut features, alive with all the vital powers of a trained intellect, were softened now by an expression of tender deference,—of gentle and glad readiness to hear."[40]

Bushnell provides his own account of his meeting with Old Law: "As I entered the room, it was quite evident that he was struggling with a good deal of mental agitation, though his manner was firm, and even dignified. He said immediately, that he had come to me 'with a message from de Lord.'" The man had heard Bushnell preach and "discovered that God was teaching me." But at the same time Old Law had been "suffering the greatest personal burdens of feeling" because he thought Bushnell was wasting his time on an unimportant project.[41]

Bushnell asked Old Law to explain, and the man answered "in a manner of the greatest deference possible, and with a most singularly beautiful skill,...straightening up his tall manly form, dropping out his Africanisms, rising in the port of his language, beaming with a look of intelligence and spiritual beauty all in a manner to second his prophetic formulas—'The Lord said to me' thus and thus; 'The Lord saint me to say.'" Fascinated, Bushnell reflected "Verily, Nathan the prophet has come again!...It was really a scene such as any painter might look a long time to find—such dignity in one so humble; expression so lofty, and yet so gentle and respectful; the air of a prophet so commanding and positive, and yet in such divine authority, as to allow no sense of forwardness or presumption."[42]

Finally Bushnell's visitor came to his point: Old Law felt that the minister was spending too much time on a public park project in Hartford and that this activity was diverting him from his proper work as a minister. Bushnell defended himself, noting the public value of the park, but his guest pressed on, arguing that other men could build parks. Finally the minister was persuaded, agreeing that he should devote more time to his writing. He came to see his work on the park—which was named for him, and still adds beauty to Hartford—as an example of the "tendency of every most earnest soul to be diverted from its aims, by things external."[43]

After Old Law left, Bushnell sought information about this prophet in Hartford's black community. The man had a reputation for being steady and honest, but hard to know. Next Bushnell visited him in a shop he ran and asked him about his communion with God. Hearing the exslave recount instances of God's communicating with him—and taking his reports seriously—Bushnell asked, "Why then does God teach you in this manner and not me?"[44]

"Ah," the old man replied, "but you have the means—you can read as I can not, you have great learning. But I am a poor, ignorant child, and God does with me just as he can." Bushnell was convinced that the man spoke truly. Here was an instance of God's conversation with the world—of the mingling of natural and supernatural. "In that humbler stratum of life," he wrote, "where the conventionalities and carnal judgments of the world have less power, there are characters blooming in the holiest type of Christian love and beauty, who talk, and pray, and, as they think, operate apostolically, as if God were all to them that he ever was to the church, in the days of her primitive grace."[45]

In such ways Bushnell believed that God's presence could be found throughout the world: in the voice of an exslave as well as in the pulpit and the Bible. Bushnell's influence over Congregational thought in the fifty years following the Civil War was as much a reflection of his personality as his thought. "One of the most remarkable things concerning him," wrote his daughter, "was that unconscious radiation of character which he was wont to call one's 'personal atmosphere.'" Born on a farm he grew up "ignorant of any but country society." He did not enter college until he was twenty-one, and by then the country "vernacular" was imbedded in his speech.[46] He grew more learned, but there remained in his speech a simplicity—the Puritans might have called it a "plain style"—that facilitated his communication with the general public.

Like the Puritan ministers of old, Bushnell spent part of his time working in the fields, even when he was a pastor in Hartford. Country metaphors colored his prose. Visiting a neighboring church and asked by the local minister whether he would like him to offer the prayer before the sermon, Bushnell replied that he would like to deliver both, saying that the prayer would "sharpen" his "scythe" for the sermon. His daughter awakened often to hear her father sharpening an actual scythe. In the fields he "swung his scythe easily, cutting rapidly a broad, clean swath." Other mornings she awoke to the sound of the "sharp ring of the ax" as he felled a tree. After working for an hour or two he would come in and offer family prayers. Then in a deep base voice he would lead the family in hymns such as "Rise My Soul and Stretch Thy Wings." In the evening his daughter sometimes saw a different man. If he had spent his whole day in the study, Bushnell would come from his "thought world...and then there was no more of the outward but of the subjective and inward life. Then his every hair stood on end, electric with thought; his eyes had a fixed and absent look, and he forgot the name of a potato."[47]

Accounts of Bushnell's life are full of anecdotes from the times when he was very much a part of the "outward" world. At Thanksgiving he thrilled his children by leaping over their heads. Fishing in Long Island Sound with clerical friends, and tempted by a cigar, he might remark to a fellow minister, "Come, Chesebrough, let's sin a little."[48] His personal charm won him many friends and elevated his spirits. His fundamental humanity is well illustrated in this letter to his wife during one of his absences:

These little times of separation seem to me to be a kind of striking part in our clock of life. If we had them not, it would run silent, and we should hardly know that it ran at all; for the soft tick-beat of ordinary experience only makes the stillness itself audible, but breaks it not. I look back now along the track of years passed by; and though it is by the tick alone that we have known each other, yet it is only by the loud strikes, here and there, of separation that I get any account or register of the minutes, and hours, and years of undistinguished comfort and unity of being in which the good Father of our life has been leading us on. What stronger evidence need we that our life has been happy, than that it is by our separations chiefly that we register its flow?[49]

Great theologians often learn as much about religion from the world as in their studies. Paul Tillich, for example, once remarked that he learned more religion from paintings than from books. Bushnell learned religion from nature. Speaking before the Beethoven Society at Yale, Bushnell discussed "the powers of music hidden in things without life." "Woods, and valleys, and mountains, and waters," he said, "are tempered with distinctions of sound, and tones to be a language to the feeling of the heart." This is true, he argued, not only when we "hear the sea roar and the floods clap their hands," but also "there is hid in the secret temper and substance of all matter a silent music, that only waits to sound, and become a voice of utterance to the otherwise unutterable feeling of our heart—a voice, if we will have it, of love and worship to the God of all."

Bushnell told the Yale students that he had heard "some fine music" of orchestras and choirs, but the "music" that moved him most came from nature.

In the lofty passes of the Alps I heard a music overhead from God's cloudy orchestra—the giant peaks of rock and ice, curtained in by the driving mist, and only dimly visible athwart the sky through its folds—such as mocks all sounds our lower worlds of art can ever hope to raise. I stood (excuse the simplicity) calling to them, in the loudest shouts I could raise, even till my power was spent, and listening in compulsory trance to their reply. I heard them roll it up through their cloudy worlds of snow, sifting out the harsh qualities that were tearing in it as demon screams of sin; holding on upon it as if it were a hymn they were singing to the ear of the great Creator....I had never any conception before of what is meant by *quality* in sound. There was more power upon the soul in one of those simple notes than I ever expect to feel from anything called music below, or ever can feel till I hear them again in the choirs of the angelic world. I had never such a sense of purity, or of what a simple sound may tell of purity, by its own pure quality; and I could not but say, O, my God, teach me this! Be this in me forever! And I can truly affirm that the experience of that hour has consciously made me better able to think of God ever since—better able to worship.[50]

A few years later he wrote in a similar vein about autumn in San Jose, California: "The colors put on a landscape would be called absurd, impossible; and yet they are fact. How many other impossible things are fact in the same manner! Distant objects, or far-off backgrounds, too, have a peculiar depth of effect; the smoky blue resting on the yellow, and gloriously lighted up by it, so that as you look you seem to hear a kind of music ringing in the colors."[51]

Impressed with the dryness of California, Bushnell suddenly understood one part of the Scriptures better. "We talk of water here just as the Scriptures do," he said. "I never could understand why so much should be made of water. But the springs, the dry brooks, the running brooks,—all these water terms come to me here with real scriptural meaning."[52]

These thoughts about landscape, music, and the Scriptures illustrate the ways that religion saturated Bushnell's life. It was fortunate for him that he derived so much satisfaction from the experiences of spirituality, for during much of his career the institutional church gave him little support. Thought of by some of his contemporaries as "the man who has dared to beard Calvinism in its own den," he was condemned and ostracized by many of his clerical colleagues.[53] A conservative periodical complained that Bushnell's "reputation as a man of genius procures him great indulgence in his eccentric flights and aberrations. He has become a sort of 'chartered libertine,' and has acquired a right to do as he likes with impunity. He may safely steal a horse from the pasture, where another man would have been hanged only for looking over the hedge. He is also much protected by the nebulosity of his ideas on the subject of *language*, enabling him, as he boasts in his recent book, to sign all the creeds he ever saw. Such a man can be held to no human accountability for anything he may choose to write. No man can tell what he means, or whether, in any respects, he is orthodox, or whatever else he is. The attempt to ascertain his opinions is like trying to pin a brilliant jack-o'lantern to the wall, or to tie up a rainbow into a true lover's knot."[54]

Bushnell may have seemed a "chartered libertine" to some, but he very nearly lost that "charter." In Connecticut the Fairfield West Association claimed that *God in Christ* was "preparing the way for a wide-spread error, captivating to the carnal mind, but destructive of the faith, and ruinous to the souls of men."[55] Reviews of his work from the orthodox theologians tended to condemn him, and the local association of churches in Hartford came close to trying him for heresy. Fortunately, Bushnell's parishioners supported him unanimously, and even withdrew from the local consociation lest their pastor be disciplined. But for many years none of the other Congregational ministers in Hartford would exchange pulpits with him, a clear sign of his ostracism.

Bushnell was afflicted with a bronchial disorder that caused him to retire from the ministry in 1861, but he continued to write, and almost half his books were published during the fifteen years between his retirement and his death in 1876. Criticisms of his works continued, and at one time the conservative outcry against *Christian Nurture* was so strong that his publisher suspended the sale of the book.

But many Congregationalists found his ideas congenial to the spirit of the age. It was partly because of Bushnell's popularity that the Congregationalists who assembled at Boston in 1865 and at subsequent national councils refused to draft rigid, conservative creedal statements. An increasing number of the church leaders in the Age of Industrialization were influenced by the tolerant spirit of Bushnell's Progressive Orthodoxy.

During the later part of the nineteenth century the foremost Congregationalists were as diverse a group of preachers as ever appeared in the church. In various ways they each benefited from the tolerant atmosphere that Bushnell did much to foster. Joseph Cook was one of the more colorful exemplars of Progressive Orthodoxy. Educated at Harvard and Andover, he declined a ministerial career to become a public lecturer. From 1874 until 1895 he led weekly Monday prayer meetings at Boston's Tremont Temple. At these gatherings he lectured on subjects as diverse as biology, socialism, and evolution. Claiming to be an authority on scientific discoveries, he broadcast information about modern thought, while assuring his audience that the best of science was compatible with the essentials of religion. Cook was enormously successful, drawing large audiences to his lectures and publishing his views widely in the United States and abroad.

George Angier Gordon, minister of Old South Church in Boston, was equally enamored with modern thought. He rejected such traditional Calvinistic doctrines as limited atonement and arbitrary election. But he maintained many elements of the traditional faith and once jokingly referred to himself as the only Trinitarian left in New England. His career furnishes a good example of the way that Congregationalists after the Civil War sought to combine orthodoxy and progress. Angier stressed the similarities between Christ and man, noting the spirituality of man and the humanity of Christ. But in *The Christ of Today* (1895), he supported the doctrine of the Trinity.

Henry Ward Beecher, the best known Congregational minister of the late nineteenth century, was equally comfortable with synthesizing tradition and modern thought. He argued that God uses natural laws to govern the universe, and so Darwinism is simply an example of the Lord's government at work. In 1885 he developed his ideas in *Evolution and Religion*. This was a popular topic, addressed by many ministers, including Lyman Abbott, who published *Theology of an Evolutionist* in 1897.

George Frederick Wright, who held the telling title of "professor of harmony of science and revelation" at Oberlin was a Congregational minister and theologian who was at the same time a leading geologist, and he argued that natural causes could be found to explain such biblical miracles as the parting of the Red Sea and the destruction of Sodom.

Progressive Orthodoxy allowed Congregationalists to feel that their religious beliefs could exist comfortably beside the new findings of science. But there was the danger that some would ignore Horace Bushnell's assertion that a supreme—and sometimes unpredictable—God ruled over the natural world. In *Nature and the Supernatural* Bushnell warned against assuming that the material world was self-determining: "And so it comes to pass that, while the physical order called nature is perhaps only a single and very subordinate term of that universal divine system, a mere pebble chaffing in the ocean-bed of its eternity, we refuse to believe that this pebble can be acted on at all from without, requiring all events and changes in it to take place under the laws of acting it has inwardly in itself."[56] During the twentieth century leading theologians would return to this fundamentally Edwardsean view of the world as "a mere pebble chaffing in the ocean-bed of its eternity."

But in the Age of Industrialization, prior to World War I, it was easy to believe that by mastering natural laws people could create a new heaven on earth. Even during the nineteenth century, however, some theologians began to question whether all was well in the world. In the wake of industrialization came new forms of poverty and ignorance, especially in the big cities. Some ministers recognized the dark side of industrialization, and would forge a new gospel, designed for the victims of material progress.

NOTES

[1] Quotation from J. William T. Youngs, *American Realities* (Boston, 1987), vol. 2: 38.

[2] On social Darwinism see Robert C. Bannister, *Social Darwinism: Science and Myth in Anglo-American Social Thought* (Philadelphia, 1979).

[3] Quotation from Youngs, *American Realities*, vol. 2, 33.

[4] Walker, *Creeds and Platforms*, xvi.

[5] Walker, *Creeds and Platforms*, 554.

[6] Walker, *Creeds and Platforms*, 555, 557.

[7] Walker, *Creeds and Platforms*, 556.

[8] Walker, *Creeds and Platforms*, 557.

[9] Walker, *Creeds and Platforms*, 558.

[10] Walker, *Creeds and Platforms*, 558.

[11] Walker, *Creeds and Platforms*, 559.

[12] Walker, *Creeds and Platforms*, 560.

[13] Walker, *Creeds and Platforms*, 561.

[14] "Burial Hill Declaration," in Walker, *Creeds and Platforms*, 564.

[15] "Burial Hill Declaration," in Walker, *Creeds and Platforms*, 563.

[16] Walker, *Creeds and Platforms*, 565.

[17] Walker, *Creeds and Platforms*, 569. The "Statement of Congregational Principles" appears in Walker, 567-68.

[18] Walker, *Creeds and Platforms*, 571.

[19] Walker, *Creeds and Platforms*, 573, 576-77.

[20] Walker, *Creeds and Platforms*, 576.

[21] Walker, *Creeds and Platforms*, 578.

[22] "The 'Commission' Creed of 1883," in Walker, *Creeds and Platforms*, 580-82.

[23] Walker, *Creeds and Platforms*, 582.

[24] Quotation from J. William T. Youngs, *Eleanor Roosevelt: A Personal and Public Life* (Boston, 1985), 42.

[25] Mary A. Bushnell Cheney, ed., *Life and Letters of Horace Bushnell* (New York, 1880), 3.

[26] Youngs, *Eleanor Roosevelt*, 42.

[27] Cayton, "Congregationalism from Independence to the Present," 491.

[28] Quotation from Charles Allen Dinsmore, "Horace Bushnell," in Allen Johnson, ed., *Dictionary of American Biography* (New York, 1929), vol. 3, 350.

[29] Quotation from H. Shelton Smith, *Horace Bushnell* (New York, 1965), 38.

[30] Quotation from Smith, *Bushnell*, 44.

[31] Dinsmore, "Horace Bushnell," 352.

[32] Cheney, *Bushnell*, 191.

[33] Cheney, *Bushnell*, 192.

[34] Smith, *Bushnell*, ix.

[35] Cheney, *Bushnell*, 193.

[36] Quotation from Smith, *Bushnell*, 24.

[37] Quotation from Smith, *Bushnell*, 22.

[38] John Cotton, "Wading in Grace," in Perry Miller and Thomas Johnson, *The Puritans*, 1, 318.

[39] Cheney, *Bushnell*, 466.

[40] Cheney, *Bushnell*, 466-67.

[41] Horace Bushnell, *Nature and the Supernatural* (New York, 1866), 486.

[42] Bushnell, *Nature and the Supernatural*, 487.

[43] Bushnell, *Nature and the Supernatural*, 488.

[44] Bushnell, *Nature and the Supernatural*, 489.

[45] Bushnell, *Nature and the Supernatural*, 489-90.

[46] Cheney, *Bushnell*, 471, 208.

[47] Cheney, *Bushnell*, 454-56.

[48] Cheney, *Bushnell*, 239.

[49] Cheney, *Bushnell*, 239.

[50] Cheney, *Bushnell*, 263-64.

[51] Cheney, *Bushnell*, 392.

[52] Cheney, *Bushnell*, 392.

[53] Cheney, *Bushnell*, 249.

[54] Cheney, *Bushnell*, 226.

[55] Cheney, *Bushnell*, 234.

[56] Bushnell, *Nature and the Supernatural*, 20-21.

9
THE SOCIAL GOSPEL

IMPOVERISHED AMERICANS

In 1890 Andrew Carnegie earned twenty-five million dollars. His workers each earned less than one thousand dollars. In such ways the Industrial Revolution created new forms of poverty as well as new forms of wealth. Wherever there were factories, mines, or cities, Americans could be found living in squalor. In New York, where millions of immigrants arrived from Europe, the poorer sections of the city "sweated humanity." In the city's Lower East Side about seven hundred people lived in each acre. Families of six or eight lived in single rooms, sharing a toilet with three or four other families.

There had always been poor Americans, but their plight had never been so desperate. In the smaller towns of eighteenth-century America, villagers generally took care of their own. Rich and poor lived in close proximity. But in industrial America whole sections of cities were given over to slums. And it was possible for the well-to-do New Yorker or Chicagoan to live within a few blocks of the poorer neighborhoods and never see them.

It was a revelation, then, to many Americans when at the turn of the century muckraking journalists began to publish accounts of slums and calls for action. The most famous of these reporters was a Danish immigrant named Jacob Riis, who came to the United States in 1870. He worked as a police reporter for the *New York Evening Sun* and came to know the tenement districts by following detectives on their cases. Riis became more interested in poverty than crime, and he began to photograph children in rags, families in tiny apartments, and adults whose bleak expressions bore witness to their desperate lives.

Riis wrote a series of articles about urban poverty and published books of photographs, including *How the Other Half Lives* (1890), *The Children of the Poor* (1892), and *Children of the Tenements* (1893). Riis naturally made enemies with his forthright accounts, but he also won supporters for reform, including Theodore Roosevelt. Thanks to Riis's work, some improvements were made in housing and recreational facilities in New York.

There and in other cities like-minded reformers tackled the problem of poverty by creating settlement houses as centers for humanitarian action. The most famous of these was Hull House, established in the Chicago slums by Jane Addams in 1889. Addams gathered around her a number of socially conscious artists and educators and provided programs for the poor. Her many articles popularized the idea of the settlement house, and her autobiography, *Twenty Years at Hull House* (1910) is a classic account of welfare activities. In 1931 she was awarded the Nobel Peace Prize.

Riis and Addams are among the most famous urban reformers of their time. But the problem of poverty required more than the individual efforts of a few dedicated Americans. In response to the urban crisis, sociology developed as a field of study, and a new movement grew within the Congregational church and other Christian denominations—the Social Gospel movement. Under the leadership of ministers like Washington Gladden, the church as a whole lent support to the reform efforts in the cities, with profound effects on the theology as well as the social program of Congregationalism.

THE SOCIAL GOSPEL

The Social Gospel, a religious movement that was particularly influential from roughly 1870 to 1920, was a distinctive Christian reaction to the problems of Industrial America. It was impossible for Congregationalists to be unaware of the changes in the world around them. In his account of the Chicago Theological Seminary, *No Ivory Tower*, Arthur Cushman McGiffert Jr. provides a colorful example of the impact of the modern city. During its first four decades the seminary had prospered in a quiet residential district of Chicago. But by the turn of the century, new immigrants had replaced the earlier settlers, tenements and warehouses were built nearby, and heavy trucks rumbled past the lecture halls. A frustrated professor, McGiffert relates, was trying to lecture above the din of the traffic and the noise of an organ-grinder on the sidewalk below the building. "That is Satan out there," he declared.[1]

One observer noted that Chicago "may promise to be a rendezvous for missionary efforts, but it promises to be a poor place for a theological seminary."[2] The Social Gospel, however, offered a way of bringing together the church and the city. Influenced by religious liberalism, the movement's leaders shared the optimism of the post–Civil War America. But their optimism was anything but glib. They were acquainted with poverty and injustice and realized that industry and the cities had created as many problems as they had solved. Walter Rauschenbusch, a Baptist leader and one of the preeminent social reformers, remarked, "If the twentieth century could do for us in the control of social forces what the nineteenth did for us in the control of natural forces, our grandchildren would live in a society that would be justified in regarding our present social life as semi-barbarous."[3] Rauschenbusch defined the Kingdom of God (in a phrase the Puritans would have applauded) as "humanity organized according to the will of God." His first congregation was a small German Baptist church near Hell's Kitchen in New York City. He preferred it to his theological seminary because "here things are tangible."[4]

While acknowledging the importance of saving souls, the movement's leaders were also interested in the impact of the environment on individuals and families. Edwin Scott Gaustad provides an apt summary of this problem: suppose a man is converted, he said, "Then let us suppose he is returned to the twelve-hour day, seven-day week at the steel mill; his wife and even his small children, taken from school, are employed elsewhere to help sustain the family; all return to a squalid, sunless, depressing tenement to make their devotions before falling wearily onto a blanket spread on a cold floor. The man's heart has been changed, but for how long and to what end?"[5] In the late nineteenth century Congregationalists, and other Social Gospellers, turned their attentions to the "tangible" urban crisis.

The deepest roots of the Social Gospel can be traced to colonial America and even to primitive Christianity. The Good Samaritan had helped his fellow, and Christ told his followers to minister unto others. Within Puritanism there had been an interest in saving society as well as individuals. In such doctrines as the one of "fair price," Puritans stressed the responsibility of merchants to deal fairly with the public at large. Although John Winthrop had declared that in any society some would be poor, he hardly believed that laborers should be faced with starvation and exploitation. Among Congregationalists the Social Gospel movement could draw on these Christian and Puritan roots, as well as the Progressive Orthodoxy of Horace Bushnell.

After the Civil War Congregationalists continued their benevolent activities as missionaries. They sent hundreds of missionaries to the South and West, more in proportion to their population than any other denomination. They were active in the field of education, and by 1867 they were supporting 528 teachers in the field, many assisting with the education of the freed men and women in the South. By 1876 they had helped create eight new institutions of higher learning, including Fisk.[6]

The church also made progress in another area of social reform, women's rights. Previous to the Civil War, women had embarked on missions only as the wives of missionaries. But the 1860s and 1870s saw the "large-scale entry" of single women into the missions. In 1861 Congregationalists formed the Women's Missionary Society for Heathen Lands. Seven years later forty Congregationalist women formed a self-governing auxiliary to the American Board of Commissioners for Foreign Missions, The Women's Board of Missions. In 1880 the Congregational Women's Home Missionary Association was formed. These groups trained women for missions, held conventions, and opened the way for fuller participation by women in the Congregational church.[7]

It is difficult to date the beginning of the Social Gospel as a distinct movement in the Congregational church. But a series of events indicated the growing interest in taking the church into social action. In 1866 Andover Seminary opened the pages of its prestigious journal, *Bibliotheca Sacra*, to social commentary. Two years later John Bascom, a professor at Williams, published in its pages "The Natural Theology of Social Science," one of the important early documents of the Social Gospel movement. Among Bascom's Pupils was Washington Gladden, who is generally regarded as the father of the American Social Gospel.

From the time he entered the ministry in 1860, Gladden was a theological liberal, and he soon became a follower of Horace Bushnell. Gladden was one of the most effective expositors of the new theology. His most popular theological works were *Who Wrote the Bible?* (1891), *How Much is Left of Old Doctrine* (1899), and *Present Day Theology* (1913). Sydney Ahlstrom compared Gladden to other liberal theologians, but noted that unlike most of them Gladden "saturated his liberalism with social concern." Ahlstrom rightly called Gladden "a major awakener of the American Protestant social conscience."[8]

In 1875 Gladden became pastor in Springfield, Massachusetts, where he became acquainted with unemployed industrial workers. There and in Columbus, Ohio, where he preached after 1882, he turned his attention to America's economic situation. Gladden argued simply, "The one thing needful is the application to all human relations of the Christian law of brotherhood."[9] Gladden studied such issues as labor, taxation, public utilities, and corporate management. Many of his dozens of books focused on social problems. Among his best are *Applied Christianity: Moral Aspects of Social Questions* (1886), *Tools and the Man* (1893), and *Social Salvation* (1902).

Many of Gladden's pronouncements suggested practical solutions to practical problems. For example, he felt that labor should be allowed to organize because business did. "In view of the stupendous combinations of capital," he said, "the refusal to permit the combination of laborers is a gross injustice."[10] But Gladden's influence on his age was as much a matter of personality as ideas. He was one of those rare individuals who reflects deeply on his own times, envisions a better world, and carries others with him. "It is often well," he once said, "to assume that what ought to be will be."[11]

WASHINGTON GLADDEN AND PROGRESSIVE ORTHODOXY

Gladden was born in Pottsgrove, Pennsylvania, in 1836. Writing his recollections more than sixty years later, he mused on how much America had changed during his lifetime. With that change came the need for the Social Gospel. Antebellum America was a rural land without a proletariat or class divisions. "Industry was still largely domestic;" Gladden wrote, "the clothing of the great majority of the people was spun and woven in their own homes....Employers generally worked with their men in small groups, and all ate at the same table; there were no social distinctions between capitalists and laborers."[12]

Gladden's picture is somewhat romanticized. Textile mills already existed in New England, and large plantations dotted the South. Mill workers and slaves hardly expected to eat with their masters. But many Americans did live in the smaller communities Gladden associated with his youth. When Gladden was born Chicago's population was a mere 550 souls. The country was connected by wagon roads and canals. As a young boy Gladden made a journey of 250 miles across Massachusetts and New York in a one-horse buggy, sitting on a picnic box that was tucked under the dashboard. The roads were rough and the inns primitive. They crossed the Hudson in a ferry worked by horses on a treadmill. Only once in the journey did they come across a railway line. "It was a sensation quite unforgettable," wrote Gladden. "Our charioteer, with exorbitant faith in the speed of his nag, spurred him into a run to keep up with the train, but soon desisted." On another journey Gladden spent about five days on a canal boat traveling from Schenectady to Syracuse: "We sat upon the deck, in the sweet October sunshine, and had time a plenty to study the landscape and chat with the natives on the farms and in the villages."

This was a land closer in social life to the world of the early Puritans than to twentieth-century America. "I have seen the forests disappear from a large part of the continent," wrote Gladden, "sometimes in a ruthless and disastrous slaughter; I have seen the wild game which once roamed everywhere driven to a few sanctuaries in the western mountains, where they cannot long survive; I have seen the population spreading through the Mississippi valley and over the plains and mountains of the great Northwest; I have seen a mighty empire spring to life upon the Pacific coast, and great cities, scores of them, rise from the heart of the forest or the sedges of the lake or the bosom of the prairie; I have seen the land, from ocean to ocean, covered with a network of steam and electric railways, whose veinings give to almost every hamlet in the land immediate and cheap access to all the rest of the world."

With the changes in the land came changes in social relationships. Gladden continued, "I have seen also as the result of multiplying machinery for shop and farm, the population steadily lessening on the farming lands and massing in the cities; and I have watched the whole of that ominous polarization of social classes—the organizers and employers of labor gathering their hoards together, and, over against them, the men who do the work becoming banded and regimented for a perennial struggle over the product of labor."

Gladden would play a role in that changed world. But his own spiritual life would change first. His spiritual biography helps us chart the progress of Horace Bushnell's influence among Congregationalists. Gladden was raised in a spiritual atmosphere that tormented his youth. He lived for a time in Massachusetts and came into contact with "the Puritanism of the New England countryside." "There was a flavor in it," he wrote, "easily enough perceptible to a boy of eight....Living in a new community is a little like learning a new language: it gives you a new set of windows, through which to look out on life." Unfortunately Gladden does not elaborate on the enduring elements of New

England Puritanism. But the religious atmosphere must have been similar in Owego, New York, where he next went to live with his uncle.

Gladden reckoned that no family in Owego went to the local Presbyterian church more regularly than his: "Rain, snow, mud, were no hindrances; we went to church as regularly as we went to dinner. The lumber farm-wagon carried us for several years; rough boards laid across the box, and cushioned with horse-blankets, furnished our chariot." The morning and afternoon service were separated by an hour and a half "recess," part of which was taken up with Sunday school. A little time was left for lunch and, in good weather, "an enlivening stroll" through the adjoining graveyard. Gladden recalled, "I could have passed an examination, *magna cum laude*, on those epitaphs."

His life was saturated with religious lessons, and yet true piety was elusive. Gladden longed for a feeling of spirituality that would tell him he was among the saved. But the church left him unfulfilled. The sermons "hardly ever touched life in the remotest way." Again and again he heard that he was under a curse and was liable to suffer "the pains of hell forever." He yearned for communion with God, and would have given up "all my boyish sports,—ball-playing, coasting, fishing" for a sense of salvation.

But the longed-for sense of communion did not come. In his memory were camp meetings he had attended with his father in Pennsylvania when he was a small boy. He recalled a country schoolhouse, lit only by one candle, where a "powerful" evangelist had preached. "Men and women were prostrate on the floor, groaning and screaming frantically; some were trying to pray; some were shouting 'Glory!' The excitement and confusion were indescribable." Gladden sat on "a low seat" watching his father, who was helping conduct the service. The elder Gladden stood in the candlelight, "perfectly silent; there were tears in his eyes, but the expression on his countenance was one of intense pain."

Despite such influences young Gladden felt no ecstasies, and the only pain he sensed, was the pain of unfulfillment. The land was saturated with religious prophets offering diverse paths to salvation, but none made sense to the boy. The local Baptists showed their hardy faith by cutting holes in the ice every winter and baptizing scores of their followers in the cold water. Millerites added excitement to Gladden's youth by predicting the imminent end of the world. When he was seven, Gladden saw a lecturer "prove with chalk upon a blackboard that the world was going to be burned up in 1843."[13] For a time it seemed that the Millerites might be right. A blazing comet appeared in the sky that winter, visible from Gladden's bed. The boy was relieved when dawn broke on the first morning of 1844.

Relieved but not redeemed. More predictions of doom followed and more fear. "I remember one October day, five or six years later," Gladden wrote, "when the haze grew dense and yellow, and the air was filled with the odor of smoke, and there were lurid spots in the sky. I was working alone in a back lot, and fear took possession of me; I thought that the Great Day had come."

A famous evangelist, Jacob Knapp, came to preach, and told in vivid detail about "the burning pit, with the sinners trying to crawl up its sides out of the flames, while the devils, with pitchforks, stood by to fling them back again." This was supposed to be a useful account, pushing sinners into the arms of the Lord. But Gladden wrote that even though he was a small boy, "I distinctly remember that it made me angry." However, the boy could not avoid a feeling of spiritual deficiency, and he was deeply troubled: "That little unplastered room under the rafters in the old farmhouse, where I lay so many nights, when the house was still, looking out through the casement upon the unpitying stars, has a story to tell of a soul in great perplexity and trouble because it could not find God."

In later years when Gladden thought back to the religious atmosphere of antebellum America he remarked that "the business of religion was to fill men with fear." Moreover, religion was "almost wholly individualistic." It did not tend "to develop an altruistic habit." Instead of teaching people to care for their fellow beings, it "concentrated the thoughts of men on their own danger and their own safety." The prevailing religious climate taught a destructive fear and a debilitating egocentrism. Society suffered from "the blighting consequences of a bad theology."

When he was eighteen, Gladden finally escaped from religious despair through the influence of "a clear-headed minister" who taught him that "it was perfectly safe to trust the Heavenly Father's love for me and walk straight on in the ways of service, waiting for no raptures, but doing his will as best I knew it, and confiding in this friendship." In that simple statement Gladden sums up a conception, new to him of what was "essential in religious experience." Although Gladden had not yet come into contact with the theology of Horace Bushnell, he was moving in a direction that would make him a follower of "the Hartford Prophet." He was coming to believe that "religion is summed up in the word Friendship—that it is just being friends with the Father above and the brother by our side."[14]

This idea seems at odds with the original Puritan conception of the estrangement between God and man. But seen another way Gladden's piety simply shows basic Puritan ideas at work in a new religious environment. When the Puritan movement grew to maturity in early seventeenth-century England, the prevailing Anglican religious ethos inculcated a glib assurance of God's approval. In that environment the idea of man's friendship with God would have sanctioned the comfortable secularism that seemed, to the Puritans, to prevail in the Anglican church. For them the path to true piety lay in realizing the awesome distance between God and man. Fear was a necessary part of conversion.

But the goal of Puritan preaching was not to leave men in a condition of *perpetual* fear. Rather it was to create an experience of communion with God, based on genuine religious feelings, rather than a superficial assurance based on a few prayers learned by rote. At the end of long periods of anxiety, many Puritans did arrive at a sense of assurance not unlike that eventually enjoyed by Congregationalists a quarter millennium later in the age of Progressive

Orthodoxy. John Winthrop, for example, could speak of being moved by the nearness of Christ.

The drama of estrangement and reunion, central to the history of Christianity, had been played out again and again in early Congregationalism. During the early nineteenth century, the prevailing theology stressed estrangement and favored reconciliation through what Gladden calls "raptures." But that attitude left many religious-minded individuals in despair. Gladden remarked, "When my ministry began I found scores of men and women who were living blameless lives, and wanted to be the friends of God, but who had given it up as an impossibility." These people did not need to be told about "sinners in the hands of an angry God." In Gladden's view, as in Bushnell's and a growing number of other Congregationalists', these despairing men and women needed to learn about God's friendship. Gladden said that such an awareness would have transformed his youth; he often looked back "with a pang to the time when such a conception, if it could have reached him, would have lifted a great load from his heart and filled the world with beauty."[15]

At about the time that Gladden was introduced to a new view of Christian spirituality, he also had his first experience with the church as an agency of social reform. He was attending the Congregational church in Owego, New York. Its pastor had been forced out of the local Presbyterian church "because he had dared to pray for the slaves." His audience consisted of former Presbyterians who had followed their minister into exile. This was the mid-1850s, and the abolitionists were still a minority in the North. Gladden was attracted to this "little Congregational church," became a member, and began to think about entering the ministry. "It was not an individualistic pietism that appealed to me," wrote Gladden, "it was a religion that laid hold upon life with both hands, and proposed, first and foremost, to realize the Kingdom of God in this world....I wanted to be—if I could make myself fit—the minister of a church like that. I could not think of any life better worth living."[16]

Some Americans at that time expected to see the Kingdom of God in a postmillennial world after the coming of Christ or in life after death; others made a false heaven out of the material wealth of industrial America. For the one the kingdom was spiritual but remote; for the other it was proximate but secular. For Gladden the kingdom would be both spiritual and temporal; and its agency would be an awakened church, devoted to a Social Gospel. Before he even entered college Gladden had arrived, thus, at two ideas that would characterize his ministry and his impact on Congregationalism: friendship between God and humanity, and stewardship of the church in the world.

Gladden attended Owego Academy and Williams College, earning his B.A. in 1859. Then in 1860 he was appointed minister to his first church, a small congregation in Brooklyn. Until then Gladden had lived in small towns. He now came face to face with another America. Every night shortly after midnight, market wagons from Long Island rattled past his house, creating a "din" on the cobblestone pavement. The city was a new reality, affecting how people lived, worked, thought. "The city," writes Gladden, "from the first day, was a thing stupendous and overpowering, a mighty monster, with portentous energies; the sense of its power to absorb human personalities and to shape human destinies was often vivid and painful. To one who had nursed his fancies for the greater part of his life in the solitude of a back country farm, and who had breasted no currents of life stronger than those which meander through the streets of a quiet village, the contact with the strenuous life of the great city was a revelation. One was standing in the center of a galvanic field, with lines of force crossing each other in every direction. Everything was alive, yet there was a vivid sense of the impersonality and brutality of the whole movement, of the lack of coordinating intelligence."[17]

From the start of his ministry Gladden was aware of "the appalling nature of the municipal problem." But at the start of the Civil War, his ministry called him away from the city to the rural suburb of Morrisania. Apart from a short stint as chaplain in Virginia, Gladden remained in Morrisania during the war. His new post allowed him time to develop his theology by reading and attending lectures at Union Theological Seminary. He was particularly impressed by the works of Horace Bushnell, whom he characterized as a man "to whom spiritual things were not traditions but living verities." Gladden was particularly influenced by Bushnell's *God in Christ*. Its introductory essay on language taught him "the futility of the ordinary dogmatic method." Other parts of the book furnished "an emancipation proclamation which delivered me at once and forever from the bondage of an immoral theology."[18]

In the 1860s Bushnell's thought was still branded as heresy. But Gladden became an adherent of the new theology, remarking that Bushnell's only "heresy" was his belief "that God is just." He had simply denied doctrines that made God unjust: "that men should be judged and doomed before they were born; that men should be held blameworthy and punishable for what was done by their ancestors; that justice could be secured by the punishment of one for the sin of another."[19]

These ideas, once the bulwarks of Congregational doctrine, seemed preposterous to Gladden, as they had to Bushnell. But Gladden realized that the prevailing religious climate was hostile to Bushnell and the Progressive Orthodoxy. "The heresy-hunters," he noted, "had not been able to dislodge him from his church, but they had filled the churches with suspicions of him, and 'Bushnellism' was a name with which no ambitious minister could afford to be branded. It was well understood that nobody suspected of that taint could hope for ordination over a Congregational church." None the less, Gladden began to preach "the heretical theory."

Fortunately the doctrines of Progressive Orthodoxy were appealing to nineteenth-century sensibilities—even if the *idea* of heresy was not. Gladden managed to preach "the heretical theory" by using Bushnell's ideas, but not his name. He tells the story of a conservative parishioner who greeted him one morning after the service, and told him, "That was a good sermon! I wish we might have more sermons like that." One can almost see the twinkle in Gladden's eye as he reported, "The good man would have been confounded if he had known that he had been listening to heresy. I did not enlighten him. Since the only bit of genuine heresy to which he had been exposed seemed so palatable to him, it would have been unkind to disturb his enjoyment of it." In such ways Bushnell's ideas fostered a quiet revolution in Congregational preaching.

In 1866 Gladden accepted a call from a church in North Adams, Massachusetts. Encouraged by a friendly congregation and angered by the news that a young Congregational minister in Illinois had been refused ordination because of his sympathy with the new theology, Gladden began to identify himself more openly with Horace Bushnell. In the *Independent*, a periodical widely read by Congregationalists, he published an article entitled, "Are Dr. Bushnell's Views Heretical?" The Illinois "heretic" had run into trouble by agreeing with Bushnell's views on atonement: sin was not a condition visited upon men by remote ancestors, rather it was a conscious act by a particular individual; Christ's atonement did not consist of paying a price to a vengeful God for Adam's sin, but served as an example of a righteous life; by drawing close to Christ in friendship a believer gained strength and acquired the power to overcome the sinful impulses in his own life.

Gladden had learned these ideas from Bushnell. By embracing them he realized that he might be branded a heretic: "'Bushnellism' was under the ban, and there were few Congregational ministers who were willing to confess their acceptance of it." But if men were to be denied the privilege of preaching Bushnell's ideas in the Congregational ministry, Gladden writes, "the sooner that fact was known the better it would be for me....If this was heresy I desired to be counted among the heretics."[20]

Shortly after the article appeared, a letter arrived in North Adams from Horace Bushnell, an old man now, in retirement. Bushnell was obviously moved by Gladden's support. The letter from him was "so cordial and grateful," wrote Gladden, "that it deeply touched me....It was good to know that a word from such a source had comforted him, but it was tragical to think that he could have needed it."

A warm friendship grew up between the two men. A few months later the time came for Gladden's installation—his formal induction into the pulpit at North Adams. He wrote Bushnell asking him to preach the sermon. Bushnell's reply is one measure of how radical the Progressive Orthodoxy still seemed in 1866: "He thought...it would put the heresy-hunters on the scent; it would be far wiser for me to invite a safer man." Gladden replied that he wanted no one else for the sermon and would take the consequences.

Bushnell was then sixty-three years old and in poor health. But he hurried up to North Adams and spent a week with Gladden before the installation ceremony. "Those were great days," wrote Gladden, "driving over the Berkshire Hills, lying in the shade, talking of things visible and invisible, meditating upon the mysteries of the heavens above and the earth beneath. Horace

Bushnell was one of the great talkers....He had a keen eye for natural beauty, and the glories of those Berkshire Hills filled him with rejoicing."

The day for Gladden's installation arrived. The installation council included several men who opposed Bushnell's ideas, but they realized that Gladden had the full support of his church, and they were unwilling to make an issue of his heretical views. But neither were they willing to tolerate explicitly his views. So in a "palpable evasion," they conducted the traditional preinstallation examination over questions that did not enter the areas of dispute. After twenty minutes they brought the examination to "an abrupt conclusion."

"I thought that you were a great heretic," one of the ministers told Gladden.

"Perhaps I am," he answered, "but you didn't bore in in the right place."

At the installation service, Horace Bushnell preached a sermon entitled, "The Gospel of the Face." Bushnell's voice was impaired by illness, and yet "one could catch even in those broken tones the ring of irresistible convictions." "Is not that the Gospel?" someone asked President Hopkins of Williams after the service. "Nothing else is the Gospel," he replied.

Horace Bushnell would live for another decade. The induction service in North Adams and his growing friendship with a young man who so boldly embraced his ideas must have cast a warm glow over the twilight of his life.

WASHINGTON GLADDEN AND THE SOCIAL GOSPEL

Washington Gladden's early career provides a measure of the success of Progressive Orthodoxy, the doctrine that would characterize much of Congregational preaching by the end of the nineteenth century—and still influences religious thought a century later. Gladden's brief ministry in Brooklyn on the eve of the Civil War had planted the seeds of another, closely related faith, the Social Gospel. New forces were at work in America. But in Morrisania and North Adams the currents of change were not so apparent. The war had brought great wealth to a few manufacturers in North Adams, but they remained close to their employees. The town was close knit, and in the finest houses Gladden rubbed elbows with mechanics and clerks as well as merchants and professional people. During the next decade, however, the relationship between capital and labor grew more strained.

Gladden would leave North Adams in 1871. Towards the end of his ministry a large shoe factory closed its doors to its employees because of a wage dispute. The lock-out lasted for several weeks, and the owners tried to run the factory with strikebreakers. But the workers met each trainload of scabs at the railway station and persuaded them to return home. Finally the superintendent of the factory collected a force of Chinese laborers in San Francisco and brought them east by rail. When the train reached North Adams, a crowd lined the streets from the railway station to the factory. The workers shouted at the immigrants, and Gladden was afraid of violence. But, he wrote, "The curiosity of the crowd was so acute that its brutality was held in check. These pig-tailed, calicofrocked, wooden-shod invaders made a spectacle which nobody wanted to miss even long enough to stoop for a brickbat."[21]

The geniality that Gladden associated with North Adams was apparent in the aftermath of the incident. The Chinese workers were boarded in the factory for safety. But the town was not disposed to molest the strangers. They were welcomed in the shops, and philanthropists made efforts to teach them English and "fit them for self-support and citizenship." The incident contrasts with the deeper divisions between capital and labor which Gladden encountered later in life.

In 1871 he left rural Massachusetts for New York City in order to serve as religion editor on the *Independent*. From a town whose public life was fundamentally sound, he moved to a city in the midst of the greatest scandal of its history. William Marcy "Boss" Tweed controlled the city and state of New York; he and his associates, the "Tweed Ring," amassed fortunes in graft by padding public works bill by as much as ninety percent. Gladden tells of a plumbing contractor who submitted a bill for $10,000 for work on a new city hall; he was told that the city could not afford the $10,000, but could pay $100,000. The man resubmitted his bill, got the money owed him, and the Tweed Ring kept the remaining $90,000. In such ways Boss Tweed and his cronies siphoned off as much as $200 million in public funds.

When Washington Gladden arrived in New York, the corruption was general knowledge, but the courts were under Tweed's control, and most of the newspaper editors were willing to look the other way in return for generous contributions. An exception was *Harper's Magazine*, which published dramatic cartoons by Thomas Nast, portraying the members of the Tweed Ring as vultures. In 1871 a disenchanted member of the ring walked into the *New York Times* offices with records detailing the corrupt practices. Tweed tried to buy off *Times* editor George Jones and cartoonist Thomas Nast with huge bribes, but neither could be bought.

That summer Washington Gladden was left in charge of the *Independent* while the editor went away for a month's vacation. The *Times* was beginning to publish its findings, but William Marcy Tweed was asking his critics defiantly, "What are you going to do about it?" For years Gladden had been moving towards the position that faith required men to take stands at just such times as these. Looking back almost forty years later, he wrote, "It was one of the times of my life when I have come across something that needed to be hit and have had the chance to strike hard. Such opportunities make life worth living."

"The gates of the Tombs," he editorialized, "have never opened to receive criminals of deeper dye than the men who compose the New York Ring. For it is not only against property, but against life and public virtue as well, that they have conspired....They make common cause with rumshops and brothels, and virtue and order cry out against their rule. If there are any criminals in the land to-day, these men are criminals. If it is worth while to punish any evil-doers whatsoever, it is worth while to punish them."[22]

The year was 1871, the place was urban America, and the writer espoused a new theology. But the words echo the cadences of the jeremiads preached two centuries before by Puritan ministers. "What are you going to do about it?" Tweed had demanded.

"We are going to turn you and all your creatures out of your offices," Gladden replied. "That we can do and shall do, please God, before the new year is a week old....At any rate, we are going to make the city and the whole country too hot for you. There is some conscience in the land yet, and you will find it out before you die. Upon you shall rest, heavy and immovable, the weight of a nation's curse. You have perverted our laws. You have corrupted our young men. You have done what in you lay to destroy our Government. There are some sins that a nation may never forgive, and yours is among them. It is our solemn charge to hold you up while you live to the scorn and contempt of mankind. God may have mercy on you; but as for us, we promise you that your ill-gotten booty shall be but a poor compensation for the inheritance of shame which shall be yours forever."[23]

Boss Tweed was tried and convicted for his crimes and died in prison in 1878. Gladden later admitted that he had been uncertain at the time that those calling for reform would be victorious. But, he wrote, "it is often well to assume that what ought to be will be." The incident strengthened his conviction that religion, the Kingdom of God, could be made a reality on earth if persons of goodwill would "strike hard" against injustice. In his moral conviction he reminds one of John Winthrop or Cotton Mather, but at the same time Gladden became increasingly explicit in his criticisms of Calvinist theology. "Every doctrine," he believed, "must have an ethical foundation."[24] And in his view, there was nothing "ethical" about the Calvinist conception of original sin.

In 1873 he wrote an editorial entitled "Immoral Theology," which explicitly rejected Calvinism:

To teach that God is a being who has a perfect right to bring into the world a creature with faculties impaired, with no power to resist temptation, utterly unable to do right, powerless even to repent of the wrong which he is fated to do, and then send to everlasting misery this helpless creature for the sin which he could not help committing,—to teach such a doctrine as this about God is to inflict upon religion a terrible injury and to subvert the very foundations of morality. To say that God may justly punish a man for the sins of his ancestors, that God does blame us for what happened long before we were born, is to blaspheme God, if there be any such thing as blasphemy. To say that any such thing is clearly taught in the Bible is to say that the Bible clearly teaches a monstrous lie. Yet such theology as this is taught in several of our theological seminaries and preached from many of our pulpits. It is idle to say that it is nothing but a philosophical refinement; that the men who come out of our theological seminaries with these notions in their heads never make any use of them in their pulpits. They do make use of them. They are scattering this atrocious stuff all over the land. They are making infidels faster than they are converting sinners. Men say, 'If this is your God, worship him, if you want to, but do not ask us to bow down to your Moloch!' Who can blame them? For our own part we say, with all emphasis, that between such a theology as this and atheism we should promptly choose the latter.[25]

Clearly Gladden had abandoned the caution of his early ministerial career. Ten years earlier a Congregationalist who characterized original sin as "atrocious stuff" would have jeopardized or ruined his ministerial career. But times were changing. Eager to return to the ministry after his stint with the *Independent*, Gladden accepted a call to North Springfield, Massachusetts. He was amused to discover that he was not the first "heretic" to serve in that part of New England. William Pynchon, who founded Springfield in 1636, was an educated layman who published a book titled *The Meritorious Price of our Redemption*. His ideas of the atonement were so shocking to Puritan sensibilities that the general court ordered the book burned on Boston Common by the hangman. A few copies survived, and after his arrival in Springfield Washington Gladden read one. He had expected "a daring denial of all that is essential in substitutionary theology." But, "instead of that," he wrote, "its orthodoxy is rock-ribbed and triple-plated; there is no Calvinistic stronghold in the land in which its doctrine would not today be deemed archaic." Pynchon's "heresy" consisted of the claim that "Christ as our substitute actually suffered the pains of hell in his soul, including the pangs of remorse."[26]

Two hundred years later the book furnished a good example of "the manner in which the heresy of one day becomes the orthodoxy of the next." When Horace Bushnell had argued that religious language is an imperfect reflection of spiritual truth, he might have cited the Pynchon controversy as an example. His disciple Gladden concluded that Springfield had learned from the episode, which "may have had some tendency to moderate the theological climate and encourage toleration in that neighborhood."[27]

In 1877, two years after he arrived in Springfield, Gladden had the opportunity to set forth his own ideas on toleration. A man named James Merriam was invited to serve as minister in the Congregational Church at Indian Orchard, near Springfield. The council called to install him hesitated because of his ideas on future punishment. He agreed with the orthodox position that all who die impenitent suffer conscious torment; but he held that those who were incorrigible might "suffer extinction." The council, including Gladden, debated the issue, and the more orthodox tried to persuade Merriam to revise his thinking. But he refused, and the majority voted against installation.

Gladden was in the minority, and in sermons to his own congregation he argued that "no interest of Congregationalism or of Christianity could be imperiled by including such men as Mr. Merriam in our fellowship." He then described the qualifications he favored for the ministry:

The man who believes in Christ, who has the spirit of Christ in him, who shows in his life the fruits of that spirit, who, denying himself and taking up his cross, is following Christ in toilsome but loving labor for the salvation of men—he is my brother, and nothing shall hinder me from offering him the right hand of fellowship. I do not care what name they call him by, whether he is a Churchman or Quaker, Universalist or Roman Catholic, he who is united to my Master shall not be divided from me. And when such a man has found a company of people who love him, not because of any brilliancy of wit that has dazzled them, nor because of any tricks of sensationalism that have amused them, but just because of the Christ life that is in him,—and want him to live among them and show them how to serve and follow Christ,—and when he asks me to come and help to join him in loving bonds as pastor to this people, I shall go, every time! My blessing is not worth much, but, such as it is, God forbid that I should withhold it! And if anybody bids me be cautious, I answer, Yes, I will be very cautious lest I hinder in his work a true servant of Jesus Christ! I will take great care always lest I exalt the letter above the spirit, the dogma above the life. For I would rather make two mistakes on the side of charity than one on the side of bigotry.[28]

This statement epitomizes the spirit of toleration and fellowship that came to characterize modern Congregationalism. In this spirit Congregationalists would form organizations for interdenominational cooperation, and in this spirit many would merge with other churches and help form the United Church of Christ. Those innovations would create controversy, just as the Merriam case and others like it provoked disputes in the nineteenth century. But the movement of the church as a whole was in the direction suggested by Bushnell and Gladden.

The emphasis on fundamental beliefs, widely shared by Christians, also facilitated the preaching of the Social Gospel. Springfield was an industrial city, and in 1875 when Gladden arrived, it was still suffering from the economic collapse of 1873. Gladden was soon active making speeches to laboring men and industrialists. He urged working men to accept menial labor, if necessary, to get the economy back on its feet, and he urged businessmen to create jobs to provide new opportunities. At his urging some of his wealthy parishioners hired unemployed men to remodel their houses. In 1876 Gladden published a book containing these and other lectures under the title, *Workingmen and their Employers*.

Gladden argued that "a great social problem....was forcing itself upon the thought of the world." The problem concerned "the relations of man to man," Gladden said, "and it is the primary business of Christianity to define and regulate these relations." He called for "the application of the Christian law to industrial society." Then as now some persons argued that "the minister has no business to bring questions of this kind into the pulpit; that his concern is with spiritual interests, and not with secular." These opponents of the Social Gospel argued that ministers should concern themselves only with saving souls; men who were saved would deal justly with their fellows. But Gladden argued that many who were supposedly "saved" were "practicing injustice and cruelty, without any sense of the evil of their conduct. They were nearly all assuming that the Christian rule of life had no application to business....Business was business and religion was religion." Gladden argued that the two realms could not be separated. "Is the man saved," he asked, "who in his dealings with his employee, or his employer, can habitually seek his own aggrandizement at the cost of the other? Is not the selfishness which is expected to rule in all this department of life the exact antithesis of Christian morality?"[29]

After serving in Springfield for seven years, Gladden accepted a call to Columbus, Ohio in 1882. By now he had acquired a national reputation for his interest in social issues. Although he often spoke out against the abuse of labor by business, he also understood the employer's need to make a profit, and accordingly he often won the trust of both sides in labor disputes. When coal miners struck in the nearby Hocking Valley, Gladden spoke with workers and the managers. When strikes occurred in Cleveland and Boston, he was called in to address both sides. Unlike the utopians who hoped to abolish pecuniary interest from the marketplace through socialism, Gladden argued that the proper business ethic would encourage both selfishness and service. The golden rule, he argued, did not demand a radical departure from man's inherent egocentrism.

"'Thou shalt love thy neighbor as thyself,'" he wrote, "is sometimes taken as a maxim of sheer altruism. But the fundamental obligation is rational self-love. That is made the measure of our love for our neighbor. How much shall I love my neighbor? As much as I love myself....I am not to degrade or destroy myself in ministering to him, nor am I to degrade and destroy him in ministering to myself; I am to identify his interest with mine, and we are to share together the good which the divine bounty distributes to all."[30]

In his most famous book, *Applied Christianity*, Gladden elaborated on the idea that "society results from a combination of egoism and altruism." He admitted that in a factory the "proportion of altruism" might be less than in the home or church, but without altruism the factory system was "a social solecism." A production based purely on greed and conflict, he argued, "is an attempt to hold society together upon an anti-social foundation."[31] Gladden favored an industrial life that would encourage workers and employers to consider each other's interests.

A century later, faced with competition from abroad, capitalists and labor unionists in the United States would begin to realize the economic value of cooperation. Gladden, too, was an economist, but his idea of "applied Christianity" was primarily spiritual in origin and purpose. Organizations that fostered cooperation would increase profits; they would also foster a healthy moral climate. Gladden described this better world:

The law of human association must be the law of Good Will. The good life is not found by those who prey upon one another or plunder one another; it is found only by those who in friendship serve one another."

The stable and fruitful social order will be that which rests on the assumption that it is every man's business to give as much as he can, prudently and safely, and with due regard to his own integrity, to all with whom he deals."

The conviction is steadily strengthening that the one thing needful is a change in the direction of the ruling motive from self-aggrandizement to service."

Swollen fortunes are the symptom of social disease; they have the same relation to social health that hydrocephalus or elephantiasis has to the health of the individual.[32]

Gladden taught by example as well as by precept. He was particularly adept at recognizing moral compromises. One of the reasons that he quit his post on the *Independent* was that it took advertisements and printed them as if they were news and commentary. In a similar spirit in 1905 he attacked the church's mission board for accepting a gift of $100,000 from Standard Oil. Gladden argued that the money had been "iniquitously gained, and that we could not accept it without being partakers of the iniquity."[33] Some church leaders joined in opposing the grant. Others agreed with Graham Taylor, professor of Christian sociology at Chicago Theological Seminary. What counted in a donation, he said, "was not its pedigree but its destiny."[34]

Hard pressed by financial needs, the mission board had already spent most of the money, but a debate developed among Congregationalists on future policy towards such grants. Gladden wrote, "It must be said that the debate revealed a widespread need of elementary instruction in the first principles of ethics." He argued that the church had become so obsessed with the need for money that it was forgetting "higher considerations."

In response others argued that "money has no moral character." "Amateur moralists," Gladden called them. One might as well argue that money contributed by "highwaymen and pirates" was good as long as it went to buying Bibles and paying missionary salaries. Sounding again like the preacher of a seventeenth-century jeremiad, Gladden argued that pirates of a sort saturated the American economy: "It is impossible to deny the existence of a considerable class of persons who have obtained great wealth by predatory methods, by evasion and defiance of law, by the practice of vast extortions, by getting unfair and generally unlawful advantages over their neighbors, by secret agreements, and the manipulation of railway and government officials;...by manifold arts that tend to corrupt the character and destroy the foundations of the social order."

These same men often sought to clear their moral debts by giving away a part of their ill-gotten gains. Needing money the churches were tempted to accept, but in doing so they undercut their own mission. Instead of forming alliances with business predators, they should, according to Gladden, make "abhorrent and detestable, in the sight of the youth, the conduct of men who are amassing great wealth by methods which tend to the overthrow of free government and the destruction of the social order. They will not fulfill this calling by building churches or endowing mission boards with money contributed by such men, or by erecting college halls that bear their names. No amount of money that such givers can contribute can compensate for the lowering of ideals and the blurring of consciences which this kind of partnership involves."

It was a high order of integrity that Gladden demanded. His arguments foreshadow debates in the 1960s about corporate contributions to American universities. At Berkeley, for example, the Crown Zellerbach corporation donated money to build a new auditorium bearing the company's name. Students discovered that Zellerbach conducted business in South Africa and protested against the university's alliance with apartheid —"tainted money." Gladden's position also echoes the debates in the early 1600s between separating and nonseparating Congregationalists. The Pilgrims argued that any association with the Anglican Church was an alliance with corruption; but the Puritans claimed that they could reform the church by avoiding an explicit break. The problem of separation entered Puritan personal lives as well: they would not withdraw into monasteries, but they would remain aloof from the world in some ways while living in it. "Wine is from God," John Winthrop had said, "but drunkenness is from the devil." Throughout its history a fundamental issue in Congregationalism had been the problem of embracing the world while avoiding its evils.

In October of 1905 the mission board met in Seattle. Washington Gladden presented a resolution "that the officers of this Board should neither invite nor solicit donations to its funds from persons whose gains have been made by methods morally reprehensible or socially injurious." The board balked at adopting this censure of its own conduct and tabled the resolution. But soon after the meeting the board members quietly agreed that the spirit of Gladden's resolution would govern their future conduct.

In the Standard Oil controversy, Congregationalists engaged in the sort of debate that had won the name Puritan for their ancestors. Puritans were accused of being too strict in their moral scruples—what did it matter whether a minister wore robes or used the sign of the cross? They and the Social Gospellers, who reflected their spirit, answered that small peccadillos prepared the way for greater sins. "The moral law admonishes us not to make our fellow man our tool, our tributary," wrote Gladden. "Disobey that law, and the consequence falls. Evade it no man ever does for so long as the wink of an eyelid. Its penalty smites him with lightning stroke; he is instantly degraded, beclouded, weakened by his disobedience. Virtue has gone out of him; the slow decay is at work by which his manhood is despoiled."[35]

"Predatory wealth" was money gained in selfish labor—whether through dishonestly manipulating railway rates or by exploiting laborers. In that age many reformers complained about the degradation of the factory worker, but fewer recognized the cruelty of racial prejudice. During the 1880s and 1890s Jim Crow laws were adopted throughout the nation. Washington Gladden showed the breadth of his moral sensitivity by condemning the mistreatment of blacks: "If the main thing to be done for the negro is to keep him in ignorance and subjection," writes Gladden:

that is a task which requires no great amount of art,—nothing but hard hearts and brutal wills. There is physical force enough in the nation to hold him down for a while; how long that dominion would last, I will not try to tell. The civilization built on that basis will fall, and great will be the fall of it. We have had our admonition already,—a war that cost six hundred thousand lives and twelve billions of dollars,—and the bills are not paid yet. That is a slice of the retribution due for trying to build a civilization on prostrate manhood. If we are not satisfied with that, if we insist on trying the same experiment over again in a slightly different form, another day of judgment will come, and will not tarry. We shall get it hammered into our heads one of these days that this is a moral universe; not that it is going to be, by and by, but that it is moral now, moral all through, in tissue and fibre, in gristle and bone, in muscle and brain, in sensation and thought; and that no injustice fails to get its due recompense, now and here.[36]

"This *is* a moral universe...." This conviction was the basis of Puritan sermons in the 1660s and the 1770s. Like the Puritans Gladden believed that a spiritual power permeated the universe, empowering people to do good, punishing them for doing evil. In a passage reminiscent of Bushnell's insistence that God must be known firsthand—and redolent too with the Puritan sense of a God present, here and now—Gladden argued against knowing God only through scripture and doctrine.

All this puts Him far away. Our religion, whatever we call it, becomes mainly a tradition. We are climbing to heaven by ladders of testimony to bring God down, we are descending into the abyss by our chains of logic to draw Him forth, when in very truth He is near us, in the very breath of our life, in the thrill of our nerves, in the pulsations of our hearts, in the movements of our minds, living and working in us and manifesting Himself in every natural force, in every law of life. This is the truth which the world is beginning to understand, the truth of the immanent God.

We hear people, in these days, denying the supernatural. It is a little as if the planets should proclaim that there is no such thing as space, or as if the rivers should proclaim that there is no such thing as water. We cannot lay our hand on life anywhere without feeling the thrill of that SOMETHING MORE which underlies all law and eludes all physical analysis.[37]

Gladden's "immanent God" entered human lives, not simply to save individual souls, but also to uplift society. The world of the spirit, Gladden argued, provides insights, aspirations, consolations, convictions, and hopes.

These things of the Spirit are the great realities. The existence of that world in which our higher nature dwells and from which we draw our inspirations is not a matter of conjecture....They are the only certainties. Everything else is fleeting and illusory. Continents subside and mountains explode and crumble, but no moment can ever come when truth will not be better than falsehood, and fidelity than treachery, and trust than suspicion. How much better? Infinitely better. No measurements can express the difference. Thus we know ourselves to be children of the Infinite; elements enter into our lives which lift us out of the realms of time and space, and reveal to us our larger parentage. It is only as we are able to draw into our life these great elements, to transfigure our human relationships and duties with the light that never was on sea or land, that life becomes significant and precious. Nothing can save our social morality but a constant infusion of this idealism. Where it is wanting, trade becomes piracy and politics plunder, the walls of the home collapse, and the state rests upon a volcano.[38]

Gladden wrote these words in the early 1900s. Forty years before he had considered himself one of a small minority within Congregationalism calling for a Progressive Orthodoxy. As his thought developed, Progressive Orthodoxy led naturally to the Social Gospel—each of the closely related philosophies depended on the belief in an immanent God, active in the world. During the 1860s and 1870s some of the more progressive Congregationalists had withdrawn from the church. Gladden characterized them as "Come-outers" and himself as a "Stay-inner."[39] But in 1904 a substantial portion of the church agreed with him, and he was elected Moderator, the symbolic leader of the Congregationalists.

By then he was an old man, with a flowing white beard. In a contemporary photograph the bald dome of his scalp suggests his active intellect. The twinkle in his eyes hints that the boy who had so longed for communion with God had at last found a spiritual life that "filled the world with beauty."

NOTES

[1] Arthur Cushman McGiffert, Jr., *No Ivory Tower: The Story of the Chicago Theological Seminary* (Chicago, 1965), 156.

[2] McGiffert, *No Ivory Tower*, 156.

[3] Walter Rauschenbusch, *Christianity and the Social Crisis* (New York, 1907), 422.

[4] Quotation from Marty, *Pilgrims in their Own Land*, 348.

[5] Edwin Scott Gaustad, *A Religious History of America* (New York, 1966), 240.

[6] Cayton, "Congregationalism," 492.

[7] Cayton, "Congregationalism," 482.

[8] Ahlstrom, *Religious History of the American People*, 794, 795.

[9] Quotation in Gaustad, *A Religious History of America*, 242.

[10] Quotation in Gaustad, *A Religious History of America*, 242.

[11] Washington Gladden, *Recollections* (Boston, 1909), 206.

[12] This quotation and the account of Gladden's youth that follows are from *Recollections*, 10-35.

[13] Gladden, the Millerites, and the evangelists: *Recollections*, 38, 59-61.

[14] Gladden, *Recollections*, 38, 39.

[15] Gladden, *Recollections*, 38, 39.

[16] Gladden, *Recollections*, 63-64.

[17] Gladden, *Recollections*, 116, 90.

[18] Gladden, *Recollections*, 91, 119.

[19] Gladden in Morrisania: *Recollections*, 119-121.

[20] Gladden in North Adams: *Recollections*, 164-68.

[21] Gladden and the shoe-factory strike: *Recollections*, 172-73.

[22] Gladden and Boss Tweed: *Recollections*, 205-6.

[23] Gladden, *Recollections*, 206.

[24] Gladden, *Recollections*, 206, 223.

[25] Gladden, *Recollections*, 224-25.

[26] Gladden, *Recollections*, 241.

[27] Gladden, *Recollections*, 242.

[28] Gladden, *Recollections*, 263-64.

[29] Gladden, *Recollections*, 251-52.

[30] Gladden, *Recollections*, 298.

[31] Gladden, *Recollections*, 299.

[32] Gladden, *Recollections*, 311, 310, 312, 315.

[33] Gladden and the Mission Board: *Recollections*, 402-7.

[34] Quotation from McGiffert, *No Ivory Tower*, 138.

[35] Gladden, *Recollections*, 371-72.

[36] Gladden, *Recollections*, 371.

[37] Gladden, *Recollections*, 427.

[38] Gladden, *Recollections*, 416-17.

[39] Gladden, *Recollections*, 430.

10
THE TWENTIETH CENTURY

THE ENDURING SOCIAL GOSPEL

During the twentieth century Congregationalism, which had its American beginnings in small wood-frame churches on the New England frontier, has taken
its place in a global community shaped by modern technology. Like other
church members, Congregationalists were brought face-to-face with the enduring
problem of evil in the world during the two great wars and the depression. The
international crises encouraged them to recognize their interdependence with
other Christians and to agree upon mergers with several other denominations.
And the social crisis of the depression, as well as the challenge of the civil
rights movement and modern environmental and social concerns, have kept
church members attuned to the problem of bringing the world closer to "the
suburbs of heaven."

At the national council meeting at Kansas City in 1913, Congregationalists
adopted a concise statement of "the things most surely believed among us concerning faith, polity, and fellowship." It is a useful description of
Congregationalism at the opening of the twentieth century:

FAITH

We believe in God the Father, infinite in wisdom, goodness and love; and in Jesus
Christ, his Son, our Lord and Saviour, who for us and our salvation lived and died and
rose again and liveth evermore; and in the Holy Spirit, who taketh of the things of
Christ and revealeth them to us, renewing, comforting, and inspiring the souls of
men. We are united in striving to know the will of God as taught in the Holy
Scriptures, and to our purpose to walk in the ways of the Lord, made known or to be
made known to us. We hold it to be the mission of the Church of Christ to proclaim
the gospel to all mankind, exalting the worship of the one true God, and laboring for
the progress of knowledge, the promotion of justice, the reign of peace, and the
realization of human brotherhood. Depending, as did our fathers, upon the continued

guidance of the Holy Spirit to lead us into all truth, we work and pray for the transformation of the world into the kingdom of God; and we look with faith for the triumph of righteousness and the life everlasting.

POLITY

We believe in the freedom and responsibility of the individual soul, and the right of private judgment. We hold to the autonomy of the local church and its independence of all ecclesiastical control. We cherish the fellowship of the churches, united in district, state, and national bodies, for council and co-operation in matters of common concern.

THE WIDER FELLOWSHIP

While affirming the liberty of our churches, and the validity of our ministry, we hold to the unity and catholicity of the Church of Christ, and will unite with all its branches in hearty co-operation, and will earnestly seek, so far as in us lies, that the prayer of our Lord for his disciples may be answered, that they all may be one.[1]

The Kansas City Statement suggests the degree to which dogmatic Calvinism had disappeared from Congregationalism. There is no discussion here of the means of grace, original sin, or predestination. On polity the declaration begins with a position congenial to early Puritanism, the affirmation of "the autonomy of the local church." But the reference to "district, state, and national bodies" suggests that Congregationalists had grown accustomed to regional associations and national bodies such as the American Board and the national council. Finally the endorsement of "wider fellowship" in the Kansas City Statement points to future, when many Congregationalists would unite with other denominations in forming new religious bodies.

The Social Gospel is sometimes thought to have gone into decline in the twentieth century. And to an extent it did. The Progressive movement, which dominated political life for the first decade and a half of the new century, brought about reforms that alleviated some of the problems the gospellers had attacked. In reaction to World War I Americans in the 1920s were less likely to support idealistic crusades than a generation before.

But religious history seldom resolves itself into crisp chronological schemes. The ideals of the Social Gospel movement continued to find support among the Congregationalists and still influence the church today. In 1919 the church's national council resolved to "work for a social order in which there will be none without opportunity to work and in which it will be impossible for idlers to live in luxury and for workers to live in poverty."[2] During the Roaring Twenties the national council went on record in favor of pacifism, labor unions, the eight-hour day, a minimum wage, unemployment insurance, and racial justice. The national council of 1925 attacked the "profit motive" itself—a position early Puritans would have found entirely congenial.

The depression reinforced Congregational interest in the social implications of their faith. A poll in 1934 showed that thirty-three percent of the clergy actually preferred socialism to capitalism. The parishioners tended to be more conservative, but the ministers were able to infuse an enduring tone of social concern into the church. In 1974 a study of United Church of Christ ministers by Harold E. Quinley revealed that they tended to be theological liberals, religious moderates, and social activists.[3]

THEOLOGICAL DEVELOPMENTS: THE EXAMPLE OF CHICAGO

The nineteenth century Congregationalist who had lamented the demise of sin would have been comforted by religious thought in the twentieth century. Particularly after World War I, theologians turned their attention once more to the problem of evil. The war with its millions of deaths had undermined naive assumptions about human perfectibility and progress. Karl Barth and Reinhold Niebuhr, pioneers of Neoorthodoxy, developed theologies that were reminiscent of Calvin and the early Puritans. They stressed humanity's limitations and the mystery of God.

Arthur Cushman McGiffert, Jr., who became professor of Christian theology at Chicago Theological Seminary in 1926, suggested the atmosphere that pervaded most Congregational households during the early twentieth century, when he described his own background. At the seminary he was the first faculty member who had been raised in a home which "took theological liberalism for granted." The family held weekly prayers and said grace at meals, and McGiffert was encouraged to learn Bible verses by heart. But he had been "largely ignorant" of orthodox Christian thought until he entered seminary, where he studied the traditional theology "much as he studied Buddhism or Hinduism, as an almost novel form of theological interpretation." He had never experienced an emotional revulsion against orthodoxy, an experience which had closed the minds of many liberals against "the faith of their fathers." As an example of the extremes to which religious rationalism had gone, McGiffert noted that "non-theistic humanists" could be found on the faculties of many seminaries. They were men who in reaction against "a popularly misconceived orthodoxy, to which they were exposed in their youth, had swung the full arc of the theological pendulum away."[4]

At the Chicago seminary and other Congregational seminaries even Bible study had lost its theological character. According to McGiffert many professors of the Bible actually drew their students away from the Bible as "the Word of God." They were so devoted to their methods of investigation that "the means of the investigation became almost ends in themselves." He noted that teachers introduced their students to the tools of research, but gave them little assistance in "getting at the basic meanings of the Biblical records."[5]

Men like Horace Bushnell and Washington Gladden had embraced Progressive Orthodoxy only after having been reared in the atmosphere of essentially

Calvinistic ideas. Their progress to a sense of friendship with God, had entailed at first a sense of unworthiness and estrangement. Although their theology stressed a proximate rather than a remote God, their experience had involved a progress from rejection to acceptance that would have been recognizable to the Puritans. This gave their faith an emotional edge that was harder to experience for men and women who had always believed God was easily accessible.

McGiffert held that many seminary students recovered a sense of the spiritual life through the study of "depth psychology." Many were influenced by Anton T. Boisen, who came to the Chicago seminary in 1927 as research associate in psychology and religion. He taught one quarter per year at the seminary, while devoting the remainder of his time to serving as chaplain of the state hospital for the emotionally disturbed at Worcester, Massachusetts. He published several books on religious psychology, including *The Exploration of the Inner World* (1936) and *Out of the Depths* (1960). Like William James, whom he admired, Boisen saw a relationship between religion and the experiences of "crazy people." He liked to point out to the skeptical that George Fox and John Bunyan had passed through mental disorders "before they finally found themselves."[6]

McGiffert noted that divinity students in the 1920s and 1930s tended to interpret human beings "as primarily minds, needing enlightenment, or as units within larger social wholes." In the process they tended to ignore "the individual's private inner life."[7] Of course, the "inner life" was exactly what had concerned the first Puritans most. Nor had such nineteenth-century liberals as Horace Bushnell and Washington Gladden rejected the religion of the heart— only the theological premises that seemed to stifle it. But in the twentieth century religious "liberalism" often meant a religion that was almost secular in orientation.

McGiffert claimed that Boisen's teaching revived the possibility of religious *experience*: "Boisen brought the individual in his tragedy and sin so poignantly and inescapably to the students' attention that the center of their concern began to shift." Many had been raised in a liberal theological tradition that tended to ignore sin and conversion. Boisen helped them understand that sin and salvation were not "outworn dogmatic terms."[8] Many years later McGiffert recalled, "Boisen's insights enabled me to move beyond a negative attitude toward orthodoxy to an appreciation of its appropriateness to some kinds of experience."[9]

Theology joined psychology at Chicago in reviving the experiential side of the Congregational tradition. The possibility of change grew with the appointment of Wilhelm Pauck to teach church history in 1927. Pauck was a brilliant young German, only twenty years old, who would become the first scholar to publish a critical study of Karl Barth in the United States. Pauck stated the Neoorthodox position clearly when he said, "I do not want to know how we can adjust our God belief to modern social or cultural life, but how we can penetrate this life with our faith." Believing that service to society had dulled the power of religion, he sought to restore "supertemporal content" of

Christianity.[10]

McGiffert described Pauck as a remarkable teacher who would begin his lecture as he entered the door and continue through the period without glancing at a note. He would single out one student, then another, to whom to speak as he walked around the classroom. A visiting student, trying to determine whether to attend the seminary, came to hear the famous professor. When Pauck shook his finger in the face of one student to emphasize a point, the visitor decided he would never attend such a doctrinaire seminary. But he changed his mind when a student talked back at Pauck "with equally emphatic voice and finger."[11]

As an apostle of Neoorthodoxy, Pauck challenged the liberalism that had come to replace Progressive Orthodoxy. But he did not retreat to the harsh dogmatism that Bushnellism had rejected. Once while visiting another seminary "of a fundamentalist persuasion" he was accosted by a student who asked him whether he had been saved. Pauck began a long list: "Do you mean saved according to St. Paul or St. Augustine or St. Jerome...."[12] Pauck embraced the Neoorthodox belief in a living God who stands outside, and sometimes against society. But in his rejection of fundamentalist self-righteousness, and in his enthusiasm for passionate dialogue he was as much the heir of Horace Bushnell as the critic of modern liberalism. (Bushnell's continuing influence is apparent also in McGiffert's statement: "My chief theological hero was Horace Bushnell."[13]) In giving credit to both liberalism and orthodoxy Pauck is representative of an important strand in twentieth century Congregationalism. Neoorthodoxy did not replace the liberalism that characterized preaching in many Congregational parishes, but it did take its place as one of the major lines of thought in modern Congregationalism. The ferment of ideas at the Chicago seminary during the 1920s and 1930s is one index of the way that psychological studies and Neoorthodoxy combined to revive in Congregationalism the spirituality and the appreciation of the supernatural that characterized the denomination during its first two and a half centuries.

CONGREGATIONAL ECUMENICALISM

From its beginning American Congregationalism exhibited contradictory tendencies in relating to other churches. The Puritans were on the one hand a particular people, proponents of *the* true church in the wilderness. They believed they were uniquely the heirs of the primitive church and that God dealt with them as he had dealt with the ancient Hebrews. Men and women who did not believe as they did were required to leave for Rhode Island or some other less holy ground.

But at the same time, the Puritans recognized their ties to other faiths. By and large, they did not think of themselves as having separated from the Church of England; they were simply the reforming *branch* of the church. They also had a certain respect for other Protestant denominations, sharing with Presbyterians an admiration for John Calvin and with Lutherans an admiration for Martin Luther. During the nineteenth century Congregationalists often co-operated with other denominations in missions, education, and social work.

In the 1871 meeting of the national council at Oberlin Congregationalists proclaimed that they were dedicated to fostering Christian unity rather than sectarian exclusiveness. The church adopted a declaration of unity that, in effect, invited other churches to federation: "We believe in 'the holy Catholic church.' It is our prayer and endeavor that the unity of the church may be more and more apparent, and that the prayer of our Lord for his disciples may be speedily and completely answered, and all be one."[14] In the years ahead Congregationalists kept alive the idea of church federation. Josiah Strong's Evangelical Alliance brought together members of many denominations in the 1880s and 1890s for cooperative efforts in fighting the evils of industrial America. Congregational minister Elias B. Stanford was instrumental in arranging a meeting at Carnegie Hall in 1905 where representatives of many denominations discussed the idea of confederation. And the principle of fellowship was reaffirmed in the Kansas City Statement of 1913.

The Congregationalists considered merging with other denominations several times before the actual mergers of the twentieth century. One of the early plans was successful. Beginning in 1852 certain Methodist churches in Georgia, Alabama, Florida, and Mississippi had withdrawn from the Methodist conference and formed the Congregational Methodist Church. In 1887 and 1888 about one-third of these churches joined the Congregationalists. Their action was not a merger in the sense of a union at the national level between two denominational administrations. Instead Congregational Methodist churches in some regions joined the local Congregational associations and have since been regarded as Congregational churches. In 1892 the national council welcomed these churches into fellowship.[15]

Other efforts in the nineteenth century were abortive. During the early nineteenth century the Plan of Union with the Presbyterians had resulted in a confederation that lasted for several decades. In 1886 the national council considered union with Free Will Baptists, an idea that fell before conflicts among the Baptists. In 1907 Congregationalists met at Chicago with Methodist and United Brethren delegates and adopted an act of union, subsequently rejected by Congregationalists because of differing views on local church autonomy. Discussions with the Episcopalians came to naught in 1923 when the Anglicans declared that only ordination by the bishops would be considered valid: historically minded Congregationalists must have recalled Archbishop William Laud and the Church of England's contribution to the Puritan migration. In 1927 Congregationalists discussed a renewed union with the Presbyterian Church, but no action followed.

Yet the ecumenical ideal remained strong. In 1895 the retiring moderator of the national council, Alonzo H. Quint, delivered an address that underscored the church's commitment to Christian union. "Congregationalism," he said, "is almost ashamed to be distinctive, and gladly it would be merged in the undivided

Church, if it found the undivided catholic Church in which to lose its name....What Congregationalism signifies to us is the absolute supremacy of the Lord Jesus Christ: the equality of all Christians in their relation to him; the responsibility and discipline of brotherhood in government....The Pilgrim principle of a spiritual kingdom, free and unshackled, carried forward by spiritual forces, and dependent upon the divine power vouchsafed to a willing church is the hope and prophecy of victory."[16]

Drawing on this ecumenical spirit, in 1927 the Congregationalists formalized a union with the Evangelical Protestant Church. It was a small pietistic denomination, Swiss and German in origin, with some six thousand members. The Evangelical Protestants embraced a liberal theology and social activism, positions congenial to the Congregationalists. An approving national council declared, "They are a very earnest body of believers, passionately devoted to the Bible only, earnestly rejecting all doctrinal creeds and statements, proclaiming Gospel liberty against all imposition of dogma."[17] The Evangelical Protestant churches were left to work out their own relationships with the Congregationalist state assemblies and were given seats on the national council. They were eager to unite with the Congregationalists in order to be part of a larger and more influential religious body. The Congregationalists, in turn, had nothing to lose by absorbing such a small and congenial denomination. In a sense, this merger "broke the ice" and established a comfortable precedent for later mergers.

Four years later, in 1931, the Congregationalists worked out a union with the Christian church. The members of this denomination were more rural than the Congregationalists and generally came from a lower economic stratum of society, but they shared many basic beliefs including local autonomy, individual freedom, and fellowship. The denomination had begun in a fashion that echoed in America Robert Browne's revolt against Anglicanism. In 1792 a Virginia Methodist minister named James O'Kelley broke away from his Methodist faith in order to replace episcopal authority with a "republican" government based on Christ and the Bible. (In seeking to discipline O'Kelley the Methodist bishop declared that "the government of this church is autocratical.")[18] He took with him about one thousand followers and twenty ministers. At first they called themselves the Republican Methodists.

Other leaders of the Christians broke away from several denominations. Rev. Abner Jones was a Vermont Baptist who insisted on being ordained simply as a Christian rather than a Baptist. He formed his first congregation at Lydon, Vermont, in 1801. Seven years latter an associate, Elias Smith, founded *The Herald of Gospel Liberty* to advertise their ideas—it has been called "the world's first religious periodical."[19] A third strand of the Christian church came from Barton W. Stone, a Kentucky Presbyterian, who was refused ordination because of an unorthodox view of the Trinity. In 1798 he was ordained by the Methodists and preached at camp meetings at Cane Ridge, Kentucky, and evangelized throughout the Midwest. He joined a group of pastors to found a church in which each member was to follow the Bible according to his own understanding, and Christian character rather than doctrinal uniformity was to be the standard of membership.

In general the Christians drew upon Baptists from New England, Methodists from Virginia and North Carolina, and Presbyterians from Kentucky. They might have gone their way as local denominations except that Smith's *Herald of Gospel Liberty* made them aware of each other, and they began to communicate and forge ties with each other. In 1820 they established an annual meeting called the United States Christian Convention. Emphasizing their independence they declared that the purpose of the meeting was to "discuss, admonish, advise and urge but [not to] command or legislate."[20] The Puritans had described their early synods in the same terms. At the turn of the century the churches formed the General Convention of Christian Churches, which included the original three groups plus a group of churches formed by freed blacks after the Civil War.

Negotiations between the Congregationalists and the Christians began in the 1890s. The two denominations proceeded cautiously, and intermittently, with the idea of a merger. For a time the Christians worried that the Congregationalists were too much a denomination—too limited by commitment to creed and polity—to suit the openness cherished by the Christians. Eventually, however, negotiations were revived and a merger was completed. In 1929 delegates from the two denominations met at Plymouth Church in Detroit and sang "Blest Be the Tie that Binds" in commemoration of their union. At the time of the merger in 1931, the Congregationalists numbered roughly 1 million, and the Christians 100,000. The new body was known as the Congregational Christian Churches, although individual parishes could still call themselves Congregationalist.

FORMING THE UNITED CHURCH OF CHRIST

Encouraged by the success of these mergers, the Congregationalists were receptive to the idea of yet another merger in the 1940s, when negotiations began with the Evangelical and Reformed church. This organization was the product of an earlier merger, in 1934, between the Reformed church in the United States and the Evangelical Synod of North America.

The history of the Reformed church in America began with the immigration of Dutch Reformed settlers to New York during the seventeenth century. A few decades later German immigrants brought the German Reformed church to America. Although the two bodies were similar in polity and theology, the difference in language kept them separate. Because German immigration during the eighteenth century outstripped Dutch immigration, the German Reformed church members outnumbered those from Holland by two to one by the end of the colonial period. A large body of German Reformed settlers went to Pennsylvania in the 1730s and later. They were at first uncomfortable with the religious diversity of Pennsylvanians. One complained that they were "living among all sorts of errorists, as Independents, Puritans, Anabaptists, the New-born, the Saturday-folks...yea, as living among some of the most dreadful heretics."[21] Because they did not immigrate as congregations, as the Puritans often did, they began with no ordained ministers. A tailor and a schoolmaster-turned-farmer were the first preachers They gained legitimacy through association with the Dutch Reformed church. The schoolmaster-farmer, John Philip Boehm, was ordained by the Dutch and is credited with founding the German Reformed Church in America. He formed a dozen churches and each month for twenty years traveled a circuit covering a hundred miles.

But by 1750 the German Reformed congregations were a force to reckon with in Pennsylvania, where they had sixty-four churches. In various ways they entered the broad stream of American life. Philip Wilhelm Otterbein led a revival corresponding to eighteenth-century awakenings in other denominations. Many Germans fought in the American Revolution. The German Reformed church at Allentown preserved the Liberty Bell in a time of crisis, and a German Reformed minister entered a camp housing Hessian prisoners of war and lectured them on the evil of serving the British.

At the meeting of the first synod of the German Reformed church, at Lancaster, Pennsylvania, in 1793, there were some fifteen thousand members of the communion in 178 churches. The members were, however, mainly of German and Swiss origin. Their adherence to the German language at first prevented them from proselytizing in the nation as a whole.[22] But as church members joined the westward migration, ministers followed, often working as circuit riders among scattered groups of German Reformed communicants. "Like the first Puritans, they preached under trees, in real barns where some of the congregation sat in hay mows. They preached in log cabins, town halls, once in a jail."[23]

In time the German Reformed church showed an aptitude for ecumenical activities. Philip Schaff, a Reformed church member and noted historian, popularized the saying: "In essentials unity; in doubtful points freedom; in all things love."[24] During the early eighteenth century the Reformed church made an effort to unite with German Lutherans in America—in Prussia the Reformed and Lutheran churches had been united by law in 1817. But the effort in America was a failure. The principal success of the church at midcentury was the uniting of the various parts of the German Reformed church itself across the United States with the formation of a general synod in 1863. In 1869 the word German was dropped from the title and the denomination came to be known as the Reformed Church in the United States. By 1884 membership had reached 150,000.[25]

In 1924 the Reformed church completed a merger with the small Hungarian Reformed church. A decade later a merger was completed with a much larger body, the Evangelical Synod of North America, whose membership totaled 250,000. They were mainly midwestern German-speaking persons, both

Lutheran and Reformed, who had completed the sort of union achieved in Prussia in 1817. The Evangelical Synod traced its origins to Luther; the Reformed church venerated Calvin and Zwingli. But the common Reformation and German heritage of both groups facilitated the merger. In 1932–33 the two denominations adopted a plan of union, declaring that they were "under the conviction that they were in agreement on the essential doctrines of the Christian faith and on the ideals of the Christian life." The new Evangelical and Reformed church had 600,000 members in three thousand parishes.[26] Its ministry included two of the giants of modern theology, Paul Tillich and Reinhold Niebuhr.

In 1942, only eleven years after the Congregationalists and Christians had merged and eight years after the Evangelical-Reformed union, representatives of both bodies began to discuss a merger. An agreement was reached in 1947, and in 1949 Congregationalists voted in support by a three-to-one margin. But merger with such a large denomination and the contemplation of a new name, the United Church of Christ, encountered stiff resistance from some Congregationalists, who felt that their traditional values would be lost in the new organization. Some Congregationalists had even objected to the much easier union with the smaller Christian church in 1931. (At that time one old-timer had allegedly complained, "I've been a Congregationalist all my life, and no one is going to make a Christian of me now."[27]) The new union was with a much larger church, whose ethnic composition was far different than the typical Congregational church. Differences of style added to the difficulties. Congregational delegates to the merger meeting complained that the Reformed and Evangelical delegates smoked too many cigars. The other side was offended by the apparent affectation in the speech of the New England Congregationalists. Even chosing a name for the national organization caused problems. The Evangelical and Reformed churches met nationally in a "synod." They had formerly used the terms coetus and classis. But one term was obscure and the other had authoritarian connotations to members of the Reformed church. So they had used the word "synod," a choice the Congregationalists eventually accepted.

In 1950 a general synod was planned, with delegates from both the Reformed and Evangelical churches and the Congregational churches. But in Brooklyn a group of Congregationalists took their case to court, claiming that essential elements of their church, especially the rights of local congregations, would be jeopardized by a merger. The court agreed, delaying the proposed merger.

Two years later, however, an appellate court reversed the lower court decision, clearing the way for the merger. Five more years were required to complete the arrangements. Then in 1957 the United Church of Christ (UCC) became a reality with a total membership of better than two million. The general council, having "directed" the Congregational church for a century, was now absorbed into the general synod of the United Church of Christ.

The Synod of 1957 began drafting a constitution, which was completed in

1961 and submitted to the churches for approval. There were dissenting votes. One of the thirty-three Evangelical and Reformed synods rejected it. The majority in thirty-five Congregational conferences approved, but substantial numbers of the member churches did not. In Massachusetts, for example, 39 of the 454 Congregational Churches rejected the constitution. Congregations that rejected the constitution went on worshipping as before and continued fellowship with other churches through ministerial associations at the regional level. But they could not be represented in the national synod. The era that brought merger also brought schism. Two dissident groups, calling themselves the Conservative Congregational Association and the National Association of Congregational Christian Churches, refused to join the United Church of Christ at all, taking with them three hundred churches. And a few other parishes remained independent of any of the denominations.

In 1959 the synod of the United Church of Christ adopted a statement of faith, emphasizing that it was not prescriptive, but a basis for study and discussion. It is marked by simplicity and brevity:

We believe in God, the Eternal Spirit, Father of our Lord Jesus Christ and our Father, and to his deeds we testify:

He calls the worlds into being, created man in his own image, and sets before him the ways of life and death.

He seeks in holy love to save all people from aimlessness and sin.

He judges men and nations by his righteous will declared through prophets and apostles.

In Jesus Christ, the man of Nazareth, our crucified and risen Lord, he has come to us and shared our common lot, conquering sin and death and reconciling the world to himself.

He bestows upon us his Holy Spirit, creating and renewing the church of Jesus Christ, binding in covenant faithful people of all ages, tongues, and races.

He calls us into his church to accept the cost and joy of discipleship, to be his servants in the service of men, to proclaim the gospel to all the world and resist the powers of evil, to share in Christ's baptism and eat at his table, to join him in his passion and victory.

He promises to all who trust him forgiveness of sins and fullness of grace, courage in the struggle for justice and peace, his presence in trial and rejoicing, and eternal life in his kingdom which has no end.

Blessing and honor, glory and power be unto him.

Amen.[28]

CONGREGATIONALISM IN MODERN AMERICA

At Chicago Theological Seminary a lovely interior courtyard bears witness to the continuity of Congregationalism from the earliest times to the present. Known as the Clarence Sidney Funk Cloisters, the memorial is in the form of stones from various historical places. The corbels are designed to represent the truths in the Kansas City Statement of Faith (1913). Some of the stones are from biblical and medieval times: one is from Solomon's quarries near Damascus, another from the Crusader Church near Bethel, Palestine. The Puritans are represented by two bricks from William Bradford's Scrooby Manor House and a fragment of Plymouth Rock. A crystal from the Rocky Mountains symbolizes the home missions, and a small stone from China represents overseas missionaries.

The United Church of Christ today is like that courtyard at Chicago. Its modern life draws on many sources—some from the Congregationalists, some from the Christians and the Evangelical and Reformed Churches. Some developments in the church, especially its current position on women, reflect changes in the modern world.

The social consciousness of the church has expanded in the twentieth century to encompass a greater role for women in the ministry. In 1893 there were only nine fully ordained women in Congregational churches. Four years before the Hartford Seminary had been the first to open its doors to women; but even there women first had to declare that they did *not* intend to be ministers. That rule lasted until 1920. During the 1910s and 1920s positions opened up for women as social workers for the church, but this was a mixed blessing, as such opportunities were often cited as justification for barring women from the ministry. By the 1950s women were admitted to United Church of Christ seminaries more frequently, but in the UCC as in other denominations their acceptance has been slow. For a time the most promising path for a woman to the ministry was to acquire her husband's parish upon his death. As recently as 1988 a historian noted that UCC women "face longer periods of unemployment, lower salaries, and less opportunity for full responsibility for parishes."[29] Nonetheless, the gradual movement in the church to embrace larger roles for women parallels that of society as a whole—slow, but steady progress.[30]

Membership in the United Church of Christ reached 2.2 million in 1960 but subsequently declined to 1.7 million in 1985. The decline follows a pattern of general membership decline among liberal Protestant denominations after 1960. Members of the United Church of Christ are associated with some six thousand religious institutions (including churches, hospitals, schools, and retirement homes) and worship under the leadership of ten thousand ministers. The highest concentration of communicants is in the Northeast and the upper Midwest. But the Church's thirty-nine subdivisions—known as conferences—cover the entire United States. The Puritan legacy of many of these churches is suggested by the frequency with which UCC churches and the independent Congregational churches incorporate Pilgrim icons into their names. For example, there are "Plymouth" churches in Stockton, California; Bellevue, Washington; Crete, Nebraska; Lawrence, Kansas; Denver, Colorado; Beaumont, Texas; and Miami, Florida, to name a few locales.[31]

Many elements in the modern church would perplex the early Puritans.

Salvation by grace is not presented in the same doctrinal framework as in Puritanism. Such doctrines as infant damnation, arbitrary election, and original sin are generally omitted from the pulpit. Horace Bushnell's revolution in religious sensibility—the Progressive Orthodoxy, infused with new life by Neoorthodoxy—has won over most modern descendents of the Congregationalists. That spirit is reflected in the writing of Douglas Horton, one of the leaders of the movement to form the United Church of Christ. In this passage he provides a striking image of the age-old Congregational concern with the relationship between work and grace:

> The fishermen off the southwest coast of England at the close of their three or four days' work often lift their sails in the evening, although on the deck of the vessel one cannot feel a breath of air stirring. Then all hands turn in, leaving only one man on deck for watch. And it is said that more time than not in the morning they find themselves closer to port, since the upper winds not felt on the deck breathe against the sails and carry the vessel homeward. So it is with each one of us: Let a man lift his sails toward the spirit of Christ; he may not at any given moment feel very different from another man who never thinks of doing so, but let ten years, twenty years, thirty years pass by: The man who has been in contact with Christ will have a poise, a master over the demons of his life.[32]

Religious ideas today are often based on a smorgasbord of sources. For many, Cotton Mather, Jonathan Edwards, and even Horace Bushnell may be less important than modern writers from a variety of religious backgrounds. Steve Coates, a minister at Eastgate Congregational Church in Bellevue, Washington, recently cited a book by Matthew Fox, a Catholic writer, as one of the books he admires most. In *The Coming of the Cosmic Christ*, Fox sets forth a "creation centered theology" that stressed the interaction between God, nature and humanity.[33] An ecological consciousness informs one of the more popular books by a Congregationalist in this century: *Other Nature Sermons* by Charles Edward Jefferson. Jefferson's subjects included grass, leaves, trees, rain, snow, brooks, rivers, dawn and dusk, and hurricanes and volcanoes.[34]

In this, as in many other areas of Congregational history, continuity exists in the midst of change. The reverence inspired by nature, for example, so apparent in the writings of Jonathan Edwards and Horace Bushnell, finds its counterpart in writings in the United Church of Christ. For example, during the summer of 1982, Jeremy Anderson, a parishioner of the United Church of Christ in Cheney, Washington, wrote these lines in a poem entitled, "The Real Reason:"

The reason I really came
Was not to enjoy mist shrouded vistas,
Nor visit alpine lakes or
Meadows ablaze with summer flowers.
I didn't come to stalk the wiley goat,
Nor gaze at doe and fawns or soaring hawks.

I didn't come to listen to conies and marmots whistle,
Or buntings twitter, camp robbers cackle or eagles scream.
I didn't come to be lulled by the roar of falling water,
Or the sooing of the wind in trees and brush.
I didn't come to smell the fragrance of pine and fir,
Or the aroma of frying fish and campfire smoke.

I didn't come to test my feet on rocky trails,
Nor my mettle on slopes of talus and scree.
I didn't come to share the comradery and
Joy of discovery with sons or boon companions.
I certainly didn't come to sleep on this hard
Ground, blasted by chill winds and driving rain.

The real reason, the only reason I came,
Was for this handful of huckleberries.[35]

The sentiment underlying the poem, that grace can be found in ordinary things, recurs often in modern preaching and writing. For Jonathan Edwards or the Puritans the "real reason" for anything was God. Their world, in which even "wine was from God," seems distant from a world in which the grape—or huckleberry—can itself be a source of gratitude. But even Edwards, and certainly Horace Bushnell, found God in nature. In each case the underlying principle is that of grace abounding, infusing the fortunate with reverence for God and for life.

This sensibility appeared in a sermon preached by Forester Freeman at the First Congregational Church in Berkeley, California in the fall of 1989. In the address, entitled "A Good Word for Mysticism," Freeman grappled with the central question that engaged the Puritans: how do you achieve communion with God? He suggested that mysticism is "the experience of the divine presence within us." And he indicated that it had probably occurred to many persons in the congregation. "For one person it happened when listening to Handel, for another person when going to a particularly gripping movie, for another watching a little child in her crib. It keeps coming in such a variety of ways that we can hardly describe it adequately. I know a man who says it has happened to him several times when he has been running....I think God in creating us built this yearning in to every human being as standard equipment just like the hunger of our bodies for food. It is expressed in all religions throughout the ages."[36]

Certainly the yearning for communion with God—and its occasional attainment—was the central fact in Puritan life. There are moments in the modern churches, like those in Puritan times or in the nineteenth century, when Washington Gladden's precept seems alive: "We know ourselves to be children of the Infinite; elements enter into our lives which lift us out of the realms of time and space, and reveal to us our larger parentage." In such encounters we may see the underlying kinship of John Winthrop, Jonathan Edwards, Mary Fish, Horace Bushnell, Douglas Horton and thousands of other Congregationalists.

NOTES

[1] "The Kansas City Statement," in Gaius Glenn Atkins and Frederick L. Fagley, *A History of American Congregationalism* (Boston, 1942), 404-5.

[2] Cayton, "Congregationalism," 494.

[3] Cayton, "Congregationalism," 494, 496.

[4] McGiffert, *No Ivory Tower*, 219, 220; letter to the author, February 5, 1990.

[5] McGiffert, *No Ivory Tower*, 227.

[6] Quotation from McGiffert, *No Ivory Tower*, 206.

[7] McGiffert, *No Ivory Tower*, 207.

[8] McGiffert, *No Ivory Tower*, 207.

[9] McGiffert, letter to the author, February 5, 1990.

[10] Quotation from McGiffert, *No Ivory Tower*, 226, 225.

[11] McGiffert, *No Ivory Tower*, 227.

[12] Quotation from McGiffert, *No Ivory Tower*, 227.

[13] McGiffert, letter to the author, February 5, 1990.

[14] Quotation from Marion L. Starkey, *The Congregational Way* (New York, 1966), 305.

[15] Fagley and Atkins, *Congregationalism*, 347.

[16] Quotation from Fagley and Atkins, *Congregationalism*, 348.

[17] "Minutes of the National Council," in Fagley and Atkins, *Congregationalism*, 351.

[18] Lowell H. Zuck, *European Roots of the United Church of Christ* (n.p., 1967), 15; Starkey, *Congregational Way*, 307.

[19] Starkey, *Congregational Way*, 307.

[20] Quotation from Starkey, *Congregational Way*, 308.

[21] Quotation from Edwin Scott Gaustad, *Historical Atlas of Religion in America* (New York, 1976), 28.

[22] Gaustad, *Atlas*, 28-29, 100.

[23] Starkey, *Congregational Way*, 312.

[24] Quotation from Gaustad, *Atlas*, 29.

[25] Gaustad, *Atlas*, 100-102.

[26] Starkey, *Congregational Way*, 315; Gaustad, *Atlas*, 102.

[27] Quotation from Starkey, *Congregational Way*, 316.

[28] "Statement of Faith" in United Church of Christ, *Who We Are, What We Believe* (New York, 1980), pamphlet, no pagination.

[29] Cayton, "Congregationalism," 496.

[30] Cayton, "Congregationalism," 481.

[31] Carolyn E. Goddard, ed., *On the Trail of the UCC: A Historical Atlas of the United Church of Christ* (New York, 1981).

[32] Douglas Horton, "Demons that Destroy Vocation," in Douglas Horton, William Blakeman Lampe, and Ernest Fremont Tittle, *Christian Vocation: A Series of Radio Sermons* (Boston, 1945). 27.

[33] Author's interview with Steve Coates, January 17, 1990.

[34] Charles Edward Jefferson, *Other Nature Sermons* (New York, 1931).

[35] Forester Freeman, "A Good Word For Mysticism," Sermon Preached at First Congregational Church, Berkeley, California, October 29, 1989 [pamphlet].

[36] Forester Freeman, "A Good Word For Mysticism," Sermon Preached at First Congregational Church, Berkeley, California, October 29, 1989 [pamphlet].

APPENDIX: CHRONOLOGY

1582	Robert Brown issues statement of Congregational principles.
1620	Pilgrims arrive in Massachusetts and found Plymouth Plantation.
1630	John Winthrop arrives in Boston with roughly one thousand followers.
1636	Harvard College founded to train Puritan ministers.
1636–37	During the Antinomian crisis spiritual-minded Puritans in Massachusetts Bay criticize the Congregational leadership. Church membership system based on testimony of conversion experience ("visible saints") begins to take hold.
1646–48	Cambridge Synod meets, drafts Cambridge Platform, containing fundamental Congregational beliefs.
1657, 1662	Congregationalists adopt the Half-Way Covenant, liberalizing requirements for baptism—many dissent.
1679–80	The Reforming Synod adopts a new confession of faith.
1692	Tensions in Puritan society lead to the execution of twenty alleged witches in region of Salem, Massachusetts.
1705	Proposals of 1705 in Massachusetts recommend firmer ministerial control of the church—not officially adopted, but clerical associations take hold anyway.
1708	Saybrook Platform guarantees ministers more authority in religious affairs in Connecticut.
1737	Jonathan Edwards publishes *A Faithful Narrative of the Surprising Work of God*, describing a revival in the Connecticut River valley.
1740	George Whitfield preaches in New England, inaugurating the Great Awakening.
1742	Charles Chauncy publishes *Enthusiasm Described and Cautioned Against*, criticizing the "excesses" of the Great Awakening.

1742   Jonathan Edwards publishes *Some Thoughts Concerning the Present Revival of Religion in New England*, defending the revival as a work of God.

1742   Jonathan Edwards publishes *A Careful and Strict Inquiry into the Modern Prevailing Notions of the Freedom of the Will*, defending Calvinistic doctrine in the language of Newton and Locke.

1784   Charles Chauncy publishes *The Mystery Hid from Ages and Generations*, a treatise on universal salvation and an indication of the growth within Congregationalism of a strain of thought that would soon lead to schism and the formation of a new denomination, Unitarianism.

1801   Plan of Union adopted with Presbyterian Church—much cooperation during next half century, especially in the West.

1805   Jedidiah Morse provokes Unitarian schism with criticism of appointment of liberal Henry Ware as Hollis Professor of Divinity at Harvard.

1810   American Board of Commissioners for Foreign Missions, composed mainly of Congregationalists, advocates missionary work abroad.

1818, 1819   Church disestablished in Connecticut and New Hampshire, respectively, requiring Congregationalists to rely on voluntary contributions.

1820   Congregationalists begin missionary work in Hawaii.

1826   American Board of Home Missions, drawing support from Congregationalists and Presbyterians, begins missionary work in the West.

1828   Nathaniel William Taylor, founder of the New Haven Theology, publishes *Concio ad Clerum*, emphasizing individual's role in salvation.

1833   Church disestablished in Massachusetts.

1836   Presbyterian heresy trial of Lyman Beecher, president of Lane Seminary, creates tension in Presbyterian-Congregational union.

1837   Conservatives gain control of Presbyterian general assembly, begin dismantling Plan of Union.

1847   Horace Bushnell publishes *Christian Nurture*, focusing on education rather than conversion as the path to salvation.

1852   Albany convention of Congregationalists from throughout the United States reflects a growing sense of denominational unity, abandons the Plan of Union with the Presbyterians.

1853   American Congregational Union formed, promotes the denomination, especially through helping to build meetinghouses.

1865   The Burial Hill Declaration of Faith, a simplified creed, reaffirms the unity of the Congregational Church.

1886   Washington Gladden publishes *Applied Christianity: Moral Aspects of Social Questions*, a classic statement of the social gospel.

1913   The Kansas City Statement rejects Calvinist tradition for liberal position on faith.

1931	Congregationalists unite with the General Convention of the Christian Church to form the Congregational Christian Churches. (The Christian Church, based in the South, had grown up in the nineteenth century with members drawn chiefly from the Baptists, Methodists, and Presbyterians.)
1957	Uniting General Synod selects 30 men and women to draw up a Statement of Faith for a new denomination, the United Church of Christ.
1961	Union with the Evangelical and Reformed Church produces the United Church of Christ. (The Evangelical and Reformed Church was itself a union of the German Reformed Church and the Evangelical Synod of North America, an assembly of German Lutheran and Reformed churches in the Midwest.)
1961-Present	Some Congregational churches are independent; some belong to the National Association of Congregational Christian Churches; most former Congregational churches now belong to the United Church of Christ.

BIBLIOGRAPHICAL ESSAY

This essay is a guide to further reading in the history of Congregationalism. Many other sources, not listed here, are available on more specialized topics. These citations will lead the interested reader to others. Further citations appear in the biographical section of the book, and should be consulted for books and articles on persons whose biographies are included.

The weighting of the bibliography to the early history of Congregationalism reflects the pattern of historical research on the denomination. Many more books and articles have been written about the first two centuries of Congregationalism in America than about the subsequent century and a half. In comparison to earlier years, the sources for twentieth-century Congregationalism are meager. In part, this is because Puritanism has exercised a spell over historians, drawing their attention to the colonial period. In part, it is because twentieth-century historians tend to emphasize broad trends in American religion rather than the story of particular denominations. In addition, the merger of 1957 that formed the United Church of Christ has tended to diminish interest in a unique Congregational history. Nevertheless, one hopes that this bibliography, which suggests the riches available for the study of early Congregationalism, will encourage others to regret the paucity of nineteenth- and twentieth-century sources and contribute to the postrevolutionary history of Congregationalism.

BIBLIOGRAPHIES AND GENERAL HISTORIES

No bibliography is complete without a list of other bibliographies—and bibliographies of bibliographies. These are especially valuable: Nelson R. Burr, *Religion in American Life* (New York: Appleton-Century-Crofts, 1971); Burr, *A Critical Bibliography of Religion in America*, 2 vols. (Princeton: Princeton University Press, 1961); Edwin Scott Gaustad, *American Religious History* (Washington, D.C.: Service Center for Teachers of History, 1966); Francis Paul

Prucha, *Handbook for Research in American History: A Guide to Bibliographies and Other Reference Works* (Lincoln: University of Nebraska Press, 1987); David L. Ammerman and Philip D. Morgan, *Books about Early America: 2001 Titles* (Williamsburg, Va.: Institute of Early American History and Culture, 1989); H. M. Dexter, *The Congregationalism of the Last Three Hundred Years as Seen in Its Literature*, 2 vols. (New York: B. Franklin, 1970; originally published London: Hodder and Stoughton, 1879); Dexter, *A Handbook of Congregationalism* (Boston: Congregational Publishing Company, 1880); John F. Wilson, ed., *Church and State in America: A Bibliographical Guide*, 2 vols. (Westport, Conn: Greenwood Press, 1986, 1987).

Several bibliographies cover all works printed in the United States prior to 1839. These include many sermons and other writings relating to the history of Congregationalism. They are especially valuable because many libraries have microcards containing the texts of the books cited. The bibliographies are: Charles Evans et al., *American Bibliography*, 14 vols. (Chicago: Blakeley Press, 1903–59) [covers 1639–1800]; Roger P. Bristol, *Supplement to Charles Evans' American Bibliography* (Charlottesville: University of Virginia Press, 1970); Ralph Shaw, *American Bibliography*, 23 vols. (New York: Scarecrow Press, 1958–1966) [covers 1801–1819]; Richard Shoemaker, *American Imprints*, 22 vols. (New York and London: Scarecrow Press, 1964–78) [covers 1821–1839].

Many Puritan manuscripts have been printed in historical journals. A useful guide to these is provided by George Selement in "A Check List of Manuscript Materials Relating to Seventeenth-Century New England Printed in Historical Collections," *Bulletin of the New York Public Library*, 79 (1976), 416-47. For manuscript records of the New England churches see: Harold Field Worthley, *An Inventory of the Records of the Particular (Congregational) Churches of Massachusetts Gathered 1620–1805* (Cambridge: Harvard University Press, 1970).

Several thousand books and articles have been written about the Congregationalists, but surprisingly few survey the whole history of the church. The exceptions are: Giaus Glenn Atkins and Frederick L. Fagley, *History of American Congregationalism* (Boston and Chicago: Pilgrim Press, 1942) [a thematic survey]; Williston Walker, *A History of the Congregational Churches in the United States* (New York: Christian Literature, 1894) [a classic account, still useful after almost one hundred years]; Marion Starkey, *The Congregational Way: The Role of the Pilgrims and their Heirs in Shaping America* (Garden City, N.Y.: Doubleday, 1966) [a colorful and impressionistic survey]. Also: A. A. Rouner, Jr., *The Congregational Way of Life* (Englewood Cliffs, N.J.: Prentice-Hall, 1960); Daniel Thomas Jenkins, *Congregationalism: A Restatement* (New York: Harper, 1954); Leonard Bacon, *The Story of the Churches: The Congregationalists* (New York: Baker and Taylor, 1904). The course of Congregational history can also be traced though an excellent collection of documents: Williston Walker, *The Creeds and Platforms of Congregationalism* (New York: Charles Scribner's Sons, 1893; and subsequent editions) is an excellent compilation of documents beginning with Richard Brown's statement of 1582.

Several general histories that provide valuable insights into the forces shaping American Christianity as a whole give the reader perspective on the history of Congregationalism: Winthrop S. Hudson, *The Great Tradition of the American Churches* (New York: Harper's Brothers, 1953; and subsequent editions); H. Richard Niebuhr, *The Kingdom of God in America* (New York: Harper & Brothers, 1937); H. Richard Niebuhr, *The Social Sources of Denominationalism* (New York: Henry Holt, 1929); Peter G. Mode, *The Frontier Spirit in American Christianity* (New York: Macmillan, 1923); William W. Sweet, *Revivalism in America: Its Origin, Growth and Decline* (New York: Charles Scribner's Sons, 1944); Bernard A. Weisberger, *They Gathered at the River: The Story of the Great Revivalists* (Boston: Little, Brown, 1958); Wilbur Edel, *Defenders of the Faith: Religion and Politics from the Pilgrim Fathers to Ronald Reagan* (Westport, Conn.: Greenwood Press, 1987); Martin E. Marty, *Pilgrims in Their Own Land: 500 Years of Religion in America* (Boston: Little, Brown, 1984); and David S. Lovejoy, *Religious Enthusiasm in the New World* (Cambridge: Harvard University Press, 1985).

CONGREGATIONAL WOMEN

Works on Congregational women are cited in the bibliographies following biographical sketches, and women appear in many other books noted on these pages. But in view of the growth of women's history as a field of scholarship, these titles are offered as an example of works available. Richard D. Shiels, "The Feminization of American Congregationalism, 1730–1835," *American Quarterly*, 33 (1981), 46-62, focuses on the increased proportion of women in the church after the Revolution and the ways that the Calvinistic message was softened to accommodate their needs. Carol F. Karlsen, *The Devil in the Shape of a Woman: Witchcraft in Colonial New England* (New York: W. W. Norton, 1987) explores why the preponderance of New Englanders accused of witchcraft were women. Judith R. Gething, "Christianity and Couverture: Impact on the Legal Status of Women in Hawaii, 1820–1920," *Hawaiian Journal of History*, 11 (1977), 188-220, discusses the impact of Congregationalism on the status of women. In "'Poor Richard' Meets the Native American: Schooling for Young Indian Women in Eighteenth-Century Massachusetts," *Pacific Historical Review*, 49 (1980), Margaret Connell Szasz shows that Eleazar Wheelock's efforts to educate Indian girls failed because of his narrow goal—teaching them housekeeping skills and elementary reading and writing so that they could support Indian husbands who would preach among the natives. Carol Kammen, "The Problem of Professional Careers for Women: Letters of Juanita Breckenridge, 1872–1893," *New York History*, 55 (1974), 281-300, tells the story of the first female graduate of Oberlin Theological Seminary, a woman of "lofty" aspirations, who was able to serve only one year as a minister. Mary Maples Dunn, "Saints and Sisters: Congregational and Quaker Women in the Early Colonial Period," *American Quarterly*, 30 (1978), 582-601, argues that Puritan women were "disciplined to silence" whereas Quaker women were encouraged to play a role in the church.

See also: "Jeanette Carter Gadt, "Women and Protestant Culture: The Quaker Dissent from Puritanism" (Ph. D. thesis, University of California, Los Angeles, 1974); Cheryl Walker, "In the Margin: The Image of Women in Early Puritan Poetry," in Peter White, ed., *Puritan Poets and Poetics: Seventeenth Century American Poetry in Theory and Practice* (University Park: Pennsylvania State University Press, 1985), 111-26; Edmund S. Morgan, *The Puritan Family: Religion and Domestic Relations in Seventeenth-Century New England* (Boston: Boston Public Library, 1944; New York: Harper and Row, 1966); Pattie Cowell, "Puritan Women Poets in America," in Peter White, ed., *Puritan Poets and Poetics*, 21-32; Sarah Moore Scott, "A Thematic Study of the Writings of Puritan Women from the Time of the Original Settlers to 1770" (Ph. D. thesis, Southern Illinois University, 1981); Linda K. Kerber, "Can a Woman Be an Individual? The Limits of Puritan Tradition in the Early Republic," *Texas Studies in Literature and Language*, 25 (1983), 165-178; Margaret Olofson Thickstun, *Fictions of the Feminine: Puritan Doctrine and the Representation of Women* (Ithaca, N.Y.: Cornell University Press, 1988).

THE ENGLISH BACKGROUND

The literature on English Puritanism—the background to American Congregationalism—is voluminous. The following titles are a small sample of available works. William Haller, *The Rise of Puritanism* (New York: Columbia University Press, 1938; 1957) gives an excellent account of the growth of Puritanism in England; scholarly and colorful. Haller's *Liberty and Reformation* (New York: Columbia University Press, 1955) describes the growth of the idea of liberty within Puritanism during the years of the English Civil Wars. M. M. Knappen, *Tudor Puritanism: A Chapter in the History of Idealism* (Chicago: University of Chicago Press, 1939) is the standard history of early Puritan dissent. See also: J. Sears McGee, *The Godly Man in Stuart England* (New Haven: Yale University Press, 1976); Patrick Collinson, *The Elizabethan Puritan Movement* (Berkeley: University of California Press, 1967); Collinson, *The Religion of Protestants: The Church in English Society 1559–1625* (Oxford: Clarenden Press, 1982); Collinson, *Godly People: Essays on English Protestantism and Puritanism* (London: Hambledon, 1983); Collinson, *English Puritanism* (London: Historical Association, 1983); Arthur Percival Newton, *The Colonizing Activities of the English Puritans* (New Haven: Yale University Press, 1914; Port Washington, N.Y.: Kennikat Press, 1966); Geoffrey Nuttall, *Visible Saints: The Congregational Way, 1640–1660* (Oxford: Blackwell, 1957); Horton Davies, *Worship and Theology in England*, 5 vols. (Princeton: Princeton University Press, 1961–75); J. J. Scarisbrick, *The Reformation and the English People* (Oxford: Blackwell, 1984); Christopher Haigh, "Some Aspects of the Recent Historiography of the English Reformation," in W. J. Mommsen, ed., *The Urban Classes, the Nobility, and the Reformation* (Stuttgart: Klett-Cotta, 1980); Dewey Wallace, "George Gifford, Puritan Propaganda and Popular Religion in Elizabethan England," *Sixteenth Century*

Journal, 9 (1978), 27-49; Wallace, *Puritans and Predestination: Grace in English Protestant Theology, 1525–1695* (Chapel Hill: University of North Carolina, 1982); Michael McGiffert, "Covenant, Crown, and Commons in Elizabethan Puritanism," *Journal of British Studies* 20 (Fall 1980), 35-52; Theodore De Welles, "Sex and Sexual Attitudes in Seventeenth-Century England: The Evidence from Puritan Diaries," *Renaissance and Reformation*, 12 (1988).

A number of books and articles touch on the problem of defining Puritanism. Some of the most noteworthy are: Charles H. George and Katherine George, *The Protestant Mind of the English Reformation, 1570–1640* (Princeton: Princeton University Press, 1961); John F. H. New, *Puritan and Anglican: The Basis of Their Opposition*" (Stanford, Calif.: Stanford University Press: 1964); Basil Hall, "Puritanism: The Problem of Definition," in G. J. Cuming, ed., *Studies in Church History* (London: Ecclesiastical History Society, 1965), vol. 2: 283-9; Timothy H. Breen, "The Non-Existent Controversy: Puritan and Anglican Attitudes on Work and Wealth, 1600–1640," *Church History*, 35 (1966), 273-87; Charles H. George, "Puritanism as History and Historiography," *Past and Present*, 41 (1968), 77-104; William Lamont, Puritanism as History and Historiography: Some Further Thoughts," *Past and Present*, 44 (1969), 133-46; Ian Breward, "The Abolition of Puritanism," *Journal of Religious History*, 7 (1972–73), 20-34; Richard Greaves, "The Nature of the Puritan Tradition," in R. Buick Knox, ed., *Reformation, Conformity and Dissent: Essays in Honour of Geoggrey Nuttall* (London: Epworth Press, 1977), 255-73; Paul Christianson, "Reformers and the Church of England under Elizabeth I and the Early Stuarts," *Journal of Ecclesiastical History*, 31 (1980), 463-84; and Patrick Collinson, "Comment," *Journal of Ecclesiastical History*, 31 (1980), 485-87.

EARLY NEW ENGLAND, 1620–1700

No American religious group has received more attention from historians and students of literature than the Puritans of colonial America. They owe this attention to their position as the first distinctively American church in the New World, to the vitality of their legacy in sermons and diaries, and to the work of one of the great figures in American studies, Perry Miller. A religious sceptic, Miller was drawn, none the less, to spend much of his intellectual life among the Puritans. His masterpiece is *The New England Mind*, a two volume work. Volume one, *The Seventeenth Century* (New York: Macmillan, 1939; and subsequent editions) discusses the major features of Puritan thought, emphasizing the tensions between piety and intellect. Volume Two, *From Colony to Province* (Cambridge: Harvard University Press, 1953; and subsequent editions) describes another tension, the conflicting demands of inherited ideals and personal experience in colonial New England. Miller did not publish his footnotes with these volumes, choosing rather to leave a copy of the notes for public consumption at the Houghton Library, Harvard. The notes for volume one became more accessible with the publication of James Hoopes, ed., *Sources for the New England Mind: The Seventeenth Century*

(Williamsburg, Va.: Institute of Early American History and Culture, 1981). In "Perry Miller: A Note on His Sources in the New England Mind: The Seventeenth Century," *William and Mary Quarterly*, 3d ser., 31 (1974), 453-64, George Selement argues that Miller's conclusions were based on a relatively small sample of available sources. (Whether that sample was typical remains to be determined.) Miller's other publications include *Orthodoxy in Massachusetts* (Cambridge: Harvard University Press, 1933; and subsequent editions), an account of the first decade of the Massachusetts Bay Colony. *Errand into the Wilderness* (Cambridge: Harvard University Press, 1956; and subsequent editions); *Nature's Nation* (Cambridge: Harvard University Press, 1967); and John Crowell and Stanford J. Searl, Jr., eds., *The Responsibility of Mind in a Civilization of Machines* (Amherst, Mass.: University of Massachusetts Press, 1979) are engaging collections of essays.

During the past twenty-five years virtually everything written about life in early New England has had some bearing on the "Miller synthesis." Social historians have questioned whether the influence of Puritanism was as pervasive as Miller claimed. Darrett B. Rutman, in *Winthrop's Boston* (Chapel Hill: University of North Carolina Press, 1965) showed that the New England metropolis has an economic history that is not simply a reflection of religious ideals. But historians have also found in land records and other nonreligious documents further evidence of the influence of Puritanism. Philip J. Greven, Jr., *Four Generations: Population, Land, and Family in Colonial Andover, Massachusetts* (Ithaca, N.Y.: Cornell University Press, 1970) and John Demos, *A Little Commonwealth: Family Life in Plymouth Colony* (New York: Oxford University Press, 1970) show the ways that Puritanism shaped village life in colonial America.

Many historians have followed Miller in exploring Puritan thought. See, for example: Norman Fiering, *Moral Philosophy at Seventeenth-Century Harvard* (Chapel Hill: University of North Carolina Press, 1981); Richard Forrer, "The Puritan Religious Dilemma: The Ethical Dimensions of God's Sovereignty," *Journal of the American Academy of Religion*, 44 (1976), 613-28; Sacvan Bercovitch, *The American Jeremiad* (Madison: The University of Wisconsin Press, 1978); Bercovitch, *The American Puritan Imagination: Essays in Reevaluation* (New York: Cambridge University Press, 1974); Robert Middlekauff, *The Mathers: Three Generations of Puritan Intellecuals* (New York: Oxford University Press, 1971); Philip F. Gura, "The Radical Ideology of Samuel Gorton: New Light on the Relation of English and American Puritanism, *William and Mary Quarterly*, 3d ser., 36 (1979), 78-100; Gura, *A Glimpse of Sion's Glory: Puritan Radicalism in New England, 1620-1660* (Middletown, Conn.: Wesleyan University Press, 1984); Michael McGiffert, "The Problem of the Covenant in Puritan Thought: Peter Bulkeley's *Gospel-Covenant*," *New England Historical and Geneological Register*, 130 (1976), 107-29; Herbert W. Schneider, *The Puritan Mind* (Ann Arbor: University of Michigan, 1961; first published 1930); Samuel Eliot Morison, *The Intellectual Life of Colonial New England* (Ithaca, N.Y.: Cornell University Press, 1956; first published 1936); James W. Jones, *The Shattered Synthesis: New England*

Puritanism before the Great Awakening (New Haven: Yale University Press, 1973); Bruce Stephens, *God's Last Metaphor: The Doctrine of the Trinity in New England Theology* (Chico, Calif.: Scholars Press, 1981); Robert Middlekauff, *Ancients and Axioms: Secondary Education in Eighteenth Century New England* (New Haven: Yale University Press, 1963); Samuel Eliot Morison, *The Founding of Harvard College* (Cambridge: Harvard University Press, 1935); James Holstun, *A Rational Millennium: Puritan Utopias of Seventeenth-Century England and America* (New York: Oxford University Press, 1987) [explores Puritan millenial rhetoric]; J. F. Maclear, "New England and the Fifth Monarchy: The Quest for the Millennium in Early American Puritanism," *William and Mary Quarterly*, 3d ser., 31 (1974), 369-406. Harry S. Stout, *The New England Soul* (New York: Oxford University Press, 1986) uses several thousand manuscript sermons as well as published works to present a picture of New England's "religious culture" that is remarkably congenial to Miller's portrait begun more than a half century earlier.

Other writers have studied the forms of worship among the Puritans. Their works include: Charles E. Hambrick-Stowe, *The Practice of Piety: Puritan Devotional Disciplines in Seventeenth-Century New England* (Chapel Hill: University of North Carolina Press, 1982); Emory Eliot, *Power and the Pulpit in Puritan New England* (Princeton: Princeton University Press, 1979); Theodore Dwight Bozeman, *To Live Ancient Lives: The Primitivist Dimension in Puritanism* (Chapel Hill, University of North Carolina Press, 1988) [emphasizes the effort by Puritans to emulate the first Christian churches]; Andrew Delbanco, *The Puritan Ordeal* (Cambridge: Harvard University Press, 1989) [focuses on the inner life of the early Puritans]; Winton U. Solberg, *Redeem the Time* (Cambridge: Harvard University Press, 1977) [how Puritans observed the Sabbath]; J. Robert Dinkin, "Seating the Meeting House in Early Massachusetts," *New England Quarterly*, 43 (1970), 450-64; Marian Card Donnelly, *The New England Meeting Houses of the Seventeenth Century* (Middletown, Conn.: Wesleyan University Press, 1968); David D. Hall, *The Faithful Shepherd: A History of the New England Ministry in the Seventeenth Century* (Chapel Hill: University of North Carolina Press, 1972).

Several historians have written about Puritan conversion experiences. Charles Lloyd Cohen in *God's Caress: The Psychology of Puritan Religious Experience* (New York: Oxford University Press, 1986) describes Puritan religious experience in the light of "God's awesome omnipotence"—"Doubt spurs the desire for assurance, which encourages deeds that increase faith, but assurance edges into presumption and inspires doubt...." Other works on Puritan religious experience include: Baird Tipson, "How Can the Religious Experience of the Past be Recovered? The Examples of Puritanism and Pietiesm," *Journal of the American Academy of Religion*, 43 (1975), 695-705; Lewis R. Rambo, "Current Research on Religious Conversion," *Religious Studies Review*, 8 (1982), 146-59 [covers history, anthropology, psychology, and sociology]; Philip Greven, *The Protestant Temperament: Patterns of Child-Rearing, Religious Experience, and the Self in Early America* (New York: Alfred A. Knopf, 1977); George Joseph Selement, "The Means to Grace: A Study of Conversion in Early New England" (Ph. D. thesis, University of New Hampshire,

1974); Daniel E. Williams, "'Behold a Tragic Scene Strangely Changed into a Theater of Mercy': The Structure and Significance of Criminal Conversion Narratives in Early New England," *American Quarterly*, 38 (1986), 827-47; Jerald C. Brauer, "Types of Puritan Piety," *Church History*, 56 (1987), 39-58. On conversion as a criteria for church membership see: Raymond Phineas Stearns and David Holmes Brawner, "New England Church 'Relations' and Continuity in Early Congregational History," *American Antiquarian Society Proceedings*, 75 (Part I- 1965), 13-45; and Edmund S. Morgan, *Visible Saints: The History of a Puritan Idea* (Ithaca, N.Y.: Cornell University Press, 1965).

Some critics of Perry Miller suggested that Puritanism must have been too complex for the ordinary New Englander. But several studies have shown that Puritanism was a "popular culture": John C. Kilman, "A Joiner Looks at Colonial New England: Edward Johnson's Special Providences," *Southern Folklore Quarterly*, 45 (1981), 135-44; George Selement, "The Meeting of Elite and Popular Minds at Cambridge, New England, 1638-1645," *William and Mary Quarterly*, 3d ser., 41 (1984), 32-48; David Hall, *Worlds of Wonder, Days of Judgment: Popular Religious Belief in Early New England* (New York: Alfred A. Knopf, 1989); Hall, "Toward a History of Popular Religion in Early New England," *William and Mary Quarterly*, 3d ser., 41 (1984), 49-55; George Selement, *Keepers of the Vineyard: The Puritan Ministry and Collective Culture in Colonial New England* (Lantham, Md.: University Press of America, 1972); Theodore Dwight Bozemen, "The Puritan 'Errand into the Wilderness' Reconsidered," *New England Quarterly*, 159 (Spring, 1986), 231-51; Teresa Toulouse, *The Art of Prophesying: New England Sermons and the Shaping of Belief* (Athens: University of Georgia Press, 1987) [explores the ways that ministers from John Cotton to Ralph Waldo Emerson shaped sermons to meet the spiritual and moral needs of their audience]; Barbara Ritter Dailey, "The Itinerant Preacher and the Social Network in Seventeenth-Century New England," *Dublin Seminar for New England Folklife* (1984), 37-48.

Studies of individual colonies, towns, or churches include: Hamilton A. Hill, *History of the Old South (Third Church) Boston, 1669–1884*, 2 vols. (Boston: Houghton, Mifflin, 1890); William G. McLoughlin, "Tiverton's Fight for Religious Liberty, 1692–1724," *Rhode Island History*, 38 (1979), 35-37 [the story of a Massachusetts town that refused for three decades to tax itself for the support of the Congregational church]; Edward Paul Rindler, "The Migration from the New Haven Colony to Newark, East New Jersey: A Study of Puritan Values and Behavior, 1630–1720" (Ph. D. thesis, University of Pennsylvania, 1977); Richard C. Simmons, "The Founding of the Third Church in Boston," *William and Mary Quarterly*, 3d ser., 26 (1969), 241-52; Richard I. Melvoin, *New England Outpost: War and Society in Colonial Deerfield* (New York: W. W. Norton, 1989); Paul R. Lucas, *Valley of Discord: Church and Society along the Connecticut River, 1636–1725* (Hanover, N.H.: University Press of New England, 1976); Sumner C. Powell, *Puritan Village: The Formation of a New England Town* (Middletown, Conn.: Wesleyan University Press, 1963); Stephen Innes, *Labor in a New Land: Economy and Society in Seventeenth-Century Springfield* (Princeton: Princeton University Press, 1983);

Kenneth A. Lockridge, *A New England Town—The First Hundred Years: Dedham, Massachusetts, 1636–1736* (New York: W.W. Norton, 1970); George D. Langdon, *Pilgrim Colony: A History of New Plymouth, 1620–1691* (New Haven: Yale University Press, 1966); Benjamin W. Labaree, *Colonial Massachusetts: A History* (Millwood, N.Y.: KTO Press, 1979); Sidney V. James, *Colonial Rhode Island: A History* (New York: Charles Scribner's Sons, 1975); Mary Jeanne Anderson Jones, *Congregational Commonwealth: Connecticut, 1636–1662* (Middletown, Conn.: Welseyan University Press, 1968).

The Puritan relationship with the Indians has been the subject of many books and articles. See for example: James Axtell, *The Invasion Within: The Contest of Cultures in Colonial North America* (New York: Oxford University Press, 1985); Axtell, "The Ethnohistory of Early America: A Review Essay," *William and Mary Quarterly*, 3d ser., 39 (1978), 110–44; Francis Jennings, *The Invasion of America: Indians, Colonialism, and the Cant of Conquest* (Chapel Hill: University of North Carolina, 1975); Alden T. Vaughan, *New England Frontier: Puritans and Indians, 1620–1675* (New York: W.W. Norton, 1979; first published, 1965); Henry Warner Bowden, *American Indians and Christian Missions: Studies in Cultural Conflict* (Chicago: University of Chicago Press, 1981); William Cronon, *Changes in the Land: Indians, Colonists, and the Ecology of New England* (New York: Hill and Wang, 1983); William S. Simmons, "Cultural Bias in the New England Puritans' Perception of Indians," *William and Mary Quarterly*, 3d ser., 38 (1981), 56–72; James P. Ronda, "'We Are Well As We Are': An Indian Critique of Seventeenth-Century Christian Missions," *William and Mary Quarterly*, 3d ser., 34 (1977), 66–82; J. William T. Youngs, "The Indian Saints of Early New England," *Early American Literature*, 16 (1981/82), 241–56; Margaret Connell Szasz, "'Poor Richard' Meets the Native American: Schooling for Young Indian Women in Eighteenth-Century Connecticut," *Pacific Historical Review*, 49 (1980), 215–35; Kathryn Zabelle Derounian, "Puritan Orthodoxy and the 'Survivor Syndrome' in Mary Rowlandson's Indian Captivity Narrative," *Early American Literature*, 22 (1987), 82–93. Three fine bibliographies on the subject are: James P. Ronda and James Axtell, *Indian Missions: A Critical Bibliography* (Bloomington: Indiana University Press, 1978); Neal Salisbury, *The Indians of New England: A Critical Bibliography* (Bloomington: Indiana University Press, 1982); and Elisabeth Tooker, *The Indians of the Northeast: A Critical Bibliography* (Bloomington: Indiana University Press, 1978).

On Salem witchcraft see: Chadwick Hansen, *Witchcraft at Salem* (New York: G. Braziller, 1969); Richard Weisman, *Witchcraft, Magic, and Religion in Seventeenth Century Massachusetts* (Amherst: University of Massachusetts Press, 1984); John Demos, *Entertaining Satan: Witchcraft and the Culture of Early New England* (New York: Oxford University Press, 1982); Richard P. Gildrie, "Visions of Evil: Popular Culture, Puritanism and the Massachusetts Witchcraft Crisis of 1692," *Journal of American Culture*, 8 (1985), 17–34; Roger Thompson, "Review Article: Salem Revisited," *Journal of American Studies*, 6 (1972), 317–36; Edmund S. Morgan, "Arthur Miller's *The Crucible* and the Salem Witch Trials: A Historian's View," in John M. Wallace, ed., *The Golden and the Brazen World: Papers in Literature and*

History, 1650–1800 (Berkeley: University of California Press, 1985); Larry D. Gragg, "Samuel Parris: Portrait of a Puritan Clergyman," *Essex Institute Historical Collections*, 119 (1983), 209-37.

Other valuable works on New England Puritanism include: Richard Dunn, *Puritans and Yankees: The Winthrop Dynasty of New England, 1630–1717* (New York, W. W. Norton, 1971; first published 1962); Roland Herbert Bainton, *Christian Unity and Religion in New England* (Boston: Beacon Press, 1964); David Cressy, *Coming Over: Migration and Communication between England and New England in the Seventeenth Century* (New York: Cambridge University Press, 1987); Thomas J. Wertenbaker, *The Puritan Oligarchy: The Founding of American Civilization* (New York: Charles Scribner's Sons, 1947); Everett Emerson, *Puritanism in America, 1620–1750* (Boston: Twayne, 1977); Emory Eliot, *Power and the Pulpit in Puritan New England* (Princeton: Princeton University Press, 1975); Robert Daly, *God's Altar: The World and the Flesh in Puritan Poetry* (Berkeley: University of California Press, 1978); Larzar Ziff, *Puritanism in America: New Culture in a New World* (New York: Viking, 1973); Ursula Brumm, *Puritanism and Literature in America* (Darmstadt, West Germany: Wissenschaftlich Buchgesellschaft, 1973); Alan Simpson, *Puritanism in Old and New England* (Chicago: University of Chicago Press, 1955); Brooks Adams, *The Emancipation of Massachusetts: The Dream and the Reality* (Boston: Houghton Mifflin, 1962; first published 1887); Kenneth B. Murdock, *Literature and Theology in Colonial New England* (Cambridge: Harvard University Press, 1949); George Lee Haskins, *Law and Authority in Early Massachusetts* (New York: Macmillan, 1960); B. Richard Burg, "Presbyterian Versus Congregationalist: A Seventeenth Century Denominational Clash," *Rocky Mountain Social Science Journal*, 7 (1970), 51-60; Paul R. Lucas, "Presbyterianism Comes to Connecticut: The Toleration Act of 1669," *Journal of Presbyterian History*, 50 (1972), 129-47; Harry S. Stout, "Word and Order in Colonial New England," in Nathan O. Hatch and Mark A. Noll, eds., *The Bible in America* (New York: Oxford University Press, 1963); Lynn Helms, "The Face of God: Puritan Iconography in Early American Poetry, Sermons, and Tombstone Carving," *Early American Literature*, 14 (1979), 15-47 [about the Puritan desire "to see God's face and visualize the invisible world"]; Francis J. Bremer, "Increase Mather's Friends: The Trans-Atlantic Congregational Network of the Seventeenth Century," *Proceedings of the American Antiquarian Society*, 94 (1984), 59-96.

Essays on the Puritans have been collected in several anthologies, including: Sydney V. James, ed., *The New England Puritans. Interpretations of American History* (New York: Harper and Row, 1968); Peter White, ed., *Puritan Poets and Poetics: Seventeenth-Century American Poetry in Theory and Practice* (University Park: Pennsylvania State University Press, 1985); David Hall, *Saints and Revolutionaries: Essays on Early American History* (New York: W.W. Norton, 1984); Hall, *Puritanism in Seventeenth Century Massachusetts* (New York: Holt, Rinehart and Winston, 1968); Michael McGiffert, *Puritanism and the American Experience* (Reading, Mass.: Addison-Wesley, 1969); Theodore P. Greene, *Roger Williams and the Massachusetts Magistrates* (Boston: D. C. Heath, 1964); T. H.

Breen, *Puritans and Adventurers: Change and Persistence in Early America* (New York: Oxford University Press, 1980).

Numerous sourcebooks make the Puritan letters, diaries, sermons, poetry, and history readily available. Among the most useful are: David Hall, ed., *The Antinomian Controversy, 1636–1638* (Middletown, Conn.: Wesleyan University Press, 1968); Alexander Young, *Chronicles of the First Planters of the Colony of Massachusetts Bay, 1623–1636* (Boston: Charles C. Little and James Brown, 1846; New York: Da Capo Press, 1970); Perry Miller, ed., *The American Puritans: Their Prose and Poetry* (Garden City, N.Y.: Doubleday, 1956); Perry Miller and Thomas Johnson, *The Puritans* (New York: American Book Company, 1938, 1963); and Everett Emerson, *Letters from New England: The Massachusetts Bay Colony* (1629–1638); Edmund S. Morgan, *Puritan Political Ideas* (Indianapolis: Bobbs-Merrill, 1965).

Several bibliographic and historiographic essays are especially useful in suggesting other readings and evaluating the major works on Puritanism: Michael McGiffert, "American Puritan Studies in the 1960s," *William and Mary Quarterly*, 3d ser., 27 (1970), 36-67; David Hollinger, "Perry Miller and Philosophical History," *History and Theory*, 7 (1968), 189-202; Richard R. Beeman, "The New Social History and the Search for 'Community' in Colonial America," *American Quarterly*, 29 (1977), 422-33; Richard S. Dunn, "The Social History of Early New England," *American Quarterly*, 24 (1972), 661-79; Jane H. Pease, "On Interpreting Puritan History: Williston Walker and the Limitations of the Nineteenth Century View," *New England Quarterly*, 42 (1969), 232-52; David D. Hall, "Understanding the Puritans," in Stanley N. Katz, ed., *Colonial America: Essays in Politics and Social Development* (Boston: Little, Brown, 1971), 31-50; Hall, "On Common Ground: The Coherence of American Puritan Studies," *William and Mary Quarterly*, 3d ser., 44 (1987), 193-229; Darrett B. Rutman, "New England as Idea and Society Revisited," *William and Mary Quarterly*, 3d ser., 41 (1984), 56-61; Allen Carden, "God's Church and Godly Government: A Historiography of Church-State Relations in Puritan New England," *Fides et Historia*, 19 (1987), 51-65. Jerald C. Brauer, "Regionalism and Religion in America," *Church History*, 54 (1985), 366-78, suggests that historians put too much emphasis on the Puritans at the expense of understanding other elements of American religious history.

PROVINCIALISM, THE GREAT AWAKENING, AND THE REVOLUTION, 1700–1789

Some of the works listed above continue into the eighteenth century. But many historians have found the year 1700 a convenient dividing line between the early history of the Puritans and a new period that brought with it new challenges, such as secularism, revivalism, and revolution. On the transition from seventeenth- to eighteenth-century Puritanism see: Richard L. Bushman, *From Puritan to Yankee: Character and the Social Order in Connecticut, 1690–1765* (New York: W. W. Norton, 1970; first published 1967); Richard R. Johnson, *Adjustment to Empire:*

The New England Colonies, 1675–1715 (New Brunswick, N.J.: Rutgers University Press, 1971); Peter Gay, *A Loss of Mastery: Puritan Historians in Colonial America* (Berkeley: University of California Press, 1966); Estelle F. Feinstein, *Stamford from Puritan to Patriot: The Shaping of a Connecticut Community, 1641–1774* (Stamford, Conn.: Stamford Bicentennial Corporation, 1976); Robert M. Bliss, "A Secular Revival: Puritanism in Connecticut, 1675–1708," *Journal of American Studies*, 6 (1972), 129-52.

The subject of the clergy has won considerable attention in this period. On the work of the ministers see: J. William T. Youngs, *God's Messengers: Religious Leadership in Colonial New England, 1700–1750* (Baltimore: Johns Hopkins University Press, 1976); Youngs, "Congregational Clericalism: New England Ordinations before the Great Awakening," *William and Mary Quarterly*, 3d ser., 31 (1974); Stephen Foster, "Prophets on a Fixed Stipend: The Congregational Ministry and the Social History of Colonial New England," *Reviews in American History*, 5 (1977), 299-307; Mary Latimer Gambrell, *Ministerial Training in Eighteenth-Century New England* (New York: Columbia University Press, 1937); Donald M. Scott, *From Office to Profession: The New England Ministry, 1750–1850* (Philadelphia: University of Pennsylvania Press, 1978); William B. Hamilton, "Preachers and Professionalism," *History of Education Quarterly*, 19 (1979), 515-22; Harry S. Stout, "The Great Awakening in New England Reconsidered: The New England Clergy," *Journal of Social History*, 8 (1974), 21-47; George B. Kirsch, "Clerical Dismissals in Colonial and Revolutionary New Hampshire," *Church History*, 49 (1980), 160-77; *Journal of Social History*, 9 (1975), 249-67; Alf E. Jacobson, "The Congregational Clergy in Eighteenth Century New England" (Ph. D. thesis: Harvard, 1962); James W. Schmotter, "Provincial Professionalism: The New England Ministry: 1692–1745" (Ph. D. thesis, Northwestern University, 1973); Schmotter, "The Irony of Clerical Professionalism: New England's Congregational Ministers and the Great Awakening," *American Quarterly*, 31 (1979), 148-68; Schmotter, "Ministerial Careers in Eighteenth Century New England: The Great Context: 1700–1740," *Journal of Social History*, 9 (1975), 453-64; Laurel Thatcher Ulrich, "Psalm-Tunes, Periwigs, and Bastards: Ministerial Authority in Early Eighteenth Century Durham," *Historical New Hampshire*, 36 (1981), 255-79; Stephen J. Stein, "The Biblical Notes of Benjamin Pierpont," *Yale University Library Gazette*, 50 (1976), 195-218 [on a young man's preparation for the ministry]; Richard D. Brown, "Spreading the Word: Rural Clergymen and the Communication Network of 18th-Century New England," *Massachusetts Historical Society, Proceedings*, 94 (1982), 1-14; Richard Warch, *School of the Prophets: Yale College, 1701–1740* (New Haven: Yale University Press, 1973); Dennis D. Martin, "Schools of the Prophets: Shepherds and Scholars in New England Puritanism," *Historical Reflections*, 5 (1978), 41-80; David Harlan, *The Clergy and the Great Awakening in New England* (Ann Arbor, Mich.: UMI Research Press, 1980); George Selement, "Publication and the Puritan Minister," *William and Mary Quarterly*, 3d ser., 37 (1980), 219-41; Winthrop S. Hudson, "Congregationalism in America: The Way of the Congregational Churches Cleared," *Encounter*, 29 (1968), 62-72 [on

Saybrook Platform of 1708 and Massachusetts Proposals of 1705]; Alonzo H. Quint, "The Origins of the Ministerial Associations in New England," *Congregational Quarterly*, 4 (1963), 293-308; Quint, "Some Account of Ministerial Associations (Congregational) in Massachusetts," *Congregational Quarterly*, 4 (1863), 293-308; J. M. Bumstead, "A Caution to Erring Christians: Ecclesiastical Disorder on Cape Cod, 1717 to 1738," *William and Mary Quarterly*, 3d ser., 28 (1971), 413-38.

On the conflict with Anglicanism in Congregational New England see: Carl Bridenbaugh, *Mitre and Sceptre: Transatlantic Faiths, Ideas, Personalities, and Politics, 1689–1775* (New York: Oxford University Press, 1962); Arthur Lyon Cross, *The Anglican Episcopate and the American Colonies* (Hamden, Conn.: Archon Books, 1964); Donald F. M. Gerardi, "Samuel Johnson and the Yale 'Apostasy' of 1722: The Challenge of Anglican Sacramentalism to the New England Way," *Historical Magazine of the Protestant Episcopal Church*, 4 (1978), 153-75; George E. DeMille and Don R. Gerlach, "Samuel Johnson and the 'Dark Day' at Yale, 1722," *Connecticut History*, 19 (1977), 38-63; Gordon E. Kershaw, "A Question of Orthodoxy: Religious Controversy in a Speculative Land Company: 1759-1775," *New England Quarterly*, 46 (1973), 205-35; David C. Humphrey, "Anglican 'Infiltration' of Eighteenth Century Harvard and Yale," *Historical Magazine of the Protestant Episcopal Church*, 43 (1974), 247-51; Bruce E. Steiner, "Anglican Officeholding in Pre-Revolutionary Connecticut: The Parameters of New England Community," *William and Mary Quarterly*, 3d ser., 31 (1974), 369-406; Bruce E. Steiner, "New England Anglicanism: A Genteel Faith?" *William and Mary Quarterly*, 3d ser., 27 (1970), 122-35; Joseph J. Ellis III, "Anglicans in Connecticut, 1725–1750: The Conversion of the Missionaries," *New England Quarterly*, 44 (1971), 66-81; Charles Clark, "A Test of Religious Liberty: The Ministry Land Case in Narragansett, 1668-1752," *Journal of Church and State*, 11 (1969), 295-319; Donald L. Huber, "Timothy Cutler: The Convert as Controversialist," *Historical Magazine of the Protestant Episcopal Church*, 44 (1975), 489-96; Harriet S. Lacy, "An Eighteenth-Century Diarist Identified: Samuel Parker's Journal for 1771," *Historical New Hampshire*, 25 (1970), 2-44 [Congregationalist who became an Anglican minister]; Bruce E. Steiner, "Connecticut Anglicans in the Revolutionary Era: A Study in Communal Tensions," (Hartford, Conn.: American Revolution Bicentennial Commission of Connecticut, 1978); Edward Bruck Tucker, "The Founders Remembered: The Anglicization of the Puritan Tradition in New England, 1690–1760" (Ph. D. thesis, Brown University, 1980); Bordon W. Painter, Jr., "The Vestry in Colonial New England," *Journal of the Protestant Episcopal Church*, 44 (1975), 381-408; Marc Alfred Mappen, "Anatomy of a Schism: Anglican Dissent in the New England Community of Newtown, Connecticut, 1708–1765" (Ph. D. thesis, Rutgers University, 1976); A. L. Cross, *The Anglican Episcopate and the American Colonies* (New York: Longmans, 1902); Joseph J. Ellis, *The New England Mind in Transition: Samuel Johnson of Connecticut, 1696–1772* (New Haven, 1973) [the career of a leading Anglican].

On relations with the Baptists and Separatists see: William G. McLoughlin, *New England Dissent, 1630–1833* (Cambridge: Harvard University Press, 1971); Michael

J. Crawford, "The Spiritual Travels of Nathan Cole," *William and Mary Quarterly*, 3d ser., 33 (1976), 89-126 [about a Congregationalist who became a Separatist]; Stephen Foster, "A Connecticut Separate Church: Strict Congregationalism in Cornwall, 1780–1809," *New England Quarterly*, 39 (1966), 309-33; William G. McLoughlin, "Barrington Congregationalists vs. Swansea Baptists, 1711," *Rhode Island History*, 32 (1973), 19-21; C. C. Goen, *Revivalism and Separatism in New England, 1740–1800: Strict Congregationalists and Separate Baptists in the Great Awakening* (New Haven: Yale University Press, 1962); James H. Barnett and Esther D. Barnett, *On the Trail of a Legend: The Separatist Movement in Mansfield, Connecticut, 1745–1769* (Mansfield, Conn.: The Mansfield Historical Society, 1978); Stephen Marini, *Radical Sects of Revolutionary New England* (Cambridge: Harvard University Press, 1982); William G. McLoughlin, *Isaac Backus and the American Pietistic Tradition* (Boston: Little, Brown, 1967).

Studies of the Awakening in New England include: Joseph Tracy, *The Great Awakening: A History of the Revival of Religion in the Time of Edwards and Whitefield* (Boston: Tappen and Dennet, 1842); Peter S. Onuf, "New Lights in New London: A Group Portrait of the Separatists," *William and Mary Quarterly*, 3d ser., 37 (1980), 627-44; Stephen A. Marini, "Evangelical Itinerancy in Rural New England: New Gloucester, Maine, 1754–1807," *Dublin Seminar for New England Folklife* (1984), 49-64; John W. Jeffries, "The Separation in the Canterbury Congregational Church: Religion, Family, and Politics in a Connecticut Town," *New England Quarterly*, 52 (1979), 522-49; James Walsh, "The Great Awakening in the First Congregational Church of Woodbury, Connecticut," *William and Mary Quarterly*, 3d ser., 28 (1971), 543-62; J. M. Bumsted, "Religion, Finance, and Democracy in Massachusetts: The Town of Norton as a Case Study," *Journal of American History*, 57 (1970), 817-31; Kenneth P. Minkema, "A Great Awakening Conversion: The Relation of Samuel Belcher," *William and Mary Quarterly*, 3d ser., 44 (1987), 121-26; Gregory H. Nobles, "In the Wake of the Awakening: The Politics of Purity in Granville, 1754–1776," *Historical Journal of Western Massachusetts*, (1980), 48-62; J. M. Bumsted, "Emotion in Colonial America: Some Relations of Conversion Experience in Freetown, Massachusetts, 1749–1770," *New England Quarterly*, 49 (1976), 97-107; Douglas H. Sweet, "One Glorious Temple of God: Eighteenth-Century Accommodation to Changing Reality in New England," *Studies in Eighteenth-Century Culture*, 11 (1982), 311-20 [argues that some ministers welcomed the new diversity and pluralism brought about by the Awakening]; John W. Jeffries, "The Separation in the Canterbury Congregational Church: Religion, Family, and Politics in a Connecticut Town," *New England Quarterly*, 52 (1979), 522-49; Christopher Jedrey, *The World of John Cleaveland: Family and Community in Eighteenth Century New England* (New York: W.W. Norton, 1979); Stephen J. Stein, "'For Their Spiritual Good': the Northampton, Massachusetts, Prayer Bids of the 1730s and 1740s," *William and Mary Quarterly*, 3d ser., 37 (1980), 261-85; J. M. Bumsted, "Orthodoxy in Massachusetts: The Ecclesiastical History of Freetown, 1683–1776," *New England Quarterly*, 43 (1970), 274-84.

On theological developments and the rise of rationalism in eighteenth-century

New England see: Conrad Wright, *The Beginnings of Unitarianism in America* (Boston: Beacon Press, 1966; first published 1955); Louis Graham, "The Scientific Piety of John Winthrop of Harvard," *New England Quarterly*, 46 (1973), 112-18; Frank H. Foster, *A Genetic History of the New England Theology* (Chicago: The University of Chicago Press, 1907); H. Shelton Smith, *Changing Conceptions of Original Sin* (New York: Charles Scribner's Sons, 1955); Conrad Wright, *The Beginnings of Unitarianism in America* (Boston, 1955); Henry F. May, *The Enlightenment in America* (New York: Oxford University Press, 1976); Gerald J. Goodwin, "The Myth of 'Arminian-Calvinism' in Eighteenth Century New England," *New England Quarterly*, 41 (1968), 213-37; Margaret Eleanor Rossen Wall, "Puritanism in Education: An Analysis of the Transition from Religiosity to Secular Morality as Seen in Primary Reading Materials 1620–1775," (Ph. D. thesis, Washington University, 1979); David Watters, "The Park and Whiting Family Stones Revisited: The Iconography of the Church Covenant," *Canadian Review of American Studies*, 9 (1978), 1-15 [Congregational controversies about the covenant and baptism found their way onto tombstones in Grafton and Rockingham, Vermont, 1770–1803].

On the connections between religion and the Revolution a number of sources are useful: Alice M. Baldwin, *The New England Clergy in the American Revolution* (Durham, N.C.: Duke University Press, 1928); Donald Weber, *Rhetoric and History in Revolutionary New England* (New York: Oxford University Press, 1988); Nathan O. Hatch, *The Sacred Cause of Liberty* (New Haven: Yale University Press, 1977); Freeman W. Meyer, *Connecticut Congregationalism in the Revolutionary Era* (Hartford, Conn.: The American Revolution Bicentennial Commission of Connecticut, 1977); Douglas Hardy Sweet, *Church and Community: Town Life and Ministerial Ideals in Revolutionary New Hampshire* (Ph. D. thesis, Columbia University, 1978); Larzar Ziff, "Revolutionary Rhetoric and Puritanism," *Early American Literature*, 13 (1978), 45-49; John G. Buchanan, "The Justice of America's Cause: Revolutionary Rhetoric in the Sermons of Samuel Cooper," *New England Quarterly*, 50 (1977), 101-24; Alan Heimert, *Religion and the American Mind: From the Great Awakening to the Revolution* (Cambridge: Harvard University Press, 1966); Perry Miller, "From the Covenant to the Revival," in Miller, *Nature's Nation* (Cambridge: Harvard University Press, 1967), 90-120; Bernard Bailyn, "Religion and Revolution," *Perspectives in American History*, 4 (1970), 87-169 [on Stephen Johnson, Jonathan Mayhew, and Andrew Eliot]; Thornton, *Pulpit of the American Revolution; or The Political Sermons of the Period of 1776* (Boston: Gould and Lincoln, 1860); Ruth H. Bloch, *Visionary Republic Millennial Themes in American Thought, 1756–1800* (New York: Cambridge University Press, 1985) [how millennial views shaped popular understanding of major events]; James W. Davidson, *The Logic of Millennial Thought* (New Haven: Yale University Press, 1977); John G. Buchanan, "Drumfire from the Pulpit: Natural Law in the Colonial Election Sermons of Massachusetts," *American Journal of Legal History*, 12 (1968), 232-44; Thomas S. Martin, "The Philosophy of Loyalism among the Ministers of Western Massachusetts," *Historical Journal of Massachusetts*, 11 (1983), 45-52;

Stephen A. Freeman, "Puritans in Rutland, Vermont 1770–1818," *Vermont History*, 33 (1965), 342-48; Gregory H. Nobles, "In the Wake of the Awakening: The Politics of Purity in Granville, 1754–1776," *Historical Journal of Western Massachusetts*, 3 (1980), 48-62; Patricia U. Bonomi, *Under the Cope of Heaven: Religion, Society and Politics in Colonial America* (New York: Oxford University Press, 1986).

CONGREGATIONALISM IN THE NEW NATION, 1789–1865

Samuel C. Pearson, Jr., "From Church to Denomination: American Congregationalism in the Nineteenth Century," *Church History*, 38 (1969), 67-87, traces the slow growth of denominational self-consciousness among the Congregationalists during the first half of the nineteenth century. In "From Church to Denomination: American Congregationalism in the Nineteenth Century," *Church History*, 38 (1969), 67-87, Samuel C. Pearson, Jr., traces the evolution of Congregationalism as a national denomination from the Plan of Union (1801) to the formation of the national council (1865). In "The Dove and Serpent: The Clergy in the American Revolution," *American Quarterly*, 31 (1979), 187-203, Emory Elliott asserts that clerical prestige declined after the revolution but returned by 1800 as ministers preached the divine mission of the new nation; Jon Butler argues for an understanding of the growth of American religion that includes a sense of its variety and complexity in *Awash in a Sea of Faith* (Cambridge: Harvard University Press, 1990).

On religion and war in the early republic see: Gary B. Nash, "The American Clergy and the French Revolution," *William and Mary Quarterly*, 3d ser., 22 (1965), 392-412; William Gribben, *The Churches Militant: The War of 1812 and American Religion* (New Haven: Yale University Press, 1973). On the social concerns of Congregationalists in this era see also James D. Essig, "Connecticut Ministers and Slavery, 1790–1795," *Journal of American Studies*, 15 (1981), 27-44.

On revivalism and the second Awakening see: Richard D. Birdsall, "The Second Great Awakening and the New England Social Order," *Church History*, 39 (1970), 345-64; Richard D. Shiels, "The Scope of the Second Great Awakening: Andover, Massachusetts as a Case Study," *Journal of the Early Republic*, 5 (1985), 233-46; Shiels, "The Connecticut Clergy in the Second Great Awakening" (Ph. D. thesis, Boston University, 1976); Doug Adams, *Meeting House to Camp Meeting: Toward a History of American Free Church Worship from 1620 to 1835* (Austin, Texas: The Sharing Company, 1981); Joseph Conforti, "Antibellum Evangelicals and the Cultural Revival of Jonathan Edwards," *American Presbyterians*, 64 (1986), 227-41; Howard Alexander Morrison, "The Finney Takeover of the Second Great Awakening During the Oneida Revivals of 1825–1827," *New York History*, 59 (1978), 27-53.

William S. Kennedy, *The Plan of Union* (Hudson, Ohio: Pentagon Steam Press, 1856) discusses Congregationalists and Presbyterians in the Western Reserve. In "'Jealousies and Contentions': The Plan of Union and the Western Reserve, 1801–37," *Journal of Presbyterian History*, 60 (1892), 130-43, Ronald H. Noricks argues that frictions between Congregationalists and Presbyterians existed from the earliest days of the Plan of Union in Ohio. On the Plan of Union see also: Earl R. MacCormac, "An Ecumenical Failure: The Development of Congregational Missions and Its Influence upon Presbyterians, Part I," *Journal of Presbyterian History*, 44 (1966), 266-85; MacCormac, "An Ecumenical Failure: The Development of Congregational Missions and Its Influence upon Presbyterians, Part II," *Journal of Presbyterian History*, 45 (1967), 8-26 [changes in the relationship between the Congregationalists' national council and the voluntary societies between 1865 and 1913].

The continuity of Puritanism into the nineteenth century is apparent in a number of sources, including: Bernard Farber, *Guardians of Virtue: Salem Families in 1800* (New York: Basic Books, 1972); Dennis Earl Minor, "The Evolution of Puritanism into the Mass Culture of Early Nineteenth-Century America" (Ph. D. thesis, Texas A&M, 1973); John S. Gilkerson, Jr., "The Rise and Decline of the 'Puritan Sunday' in Providence, Rhode Island, 1810-1926," *New England Quarterly*, 59 (1986), 75-91; Joseph Conforti, "David Brainerd and the Nineteenth Century Missionary Movement," *Journal of the Early Republic*, 5 (1985), 309-29; Regina Siegfried, "Conspicuous by Her Absence: Amherst's Religious Tradition and Emily Dickinson's own Growth in Faith" (Ph. D. thesis, St. Louis University, 1982); Doug Adams, *Humor in the American Pulpit from George Whitefield through Henry Ward Beecher* (Austin, Texas: The Sharing Company, 1975); Richard Rabinowitz, *The Spiritual Self in Everyday Life: The Transformation of Religious Experience in Nineteenth-Century New England* (Boston: Northeastern University Press, 1989); Donald M. Murray and Robert M. Rodney, "Sylvia Drake, 1784-1868: The Self Portrait of a Seamstress of Weybridge," *Vermont History*, 34 (1966), 125-35; James Hoopes, *Consciousness in New England: From Puritanism and Ideas to Psychoanalysis and Semiotic* (Baltimore: Johns Hopkins University Press, 1989); William C. Spengemann, "Puritan Tradition in American Literature," *Early American Literature*, 16 (1981), 175-86 [review essay]; Wesley T. Mott, "Emerson and Antinomianism: The Legacy of the Sermons," *American Literature*, 50 (1978), 369-97; Richard Forrer, *Theodicies in Conflict: A Dilemma in Puritan Ethics and Nineteenth-Century American Literature* (Westport, Conn.: Greenwood Press, 1986); Mark Kaplanoff, *From Yankee to Puritan: Economic Change, Religious Revivals, and Desecularization in Early Nineteenth-Century New England* (Boston: Northeastern University Press, 1990); Edward Byers, *The Nation of Nantucket: Society and Politics in an Early American Commercial Center, 1660-1820* (Boston: Northeastern University Press, 1987); Michael T. Gilmore, *The Middle Way: Puritanism and Ideology in American Romantic Fiction* (New Brunswick, N.J.: Rutgers University Press, 1977); Wesley Theodore Mott, "Emerson and Thoreau as Heirs to the Tradition of New England Puritanism" (Ph. D. thesis, Boston University, 1975).

Theological developments and the Unitarian controversy are the subject of: George N. Broadman, *A History of the New England Theology* (Chicago: University of Chicago Press, 1907); Philip F. Gura, "The Reverend Parsons Cook and Ware Factory Village: A New Missionary Field," *New England Historical and Genealogical Register*, 135 (1981), 199-212 [conflict between Congregationalists and Unitarians in Ware]; Daniel Walker Howe, *Unitarian Conscience: Harvard Moral Philosophy, 1805–1861* (Cambridge: Harvard University Press, 1970) [the Unitarian side of the divide, liberal thinking, esp. moral philosophy].

On the westward movement of Congregationalism see: David French, "Puritan Conservatism and the Frontier: The Elizur Wright Family on the Connecticut Western Reserve," *Old Northwest*, 1 (1975), 85-95; Donald B. Marti, "The Puritan Tradition in a 'New England of the West,'" *Minnesota History*, 40 (1966), 1-11; Virginia Ward Duffy McLoughlin, ed., "Establishing a Church on the Kansas Frontier: The Letters of the Rev. O. L. Woodford and His Sister Henrietta, 1857–1859," *Kansas Historical Quarterly*, 37 (1971), 153-91; J. Fraser Cocks III, "George N. Smith: Reformer on the Frontier," *Michigan History*, 52 (1968), 37-49; Dewey D. Wallace, Jr., "Charles Oliver Brown at Dubuque: A Study in the Ideals of Midwestern Congregationalists in the Late Nineteenth Century," *Church History*, 53 (1984), 46-60; Beverly Seaton, "'In Canaan's Land': Images of Granville, Ohio," *Old Northwest*, 5 (1979), 3-17; William W. Sweet, ed., *Religion on the American Frontier: The Congregationalists*, vol. 3 (Chicago: University of Chicago Press, 1939); Dorothea R. Muller, "Church Building and Community Making on the Frontier, A Case Study: Josiah Strong, Home Missionary in Cheyenne, 1871–1873," *Western Historical Quarterly*, 10 (1979), 191-216; Paul Jeffrey Potash, "Welfare of the Regions Beyond," *Vermont History*, 46 (1978), 109-28 [Connecticut evangelists on the Vermont frontier]; William Warren Sweet, ed., *The Congregationalists, a Collection of Source Materials* (Chicago: Chicago University Press, 1939) [focuses on the expansion of home and Indian missions]; John Randolph Willis, *God's Frontiersman: The Yale Band in Illinois* (Washington: University Press of America, 1979); Robert J. Plumb, "The Alcalde of Monterey," *US Naval Institute Proceedings*, 95 (1969), 72-83 [about Walter Colton, Congregational chaplain on board Commodore Robert F. Stockton's flagship when the United States occupied California—he served for three years as mayor of Monterey].

On most topics the literarure on nineteenth century Congregationalism is sparse. The major exception is on the subject of overseas missions. These are some of the most important works: Lois K. Matthews Resenberry, *Expansion of New England* (Boston: Houghton, Mifflin, 1909); Myra Dinnerstein, "The American board Mission to the Zulu, 1835–1900" (Ph. D. thesis, Columbia, 1971); Sandra E. Wagner, "Mission and Motivation: The Theology of the Early American Mission in Hawaii," *Hawaiian Journal of History*, 19 (1985), 62-70 [the "Puritan Calvinism" of the missions]; Rufus Anderson, *History of the Missions of the American Board of Commissioners for Foreign Missions in India* (Boston: Congregational Publishing Society, 1874) [an "official" history written by the secretary of the board]; Rufus Anderson, *A Heathen Nation Evangelized: History of the Sandwich Islands Mission* (Boston: Congregational Publishing Society, 1870); Gavan Daws, "The Decline of Puritanism at Honolulu in the 19th Century," *Hawaiian Journal of History*, 1 (1967), 31-42 [declining influence of religion in Honolulu's social life]; Clifton Jackson Phillips, *Protestant America and the Pagan World: The First Half-Century of the*

American Board of Commissioners for Foreign Missions, 1810–1860 (Cambridge: Harvard University Press, 1969); John A. Andrew III, *Rebuilding the Christian Commonwealth: New England Congregationalists and Foreign Missions, 1800–1830* (Lexington: University of Kentucky Press, 1976) [Congregational missionaries, 1800–1830, hoped to restore the early vitality of Puritanism]; William R. Hutchison, *Errand to the World: American Protestant Thought and Foreign Missions* (Chicago: University of Chicago Press, 1987); Alan F. Perry, "The American Board of Commissioners for Foreign Missions and the London Missionary Society in the Nineteenth Century: A Study of Ideas" (Ph. D. thesis, Washington University, 1974); Harold Whitman Bradley, *The American Frontier in Hawaii* (Palo Alto, Calif.: Stanford University Press, 1942) [missionaries and other Americans in Hawaii, 1789–1843]; Albertine Loomis, *Grapes of Canaan* (New York: Dodd, Mead, 1951) [early mission years in Hawaii, based on papers of missionary-printer Elisha Loomis]; Thomas E. Korson, "Congregational Missionaries in Foochow During the 1911 Revolution," *Chinese Culture*, 8 (1967), 44-103; William Ellsworth Strong, *The Story of the American Board* (Boston: Pilgrim Press, 1910) [centennial history by a member of the board]; Kenneth Scott Latourette, *A History of the Expansion of Christianity*, 7 vols. (New York: Harper Brothers, 1937–1945) [volume 5 deals with the Congregationalists in Hawaii]; Louis B. Wright and Mary Isabel Fry, *Puritans in the South Seas* (New York: H. Holt and Company, 1936) [English and American missionaries in the Pacific]; Jean F. Hobbs, *Hawaii: A Pageant of the Soil* (Palo Alto, Calif.: Stanford University Press, 1935) [argues against the notion that "land-hungry" Yankee evangelists expropriated the soil].

Works on Indian missions include: Robert S. Walker, *Torchlights to the Cherokees* (New York: Macmillan, 1931) [history of the Brainard mission to the Cherokees]; Robert F. Berkhofer, Jr., *Salvation and the Savage* (Lexington, Ky.: University of Kentucky Press, 1965) [argues that the Indians were slow to respond to Protestant missionary activities, 1787–1862]; Robert W. Bullen, "Joseph Bullen, Some Biographical Notes," *Journal of Mississippi History*, 27 (1965), 265-67 [describes New England background of Congregationalist who ministered to the Chickasaw Indians in Mississippi]; Colin Brummitt Goodykoontz, *Home Missions on the American Frontier* (Caldwell, Idaho: Caxton Printers, 1939); William G. McLoughlin, "The Choctaw Slave Burning: A Crisis in Mission Work Among the Indians," *Journal of the West*, 13 (1974), 113-27; James Findlay, "The Congregationalists and American Education," *History of Education Quarterly*, 17 (1977), 449-54 [discusses work of the American Education Society in the West]. See also Joe M. Richardson, "The Failure of the American Missionary Association to Expand Congregationalism Among Southern Blacks," *Southern Studies*, 18 (1979), 51-73; Richardson, *Christian Reconstruction: The American Missionary Association and Southern Blacks, 1861-1890* (Athens: University of Georgia Press, 1986).

For the sort of local history that is common in colonial religious studies but rare in nineteenth-century Congregationalism see: Maryann Rossi, "The Congregational Church Membership of Westport, Connecticut: 1835–1880" (Ph. D. thesis, Saint

Louis University, 1983).

LIBERALISM AND CONSOLIDATION—INDUSTRIAL AMERICA

On the church and the Social Gospel see Henry F. May, *Protestant Churches and Industrial America* (New York: Octagon Books, 1949); Charles Howard Hopkins, *The Rise of the Social Gospel in American Protestantism: 1865–1915* (New Haven: Yale University Press, 1940). Intellectual currents in this period are the subject of: Jon H. Roberts, *Darwinism and the Divine in America: Protestant Intellectuals and Organic Evolution, 1859–1900* (Madison: University of Wisconsin Press, 1988) [comprehensive overview of the many ways in which evolution theory shaped theological discourse in late nineteenth century]; Sandra Sizer Frankiel, *California's Spiritual Frontiers: Religious Alternatives in Anglo-Protestastism, 1850–1910* (Berkeley: University of California Press, 1988) [social and cultural milieu of California fostered religious liberalism and openness, as well as mystical communion with nature]; Jack C. Lane, "Liberal Arts on the Florida Frontier: The Founding of Rollins College, 1885–1890," *Florida Historical Quarterly*, 59 (1980), 144-64; John W. Cresswell, "Character Building at Kingfisher College, 1890–1922," *Chronicles of Oklahoma*, 55 (1977), 266-81; Jan C. Dawson, "Puritanism in American Thought and Society: 1865–1910," *New England Quarterly*, 53 (1980), 508-26 [argues that a diluted form of Puritanism helped Americans keep their moral bearings during the half century following the Civil War].

Studies of local parishes include Charles D. Broadbent, "A Brief Pilgrimage: Plymouth Church of Rochester," *Rochester History*, 40 (1978) 1-22; Margaret Connell Szasz, "Albuquerque Congregationalists and Southwestern Social Reform, 1900–1917," *New Mexico Historical Review*, 55 (1980), 231-52; Paul R. Lucas, "The Church and the City: Congregationalism in Minneapolis, 1850–1890," *Minnesota History*, 44 (1974), 55-69; Robert W. Lovett, "A Parish Divided and Reunited, The Precinct of Salem and Beverly 1813–1913," *Essex Institute Historical Collections*, 99, 203-36; Genevieve C. Weeks, *Oscar Carleton McCulloch, 1843–1891: Preacher and Practitioner of Applied Christianity* (Indianapolis: Indiana Historical Society, 1976); Weeks, "Oscar McCulloch Transforms Plymouth Church, Indianapolis, Into an 'Institutional' Church," *Indiana Magazine of History*, 64 (1968), 87-108; Weeks, "Religion and Social Work as Exemplified in the Life of Oscar C. McCulloch," *Social Service Review*, 39 (1965), 38-52; Mabel C. Skjelver, "Randall's Congregational Church at Iowa City," *Annals of Iowa*, 42 (1974), 361-70; Frances Hurd Stadler, "Pilgrim Congregational Church: The First 100 Years," *Bulletin of the Missouri Historical Society*, 23 (1966), 21-51 [1866–1966]; Charles C. Cost, "Edna Dean Proctor, Poetess of the Contoocook," *Historical New Hampshire*, 21 (1966), 2-30 [about a writer who was a member of Henry Ward Beecher's Plymouth Congregational Church]; Annadora F. Gregory, "The Reverend Harmon Bross and Nebraska Congregationalism, 1873–1928," *Nebraska History*, 54 (1973), 445-74; Keith A. Murray, *Centennial Churches of Washington's "Fourth Corner"* (Bellingham: Western Washington University, Center for Pacific Northwest

Studies, 1985) [includes Bellingham's First Congregational Church, 1883–1984]; Egbert S. Oliver, *Saints and Sinners: The Planting of New England Congregationalism in Portland, Oregon, 1851–1876* (Portland, Ore.: HaPi, 1986); Dorothea R. Muller, "Church Building and Community Making on the Frontier, A Case Study: Josiah Strong, Home Missionary in Cheyenne, 1871–1873," *Western Historical Quarterly*, 10 (1979), 191-216.

Disputes about doctrine and social values led to stormy careers for some ministers: "F. E. Maddox: Chaplain of Progress, 1908," *Arkansas Historical Quarterly*, 38 (1979), 146-66, tells the story of a southern Presbyterian minister in Texarkana, Arkansas, whose modernist theology led to his conviction of heresy. He founded a Congregational church in town, and three-quarters of his former parishioners followed him; in "George D. Herron in the 1890s: A New Frame of Reference for the Study of the Progressive Era," *Annals of Iowa*, 42 (1973), 81-113, Robert M. Crunden tells the story of a minister who argued that "economic competition was always opposed to moral development"—and was expelled from his church for radical socialism.

Several essays explore the position of the Congregational church among African Americans in this period. George A. Rogers and Frank R. Saunders, Jr., "The American Missionary Association in Liberty County, Georgia: An Invasion of Light and Love," *Georgia Historical Quarterly*, 62 (1978), 304-15, explores the role of the Congregational church in helping freed men and women in Liberty County, Georgia. Thomas F. Armstrong, "The Building of a Black Church: Community in Post Civil War Liberty County Georgia," *Georgia Historical Quarterly*, 66 (1982), 346-67, describes a conflict between the American Missionary Association and a local church leader. Benjamin D. Berry, Jr., "The Plymouth Congregational Church of Louisville, Kentucky," *Phylon*, 42 (1981), 224-232, describes a church that between 1877 and 1930 became a gathering place for black professionals and educators in Louisville; A. Knighton Stanley, *The Children is Crying: Congregationalism Among Black People* (New York: Pilgrim Press, 1979) covers the southern experience, 1861–1926; Richard B. Drake, "The Growth of Segregation in American Congregationalism in the South," *Negro History Bulletin*, 21 (1958), 135-37, argues that the integrated churches planted by the American Missionary Association during Reconstruction were superceded by segregated congregations during the 1880s.

MERGERS AND MODERN AMERICA

On the general history of twentieth-century religion in America see: Gaius Glenn Atkins, *Religion in Our Times* (New York: Round Table Press, 1932); Thomas J. J. Altizer and William Hamilton, *Radical Theology and the Death of God* (Indianapolis: Bobbs-Merrill, 1966); Daniel Callahan, ed., *The Secular City Debate* (New York: Macmillan, 1966), Paul A. Carter, *The Decline and Revival of Social Gospel, 1920–1940* (Ithaca, N.Y.: Cornell University Press, 1956); Harvey Cox, ed., *The Situation Ethics Debate* (Philadelphia: Westminster Press, 1966); Carl F. H. Henry, *Fifty*

Years of Protestant Theology (Boston: W. A. Wilde, 1950); Will Herberg, *Protestant, Catholic, Jew: An Essay in American Religious Sociology* (Garden City, N.Y.: Doubleday, 1955); George M. Marsden, *Fundamentalism and American Culture: The Shaping of Twentieth-Century Evangelicalism* (New York: Oxford University Press, 1970); Martin E. Marty, *The New Shape of American Religion* (New York: Harper and Brothers, 1959); Marty, *A Nation of Behavers* (Chicago: University of Chicago Press, 1976); Robert M. Miller, *American Protestantism and Social Issues, 1919–1939,* (Chapel Hill: University of North Carolina Press, 1958); Arnold S. Nash, ed., *Protestant Thought in the Twentieth Century* (New York: Macmillan, 1951).

On twentieth-century ecumenicalism see: George K. A. Bell, *The Kingship of Christ: The Story of the World Council of Churches* (Baltimore: Penguin Books, 1954); Samuel McCrea, *The American Churches in the Ecumenical Movement, 1900–1968* (New York: Association Press, 1968); Robert Lee, *The Social Sources of Church Unity* (Nashville: Abingdon Press, 1960); Ruth Rouse and Stephen C. Neill, *A History of the Ecumenical Movement, 1517–1948* (Philadelphia: Westminster Press, 1954). These sources describe the formation of the United Church of Christ: Douglas Horton, *The United Church of Christ: Its Origins, Organization, and Role in the World Today* (New York: T. Nelson, 1962); William G. Chrystal, "German Congregationalism," *Journal of the American Historical Society of Germans from Russia,* 6 (1983), 31-29 [on the appeal of American Congregationalism for Russian-German refugees]; Louis Gunnemann, *Shaping of the United Church of Christ* (New York: United Church Press, 1977) [history of the merger with essays on the history of Congregationalism and the Evangelical and Reformed churches]; Division of Publications, United Church Board for Homeland Ministries, *United Church of Christ: History and Program* (New York: United Church Press, 1982) [brief history of the UCC and its parent churches with a description of the current organization of the UCC]; Barbara Brown Zikmund, "Issues Relevant to Union in the History of the United Church of Christ," *Encounter,* 41 (1980), 25-36. Malcom King Burton, a leading opponent of the Mergers has published numerous books on the subject including: *Destiny for Congregationalism* (Oklahoma City: Modern Publishers, 1953) and *Disorders in the Kingdom,* (New York: Vantage Press, 1980). An article on the legal efforts to block the merger is Charles E. Harvey, "Congregationalism on Trial, 1949–1950: An Account of the Cadman Case," *Journal of Church and State,* 12 (1970), 255-72.

On the background of the denominations that united with the Congregationalists these books are useful. On the Christians see: Frederick Louis Fagley, *Story of the Congregational Christian Churches* (Boston and Chicago: Pilgrim Press, 1941); T. E. MacClenny, *The Life of Rev. James O'Kelley and the Early History of the Christian Church in the South* (Raleigh, N.C.: Edwards and Broughton, 1910); W. G. West, *Barton Warren Stone* (Nashville: Disciples of Christ Historical Society, 1954); and Charles G. Ware, *Barton Warren Stone* (St. Louis: Bethany Press, 1932). On the Evangelical and Reformed church see: David Dunn et al., *A History of the Evangelical and Reformed Church* (Philadelphia: Christian Education Press, 1961);

Julius Herman Edward Horstmann and Herbert H. Wernecke, *Through Four Centuries: The Story of the Beginnings of the Evangelical and Reformed Church* (St. Louis: Eden Publishing House, 1938); Joseph H. Dubbs, *A History of the Reformed Church, German* (New York: no publisher, 1985); Barbara Brown Zigmund, *Hidden Histories in the United Church of Christ*, 2 vols. (New York: United Church Press, 1984) contains useful essays on various strands of the denomination's history.

Important sidelights on Congregational ecumenicalism appear in several articles. Peter G. Gowing, in "Newman Smyth and the Congregational-Episcopal Concordat," *Church History*, 33 (1964), 175-91, tells the story of cooperation between Congregtionalists and Episcopalians on the matter of ordination and the ministry. In "The Utah Gospel Mission, 1900–1950," *Utah Historical Quarterly*, 44 (1976), 149-55, Stanley B. Kimball describes the efforts of Congregational missionaries to convert Mormans in Utah, Idaho, Wyoming, and Montana. Gary Topping tells a similar story in "The Ogden Academy: A Gentile Assault on Mormon Country," *Journal of the West*, 23 (1984), 37-47. See also Elaine Bauer, "Family Register, United Church of Christ, Menno, South Dakota," *Heritage Review*, 15 (1985), 12-18 [covers 1828–1954, many members born in Russia]; Dwyn Mecklin Mounger, "Samuel Hanson Cox: Anti-Catholic, Anti-Anglican, Anti-Congregational Ecumenist," *Journal of Presbyterian History*, 55 (1977), 347-61.

Several historians have considered the role of Puritanism in modern American society and culture. Sometimes they use the word "Puritan" in ways that would surprise the first New Englanders; but these articles deal with aspects of the original Puritanism in contemporary life. Richard L. Johannesen, "The Jeremiad and Jenkin Lloyd Jones," *Communication Monographs*, 52 (1985), 156-72, argues that the Puritan Jeremiad tradition finds its way into twentieth century rhetoric. George Malcolm Stephenson, *The Puritan Heritage* (New York: Macmillan, 1952) explores the role of Puritanism in the growth of civil liberties in America. Robert D. Linder, "Religion and the American Dream: A Study in Confusion and Tension," *Mennonite Life*, 38 (1983), 17-22, traces the Puritan idea of mission to contemporary America. Wesley C. McNair, "The Secret Identity of Superman: Puritanism and the American Superhero," *American Baptist Quarterly*, 2 (1983), 4-15, argues that the morality and rugged individualism of the Puritan pioneers finds its way into modern superheroes and their commitment to good; Norman Pettit, "The Puritan Legacy," *New England Quarterly*, 48 (1975), 283-94, discusses the idea, promulgated by Sacvan Bercovitch, that the Puritan legacy to American culture lies "in the realm of the imagination." Kathleen Verduin, "Religious and Sexual Love in American Protestant Literature: Puritan Patterns in Hawthorne and John Updike" (Ph. D. thesis, Indiana University, 1980) explores Puritan themes in American literature. Wade Tyree, "Puritan in the Drawing-Room: The Puritan Aspects of Edith Wharton and Her Novels" (Ph. D. thesis, Princeton University, 1980) covers the years 1902 to 1930; Daniel B. Shea, Jr., "B. F. Skinner: The Puritan Within," *Virginia Quarterly Review*, 50 (1974), 416-37, finds similarities between Skinner and Jonathan Edwards; William J. Scheick, "Puritanism and the New Left," *Thought*, 46 (1971), 72-82, argues that the two groups exhibit a similar view of the individual and history;

Winthrop S. Hudson, "Congregationalism in America: Popular Congregationalism," *Encounter*, 29 (1968), 62-72, traces the influence of congregational polity on other denominations; Darrly Baskin, "The Congregationalist Origins of American Pluralism," *Journal of Church and State*, 11 (1969), 277-93.

On the modern social concerns of Congregationalists see: Wesley A. Hotchkiss, "Congregationalism and Negro Education," *Journal of Negro Education*, 29 (1960), 289-98; Lawrence Neale Jones, *From Consciousness to Conscience: Blacks and the United Church of Christ* (n.p.: United Church Press, 1976); Edyth L. Ross, "Black Heritage in Social Welfare: A Case Study of Atlanta," *Phylon*, 37 (1976), 297-307, traces the role of Atlanta's First Congregational Church in providing for the welfare of urban blacks; Roland Edward Holstead, "The Differential Responses of Protestant Church Polities to Racial Change in an Urban America" (Ph. D. thesis, University of Connecticut, 1982) focuses on Episcopal Church and United Church of Christ.

Other sources on the recent history of Congregationalism and the United Church of Christ include: Arthur Cushman McGiffert, Jr., *The Story of Chicago Theological Seminary* (Chicago: Chicago Theological Seminary, 1965); William McKinney and Dean R. Hoge, "Community and Congregational Factors in the Growth and Decline of Protestant Churches," *Journal for the Scientific Study of Religion*, 22 (1983), 51-66 [explores reason for decline in membership in the United Church of Christ]; Jamet E. Heininger, "Private Positions Versus Public Policy: Chinese Devolution and the American Experience in East Asia," *Diplomatic History*, 6 (1982), 287-302 [Congregational missionaries in China, 1910–1948]; Lawrence Arnold Washburn, *Peace Dale House: Church-Sponsored Elder Housing* (Ph. D. thesis, Hartford Seminary, 1980); Carolyn E. Goddard, *On the Trail of the UCC: A Historical Atlas of the United Church of Christ* (New York: United Church Press, 1981) [contains maps of the thirty-nine conferences of the UCC and lists each of the parishes]; Duane Warner Smith, "The Social Sources of Congreional Ministry" (Ph. D. thesis, New York University, 1980) [1865–1980]; Edward C. Ehrensperger, *History of the United Church of Christ in South Dakota, 1869–1976* (Freeman, S. D.: Pine Hill, 1977); William G. McLoughlin, "The Relevance of Congregational Christianity: Barrington Congregational Church, 1717–1967," *Rhode Island History*, 29 (1970), 63-81.

INDEX

About the Author

J. WILLIAM T. YOUNGS is Professor of History at Eastern Washington University. He is the author of three books, including Eleanor Roosevelt, and has written numerous journal articles.